The **End of Sacrifice**

"A welcome resource to help Christians grapple with the morality of capital punishment. John Nugent helps readers see how Yoder's contributions to the debate about capital punishment are integral to his theology of reconciliation."
—Michael G. Cartwright, Dean of Ecumenical and Interfaith Programs University of Indianapolis

Yoder leads us into crucial issues of how to read the Old and New Testaments together in the light of Christ, how to think about punishment and forgiveness, and so many other timely concerns for the church in our day.
—Michael L. Budde, Professor of Political Science and Catholic Studies DePaul University

The death penalty is dying; *The End of Sacrifice* gives us the most powerful Christian reasons why.
—Glen Stassen, author of Living the Sermon on the Mount and Smedes Professor of Christian Ethics, Fuller Theological Seminary

This book is about far more than capital punishment. It is a rich exploration of the way practices of violence are grounded in a logic of sacrifice that has been overcome in the cross and resurrection of Christ.
—Chris K. Huebner, Associate Professor of Theology and Philosophy, Canadian Mennonite University

The End of Sacrifice is classic Yoder: biblically formed, sociologically informed, politically engaged, and theologically provocative. It illustrates how profoundly we have ignored some of the most obvious implications of a claim that a crucified Messiah now reigns as Lord.
—Lee Camp, Professor of Theology and Ethics, Lipscomb University

The End of Sacrifice

The Capital Punishment Writings of John Howard Yoder

Edited by John C. Nugent

Herald Press

HV
8694
.Y63
2011

Library of Congress Cataloging-in-Publication Data

The end of sacrifice : the capital punishment writings of John Howard
Yoder / edited by John C. Nugent.
    p. cm.
    Includes bibliographical references and index.
    ISBN 978-0-8361-9464-7 (pbk. : alk. paper)
    1. Capital punishment—Religious aspects—Christianity. 2. Capital punish-
ment. 3. Yoder, John Howard. I. Yoder, John Howard. II. Nugent, John C.,
1973-
    HV8694.E53 2011
    261.8'3366—dc23
                                                2011023570

THE END OF SACRIFICE
Copyright © 2011 by Herald Press, Harrisonburg, VA 22802
        Released simultaneously in Canada by Herald Press,
        Waterloo, Ont. N2L 6H7. All rights reserved
International Standard Book Number: 978-0-8361-9464-7
Library of Congress Control Number: 2011023570
Printed in the United States of America
Cover design by Merrill Miller
Interior design by Joshua Byler

18 17 16 15 14 13 12 11   10 9 8 7 6 5 4 3 2 1

To order or request information please call 1-800-245-7894
or visit www.heraldpress.com.

TABLE OF CONTENTS

Permissions

Several of the chapters of this book were previously published in journals and books; others were informally published online or circulated in unpublished form. The editor and publisher here express our gratitude to John Howard Yoder's daughter, Martha Yoder Maust, and the various publishers indicated below for permission to gather and re-present that work in this volume.

Please see "Editorial Concerns" on page 23 for an explanation of the further editorial work done on these pieces.

Chapter 1, "Capital Punishment and the Bible," was previously published in *Christianity Today* 4 (February 1960): 3-6.

Chapter 2, "The Christian and Capital Punishment," was previously published in pamphlet form by Faith and Life Press, Newton, Kan., 1961.

Chapter 3, "Capital Punishment and Our Witness to Government," was previously published in *The Mennonite* 78, no. 24 (June 1963): 390-94.

Chapter 4, "Against the Death Penalty," was previously published in H. Wayne House and John H. Yoder, *The Death Penalty Debate: Two Opposing Views of Capital Punishment*. Dallas, Tex.: Word Books, 1991.

Chapter 5, "You Have It Coming: Good Punishment," was previously published online as "You Have It Coming: The Cultural Role of Punishment, An Exploratory Essay." Shalom Desktop Publications, 1995. http://theology.nd.edu/people/research/yoder-john/ [accessed Jan 1, 2011].

The Appendix, "The Wrath of God and the Love of God," is a previously unpublished lecture that Yoder originally prepared for the Historical Peace Churches and International Fellowship of Reconciliation Conference, Beatrice Webb House, England, Sept. 11-14. Basel: Mennonite Central Committee, 1956.

Foreword

On more than one occasion John Yoder expressed frustration that his critics too often seemed unaware that the first book he wrote (apart from his doctoral thesis) was *The Christian Witness to the State*.[1] This book, he thought, should challenge the stereotypical notion that he as a Mennonite was (ever) "sectarian" and thus unconcerned about the social order. It is, I believe, less common in the year 2011 that Yoder is cavalierly dismissed as a sectarian. However, it is still the case that many are, understandably, unaware of the specifics of Yoder's attempts to reflect theologically on engagement with the social order and to address specific social issues.

The topic of the Christian and the church's relationship to the social order is something to which Yoder returned throughout his career. It was also one of the earliest sets of issues he would confront. From the mid-1950s through the first half of the 1960s, John Yoder undertook a serious study of the Christian witness to the social order.[2] In March of 1955, he produced a 27-page essay, "The Theological Basis of the Christian Witness to the State."[3] In 1957 he produced at least three lectures along similar lines: "The State in the New Testament,"

---

1. By the third "printing" in 1977, clearly some footnotes were added—footnotes that referenced some of Yoder's more recent writings. This book has been in and out of print. It was reissued in 2002 by Herald Press.
2. The following listing does not include lectures/essays Yoder wrote on social ethics in relation to Reinhold Niebuhr (1954), Karl Barth (1957), and H. Richard Niebuhr (1958).
3. Excerpts from this were published as John Howard Yoder, "The Theological Basis of the Christian Witness to the State," in *On Earth Peace*, ed. Donald F. Durnbaugh, 136-43.

"Following Christ as a Form of Political Responsibility," and "The Politics of the Messiah."[4] In the summer of 1957, Yoder returned to the U.S. after eight years in Western Europe. In 1958-59 he was involved in a study assignment funded by the Institute of Mennonite Studies. During this time, in collaboration with an advisory group, Yoder did further research and rewrote some of his earlier material. The most obvious product of this work was the aforementioned 1964 book, *The Christian Witness to the State.*

Yoder also apparently decided that capital punishment would be the specific social issue he would focus on most during his study assignment of 1958-59. In 1959 he produced three separate reports on his research on the death penalty. It is obvious from these reports that he did a serious study of the most relevant biblical texts as well as the theological and pragmatic issues related to capital punishment in the U.S. in the late 1950s.[5] The first three chapters of the present book were originally products of this work.

As it happens, I was loosely connected to some of the research Yoder did for his part of the debate with H. Wayne House—research done in the late 1980s, represented here in chapter 4. In the fall of 1989, when I was a student in Indianapolis, Yoder experienced a serious automobile accident and was hospitalized for some weeks in Indianapolis. Since he was determined to continue working while in the hospital, I was able to do some research for him in our library. After Yoder's death (Dec. 30, 1997), I visited his widow, Annie, a number of times, the first few times in the home they had shared together for many years. I was amazed at the number of file cabinets John used to store his research material. Specifically I noticed how much

---

4.   These lectures were published in German in 1964. The English translation was published as *Discipleship as Political Responsibility*, trans. Timothy J. Geddert.

5.   These reports, adding up to 26 pages of summarizing, are available at The Archives of the Mennonite Church, Goshen, IN, Hist. MSS 1-48, Box 84, folder 13.

material he acquired on topics he cared about, including several inches of files on the death penalty.

For Yoder an issue like capital punishment was primarily decided theologically, with a significant engagement of biblical texts—as is obvious by the collection of essays assembled in this book. But the references to statistics as well as his experimental use of Girard to reflect on punishment also demonstrate Yoder's attempt to engage a broad range of resources pertaining to this serious issue. John Nugent has thus done us a great service in cleaning up some of Yoder's rather raw unpublished work (especially the Girard material) and bringing his writings on capital punishment together in one volume. Moreover, I am grateful that this gives readers of Yoder's writings a brief introduction to one of the brightest, most astute young interpreters of Yoder's writings. Keep alert for Nugent's other writings on Yoder, including his forthcoming book *The Politics of Yahweh*.

—*Mark Thiessen Nation, Professor of Theology*
Eastern Mennonite Seminary
Harrisonburg, Virginia

Editor's Preface and Acknowledgments

When I was first introduced to Christ, I thought I knew what the end of sacrifice meant. I learned that Jesus died so humans would not have to suffer because of their sins; he gave himself to suffer on our behalf. In the course of reading John Howard Yoder's writings on capital punishment, I learned that it also means the end of sacrificing others because of their sins. As it turns out, Jesus died for them, too. So it is tempting to think that the only sacrifice that remains is the "self-sacrifice" we offer as we pour out our lives in service to others. Yet, as Professor Rollin Ramsaran once taught me, even this notion of sacrifice is misguided because "self - self = zero." Christ did not die so that we might become nothing, but that we might live life to the fullest. What Christians do as we love and serve one another is better understood as "self-giving." Following Christ's example, we freely give of ourselves and God replenishes our supply with his super-abundant grace that never runs out.

I am still learning what this might mean, and I continue to be taught by friends and family who have given freely of their time, energy, and resources to make my work possible. One such teacher is Mark Thiessen Nation, who encouraged me to pursue this project, gathered electronic files for most of the essays, and composed a foreword that locates this work within the context of Yoder's life. I have also learned much from Branson Parler and Ted Troxell whose careful reading of my work and that of Yoder have made me a better writer, editor, and thinker. John Gleason and Joel Ickes also gave a great deal of time helping me work through the index, as well as Heather Bunce, who carefully proofread the footnotes and caught several errors that had escaped my notice. Yet the person from whom I have learned the most about what it means to give freely of oneself is my wife, Beth. She and my daughters—Alexia, Sierra, and Alissa—not only give generously of their time with me, but continue to give me joy for life in times of work, rest, and play.

—John C. Nugent

INTRODUCTION

The End of Sacrifice

John Howard Yoder engaged the topic of capital punishment throughout his prolific literary career. He began publishing on it in 1959 and continued exploring and articulating his position until his death in 1997.[1] Surprisingly, over the course of these four decades we see no significant change in his position. Instead, we see Yoder deepening his position and broadening its scope. Central to this position is his conviction that both biblically and culturally, from ancient society until today, capital punishment is an inherently cultic or ritual practice.[2] It is a sacrifice, the performance of a sacred rite, whether performed by religious specialists or public servants.[3] This understanding is critical to Yoder's core thesis: since the death of Jesus brought

---

1. Yoder's first published piece was "The Death Penalty," *The Mennonite* (Nov. 1959): 724-25. Yoder's last piece was an unpublished addendum in 1997 to a work he published online through Shalom Desktop Publications, titled "You Have It Coming: Good Punishment. The Legitimate Social Function of Punitive Behavior" (1995), included as chapter 5 of this collection.

2. This is why Yoder's final work on capital punishment, an engagement of the cultural role of punishment (ch. 5 of this collection), is not merely tangential to Yoder's project. By unmasking the sacrificial component of the public practice of capital punishment, Yoder is calling Christians to own up to their core theological commitment to the finality of Christ's sacrifice to atone for sin.

3. The term "religious specialist" or "professional religionist" is Yoder's way of describing sociologically those persons that all cultures have appointed to carry out their sacred rituals. Cf. *The Fullness of Christ: Paul's Vision of Universal Ministry* (Elgin, Ill.: Brethren Press, 1987), 1-8.

a decisive end to sacrifices for sin, Christians should proclaim its abolition, and death penalty advocates should no longer claim biblical validation. In Yoder's words,

> It is the clear testimony of the New Testament, especially of the epistle to the Hebrews, that the ceremonial requirements of the Old Covenant find their end—both in the sense of fulfillment and in the sense of termination—in the high-priestly sacrifice of Christ. "Once for all" is the good news. Not only is the sacrifice of bulls and goats, turtledoves and wheatcakes at an end; the fact that Christ died for our sins, once for all, the righteous one for the godless (Heb 9:26-28; 1 Pet 3:18), puts an end to the entire expiatory system, whether it be enforced by priests in Jerusalem or by execution[ers] anywhere else.[4]

The title of this collection, *The End of Sacrifice*, is derived from the double entendre that Yoder identifies in this quote. Jesus is the "end" of sacrifice in both a teleological and a chronological sense. Teleologically, Jesus' death fulfills the ultimate purpose (*telos*, or end) that the death penalty first served: to atone for the "cosmic, ritual, religious evil" of taking the life of a fellow human who was created in God's image (Gen 9:6).[5] Chronologically, Jesus' death strictly forbids and therefore terminates all future bloodletting in order to atone for sin (Heb 9:26-28).[6]

---

4. "Against the Death Penalty," p 102 below, originally published in H. Wayne House and John Howard Yoder, *The Death Penalty Debate: Two Opposing Views of Capital Punishment*, 128.

5. "Against the Death Penalty," p 98 below.

6. At a dissertation defense, I heard Richard Mouw quip that Yoder had no theology of atonement—no notion that the cross did anything to deal with human sin. Despite knowing Yoder well, Mouw assumed this because many of Yoder's writings focus on showing that Christ's death meant more than atonement for sin; e.g., it meant an end to enmity between Jews and Gentiles and victory over the powers and principalities. It is typical of Yoder to focus most on

Yoder does not presume to be original in asserting the implications of Christ's death for the practice of capital punishment. He credits Karl Barth for expressing similar sentiments.[7] Nonetheless, Yoder brings a level of interdisciplinary awareness, hermeneutical sophistication, and critical analysis to this topic that provokes fresh insight and casts due suspicion on long held positions. Yoder also brings a firm commitment to his Mennonite heritage. This does not mean that he was simply justifying the stance of his own tradition; it means that he made his case with a keen eye toward challenging problematic tendencies *within* his tradition. Toward this end, he rejected the false choice between articulating a faith-based position and speaking relevantly into the realm of world governance. He refused to espouse an official position for Christians and then leave it to unbelieving public authorities to establish their own position without having the opportunity to receive guidance from the church. On the contrary, he insisted that it is the church's responsibility to proclaim Christ's lordship and its implications to everyone since everyone lives under Christ's jurisdiction, regardless of whether they submit to his lordship. For Yoder, the end of sacrifice is not only true for believers and binding on the believing community; it is true for the cosmos and binding on all rulers and authorities, powers and principalities.

Beyond the above summary, this introduction makes no attempt to weave together all the diverse threads of Yoder's thought on capital punishment. To do so would be redundant because Yoder himself does so in chapter 2 of this collection[8]. Instead, it will facilitate an informed reading of Yoder's essays by surveying the circulation and reception of Yoder's works on capital punishment, introducing the nature and previewing the

---

neglected matters in theology. This collection should put to rest the notion that Yoder had no theology of atonement

7.   Cf. p 103 below, n. 27.
8.   I was, however, asked to present a synopsis of Yoder's position at the 2011 Christian Scholars Conference. It is available at www. walkandword.com/writings/?cat=1&id=1.

content of the included essays, explaining the editorial decisions behind the current collection, and introducing Yoder's
basic approach to Scripture without which some of his arguments may be difficult to grasp.

Circulation and Reception

Yoder's work on capital punishment has enjoyed widespread
circulation. It has circulated among Anabaptists as articles in a
Mennonite magazine, a conference proceedings handbook, and
a pamphlet series.[9] It entered the broader evangelical tradition
in the form of a popular Christian magazine article, an essay in
a Christian ethics textbook, and a published debate with well-
known evangelical theologian H. Wayne House.[10] It also broke
well beyond Christian circles into two editions of Hugo Adam
Bedau's broadly circulated series of *Death Penalty in America*
anthologies.[11] If that was not enough, Yoder's most recent work
has been available since 1995 as a Web-based desktop publication for anyone who manages to find it on the University of
Notre Dame website.[12]

  With all of this exposure, one would expect that Yoder
would be one of the leading voices in recent conversations about

---

9.   "The Death Penalty," in *The Mennonite* (Nov. 1959): 724-25;
      "Capital Punishment and Our Witness to Government," in *The
      Mennonite* 78, no. 24 (June 1963): 390-94; "The Death Penalty: A
      Christian Perspective," in Capital Punishment Study Guide, 44-49;
      and *The Christian and Capital Punishment* pamphlet series.

10.   "Capital Punishment and the Bible," in *Christianity Today* 4 (Feb.
      1960): 3-6; "Noah's Covenant and the Purpose of Punishment,"
      in *Readings in Christian Ethics*, vol. 2, *Issues and Application*,
      eds. David K. Clark and Robert V. Rakestraw, 471-81; and H.
      Wayne House and John H. Yoder, *The Death Penalty Debate: Two
      Opposing Views of Capital Punishment*.

11.   Hugo Adam Bedau, ed. *The Death Penalty in America* and *The
      Death Penalty in America: Current Controversies*.

12.   John Howard Yoder, "You Have It Coming: The Cultural Role of
      Punishment, An Exploratory Essay." (Shalom Desktop Publica-
      tions, 1995), http://theology.nd.edu/people/research/yoder-john/
      [accessed Jan. 1, 2011].

capital punishment, at least among Christians. Yet this is not so. Though several essays briefly cite his work, few engage it in a substantial way, and none acknowledge the broad range of his writings on this subject.[13] This is largely Yoder's fault. Though he wrote prolifically, he did little to make his work readily accessible to those researching in areas of his specialty. His highly informative pamphlet circulated mostly among Mennonites, his Web publication was never polished, and he failed to bring the insights of his various works together into one easily accessible book. As a result, few scholars are aware of and even fewer have had access to the breadth of Yoder's work on this subject.[14]

---

13. Stanley Hauerwas offers the most sustained engagement in "Punishing Christians: A Pacifist Approach to the Issue of Capital Punishment," in *Religion and the Death Penalty: A Call for Reckoning*, eds. Erik C. Owen, John D. Carlson, and Eric P. Elshtain, 57-72. Recent texts that also recognize his work in this area include Darrin W. Snyder Belousek, "Capital Punishment, Covenant Justice and the Cross of Christ: The Death Penalty in the Life and Death of Jesus," in *Mennonite Quarterly Review* 83, no. 3 (2009): 375-402; Millard Lind, *The Sword of Sheer Silence and the Killing State: The Death Penalty and the Bible*, 141-44; Glen H. Stassen, "Biblical Teaching on Capital Punishment," *Review and Expositor* 93 (1996): 485-96; and Michael L. Westmoreland-White and Glen H. Stassen, "Biblical Perspectives on the Death Penalty," in *Religion and the Death Penalty*, 123-38. Most works, however, ignore him altogether. See, for example, most of the articles in *Religion and the Death Penalty*; Glen H. Stassen, ed., *Capital Punishment: A Reader*; and two recent books whose basic arguments have not taken seriously the position Yoder articulates: Ron Gleason, *The Death Penalty on Trial: Taking a Life for a Life Taken*; and Oliver O'Donovan, *The Ways of Judgment*. Gleason's exegetical leap from Genesis 9:6 to Romans 13 is a classic example of the sort of undisciplined hermeneutical sleight of hand that Yoder exposes throughout his works on capital punishment. Though far more disciplined, O'Donovan's approach continues to operate with a division of spheres mentality that, while claiming with Yoder that Christ's reign is relevant to all spheres of life, nonetheless enjoins Christian statesmen to do the opposite of what Christ taught as a sort of reverse prophetic statement (ch. 6).

14. The Yoder Index project will make Yoder's work far more accessible: www.yoderindex.com.

The Nature of This Collection

This collection of Yoder's writings on capital punishment is not exhaustive. Several essays have been intentionally omitted because they primarily repackage old material for new contexts.[15] Nonetheless, considerable overlap still remains. Readers who are concerned to minimize redundancy are advised to skip chapter 2, since all of its material is present in chapter 4. The former remains in the collection because it furnishes a thorough and relatively concise introduction to Yoder's thought, such that when one is looking for a single chapter to quickly brush up on Yoder's position, chapter 2 would be the best.

The essays have been arranged chronologically. One by-product of this arrangement is that each successive essay, with the exception of chapter 3, is longer and more detailed than those that precede it. Those who read all of the texts in their current order will see a core position articulated early that is further expounded upon in each successive essay.

The collection begins with a relatively simple piece, "Capital Punishment and the Bible." This piece was published in *Christianity Today* in 1960. Though its basic argument is repeated in later essays, it stands out in how Yoder frames

---

15.   For example, Yoder's first and briefest article, "The Death Penalty" (in *The Mennonite*), duplicates the first two sections of the *Christian and Capital Punishment* pamphlet (1961). Though Yoder's pamphlet was published two years after the article, it appears to have existed in some form beforehand because the latter is prefaced by the explanatory note "from an extensive study on the subject of capital punishment" (724). Yoder's brief article "The Death Penalty: A Christian Perspective" (*The Interpreter* [Jan. 1979]), is a condensed version of his *Christian and Capital Punishment* pamphlet. It was reprinted shortly thereafter in Capital Punishment Study Guide, 44-49, and in the third edition of Bedau's *The Death Penalty in* America, 370-75. Likewise, Yoder's contribution to the 1997 edition of Bedau's anthology is identical to chapters 2 and 4 of his *Death Penalty Debate* with H. Wayne House. Chapter 2 is also re-published in *Readings in Christian Ethics*, 471-81. These chapters are reproduced in chapter 4 of the current book; see pp. 77-152.

the hermeneutical challenges inherent in discerning Scripture's teaching on capital punishment. Consequently, it ideally sets the stage for the following chapters.

The collection continues in chapter 2 with "The Christian and Capital Punishment." This pamphlet was the most complete early articulation of Yoder's position for three decades (from 1961-1991). In it, one is exposed to Yoder's biblical argumentation as well as his practical and sociological case for abolishing capital punishment.

Chapter 3, "Capital Punishment and Our Witness to Government," is the transcript of a live interview with Yoder at Bethel College in 1963. Since Yoder was engaging an in-house audience that already had access to the above pamphlet, he quickly summarized his position and fielded multiple questions in question and answer format. This relatively brief piece is therefore unique in its informal tone and insightful in how Yoder answers questions that his other writings raise but do not necessarily answer.

Chapter 4, "Against the Death Penalty," makes available Yoder's half of a published dialogue with H. Wayne House. Though Yoder repackages most of his 1961 pamphlet in this 1991 work, it also bears the mark of three decades of additional research and reflection. The result is nine chapters (called "parts" in this volume) of detailed exegetical and sociological analysis. It thus surpasses Yoder's pamphlet as the most complete single-work summary of his thought on capital punishment.

The final chapter, "You Have It Coming: Good Punishment," is Yoder's most narrow, technical, and perhaps pioneering analysis. In this fresh work, Yoder engages and extends the thought of René Girard in order to analyze the punitive character of our world's social structures and to expose the ritual, cultic functions of punishment both in ancient societies and today. Though this 13-part study has been available online since 1995, Yoder never polished it for formal publication.[16] Since then, others have explored the

---

16.   This work therefore does not bear all the marks of consistency and refinement that one would expect in a published work. Yoder describes it in his preface as "heterogeneous and incomplete," but nonetheless "worth circulating for critique" (153).

implications of Girard's work for the present subject, apparently oblivious to Yoder's contributions.[17] This work also stands out in this collection because in it Yoder self-consciously operates from a cultural-scientific perspective and not a specifically Christian one. His 1997 addendum makes clear that Yoder did not do so because he had abandoned a Christian perspective but in order to engage his interlocutors (including Socrates, Antisthenes, Marcus Aurelius, Dürkheim, and Girard) in their own terms.[18] This addendum indicates the kind of perspective Yoder believed Christian faith brings to such analysis.

The appendix of this collection contains one more article from Yoder, although not on the subject of capital punishment. Instead, "The Wrath of God and the Love of God" showcases Yoder's exploration of important theological themes such as divine love, wrath, human freedom, and hell. It is published here both to make available an important, previously unpub-

---

17.   Cf. James McBride, "Capital Punishment as the Unconstitutional Establishment of Religion," 263-87; Brian K. Smith, "Capital Punishment and Human Sacrifice," 3-25; and Sandra M. Levy, "Primitive Symbolic Consciousness and the Death Penalty in American Culture," 717-34.

18.   Yoder sought to understand how and why lethal punishment plays an important role in society out of the conviction that empathizing nonjudgmentally is necessary for those who would advocate positive change (see ch. 5, part 5 of this volume). Importantly, Yoder concludes in this study that the "good" function that punishment still serves in unbelieving society is analogous to its most ancient function: "I reiterate here...that our society's very modern and very pragmatic concern to punish stands in some kind of strong analogy to very ancient notions of a divine order in which innocent sacrifice is a moral demand of the cosmos" (186). This is important to Yoder because he believes that the death of Christ satisfied once and for all the demands of that order. Those who reject Christ will therefore seek some other means of satisfaction, so Christians should not be surprised when unbelievers continue advocating capital punishment over against all evidence contrary to its efficacy as a deterrent (on 227 below, Yoder acknowledges its resurgence in the 1990s). Their core need is therefore not enlightenment, but reconciliation (228).

lished 1956 essay and to give readers who are less familiar with Yoder's broader theological project some basic acquaintance with his thought. Further information about the background and provenance of the chapters of this collection will be provided in the first footnote of each one.

This collection is designed to serve the needs of various readers. Those interested in exploring the various Christian perspectives on capital punishment will find a robust and coherent position that is certain to enrich their understanding. Those wrestling with macro issues of church and state relations will find a challenging position that will call them to remain steadfast in their faith convictions without remaining silent as to their social implications. Those seeking to better understand Yoder's theology will find extended reflection on topics that are seldom addressed elsewhere, including atonement, the state's origins, exegesis of a variety of biblical texts, how to address empirical evidence without allowing it to take over, divine wrath, the nature of hell, primeval matriarchy, and God's nature with respect to human freedom. Those seeking to discern whether Yoder's theology evolved over time will be given a perfect test case for evaluating the consistency of his thought.

Editorial Concerns

This collection was edited with an eye toward preserving Yoder's unique voice and writing style. For the most part, we resisted the temptation to "make Yoder a better writer," but for the sake of clarity it was often necessary to smooth out long and unwieldy sentences and to eliminate unhelpful redundancy. More often than not, this was accomplished simply by altering punctuation marks and coordinating conjunctions. Occasionally, it required breaking up long sentences. Where word changes were deemed necessary for clarity, brackets were inserted to indicate such interventions. Specific changes and additions were also necessary for the sake of uniformity and in keeping with Herald Press's publishing standards. Following Yoder's own inclinations later in life, his essays were conformed to gender neutrality, except with reference to

God. Scripture citations and Bible versions were added when not supplied by Yoder himself. References in footnotes were filled out to the extent possible and sometimes created from scratch. Editorial notes that go beyond simply filling out Yoder's work are placed in brackets to clearly distinguish them from Yoder's own notes. Many words—including "state," "world," "church," and pronouns referring to deity—were decapitalized, except when retaining capitalization significantly aided the reader.

The two larger works within this collection require special mention. As noted above, chapter 4, "Against the Death Penalty," was originally a series of chapters in a book co-authored with H. Wayne House.[19] Only Yoder's chapters, excluding his 12-page response to House's argument, have been included in this book. These chapters are called "parts" in this volume because we identify the separate works that comprise *The End of Sacrifice* as "chapters." The other large work, chapter 5, required the most editorial attention. As Yoder notes in his preface to "You Have It Coming: Good Punishment," this work was not intended to be a formally published book, but a coherent package of subject matter worth circulating for critical engagement.[20] As such, it was far from polished and required heavier editing. Footnotes were generated to adequately cite sources. Occasional redundancies were eliminated to foster a smoother reading. Chapters were renamed "parts," one of which was moved to occupy a place more appropriate to the argument, and another that Yoder added two years later was included as an addendum. A few of the internal references within the document were eliminated, having been made redundant by the addition of an index to the collection. The end result is that the genius of Yoder's own argument is more clearly visible.

Yoder's Approach to Scripture

Although most Christian positions on capital punishment engage key biblical texts (e.g., Gen 9:6; John 8), Yoder's position tends to broader hermeneutical factors to such an extent that those

---

19.   *The Death Penalty Debate.*
20.   Cf. 153 below

unfamiliar with his basic approach to Scripture may be at a disadvantage in seeking to understand his stance. The remainder of this introduction briefly sketches Yoder's approach so as to remove this disadvantage.

All who draw ethical guidance from the totality of Scripture, as Yoder does, must come to grips with the perennial problem of how to relate the Old and New Testaments to each other.[21] This is especially so for those interested in biblical backgrounds to capital punishment, because surface readings often yield contradictory findings. In the Old Testament, God appears as a stern judge who decisively punishes, often by death, those who do wrong. In the New Testament, God offers the life of his only son precisely so the guilty would not have to pay for their transgressions. The God of the Old Testament appears to demand blood for blood (Gen 9:6); the God of the New Testament pardons a woman who has clearly committed a capital offense (John 8).

Classical dispensationalism offers a thoughtful solution to this thorny problem. Its proponents affirm that God is sovereign over world history and that he has chosen to relate to different people in different ways during different times.[22] Not only was God free to work through violent means in one testament and not the other, but each testament is itself divided into multiple dispensations during which God reserves the right to alter his means and measures. Yoder was not satisfied with that answer, nor was he content with approaches that deal with transtestamental tension by narrating differences in terms of

---

21. For a more detailed summary of Yoder's approach to Scripture, as well as an overview of how he interprets the grand narrative of the Old Testament, see John C. Nugent, "The Politics of YHWH," 71–99. This material will be presented in much greater detail in my forthcoming book, *The Politics of Yahweh* [tentative title], Theopolitical Visions Series (Eugene, Ore.: Cascade Books).

22. See Charles C. Ryrie, *Dispensationalism*, 27-50. For a select annotated bibliography, see 249-55. For a more detailed explanation of dispensational roots, see Clarence B. Bass, *Backgrounds to Dispensationalism: Its Historical Genesis and Ecclesiastical Implications*.

progressive revelation, attributing discrepancies to pedagogical concessions, or positing a split between various realms or vocations and assigning the teachings of the Old Testament to some and the New Testament to others.[23] Yoder rejected all of these approaches because he denied their shared premise, namely, that there is, in fact, sharp discontinuity between Old and New Testament ethical teaching.

Yoder's case for Scripture's continuity combines two approaches: biblical realism and directional fulfillment.[24] Biblical realism is a hermeneutical sensibility that entails reading Scripture in its final canonical form *with* the help of historical-critical tools and *without* the skeptical bias that often accompanies historical criticism. Biblical realists do not deny that multiple sources and even ahistorical legends may stand behind some books of the Bible, nor do they assume that the persons traditionally identified as biblical authors are the actual authors. Nonetheless they prefer to use historical-critical tools not to establish the various histories of and behind biblical texts, but to discern the meaning of the texts as they stand. This approach should not be confused with naïve biblicism. Yoder insists that it is a post-critical phenomenon: "What is at stake is not whether the Bible can be interpreted at a great distance without linguistic and hermeneutic tools, but whether, at those points where it is clear in what it says, we are going to let that testimony count rather than subjecting it to the superior authority of our own contemporary hermeneutic framework."[25]

Yoder's Anabaptist heritage also led him to read Scripture

---

23.   Yoder engages dispensationalism and these other approaches in "If Abraham Is Our Father," in *The Original Revolution*, 91-100; *Christian Attitudes to War, Peace, and Revolution*, eds. Theodore J. Koontz and Andy Alexis-Baker, 321-27.

24.   Elsewhere, I use the term "canonical-directional" to summarize the particular way Yoder melds together these approaches. Cf. John C. Nugent, "The Politics of YHWH," 71–99.

25.   Yoder, "The Use of the Bible in Theology," in *To Hear the Word*, 89.

directionally.[26] This means reading it forward—from Old Testament to New and not vice versa—*and* interpreting Old Testament persons and events in light of the New Testament.[27] How can Yoder do this without contradicting himself? He does so by affirming Scripture's promise-fulfillment structure. Since Jesus is the fulfillment of the Old Testament narrative, he provides the interpretive key for distinguishing between Old Testament developments that constituted harmful deviations (e.g., the monarchy) and those that constituted genuine progress (e.g., the diaspora).[28] It also enabled Yoder to discern the meaning of Old Testament laws and practices that are misunderstood when divorced from their fulfillment in Christ. So when Torah dictates that life be taken for life, this ought not be interpreted as contradicting the gospel mandate to repay evil with good and not evil. Since Jesus is the fulfillment of Torah, this precept is properly interpreted as a contextually appropriate first step *away from* the ancient pattern of endless escalating vengeance. In limiting retaliation to equal recompense, God countered the debilitating cycle of revenge by steering his people in the direction of overcoming evil with good. Far from negating the older law, the gospel mandate completes the movement that Torah began.[29]

---

26. See Yoder, *The Priestly Kingdom*, 9; *Anabaptism and Reformation in Switzerland*, 169-72; and "The Hermeneutics of the Anabaptists," in *To Hear the Word*, 217-37. Yoder was well aware, however, that Anabaptists were not alone in reading Scripture directionally (see Richard J. Mouw and Yoder, "Evangelical Ethics and the Anabaptist-Reformed Dialogue," 132-33).

27. Yoder's insistence on *not* reading backward is seen clearly in "If Abraham Is Our Father," in *The Original Revolution*, 100.

28. Yoder sets forth his positive assessment of the diaspora in several places, including "Exodus and Exile: The Two Faces of Liberation," in *Cross Currents*, 297-309, and "See How They Go with Their Face to the Sun," in *The Jewish-Christian Schism Revisited*, 183-202.

29. Cf. Yoder, "'Thou Shalt Not Kill' (Exod 20:13)," in *To Hear the Word*, 38-46.

In granting the benefit of the doubt to the conceptual world of the texts as they stand, Yoder thus saw in Scripture a coherent narrative that spans both testaments and finds its fulfillment in Christ. Rather than rip Old Testament laws and New Testament councils out of their narrative contexts and highlight their differences, he locates all passages in the continuous story of how, beginning with one man and his wife, God was forming a people in this world who would become his vessel for carrying his vision of justice to the ends of the earth. This vision of justice, Yoder argues, was most concretely revealed in and through Jesus of Nazareth. It is the single vision that was in view from the very beginning, and each step of the way the narrative depicts God as directing his people from where they were at a given time toward that single end. The resulting narrative is not, however, a paragon of consistent forward progress. As genuine partners in their own formation, God's people had the ability to resist God's direction in ways that derailed them from their appointed end. The narrative thus portrays God's people navigating through self-inflicted detours with the result that he is compelled to graciously intervene on multiple occasions in order to redirect their paths.

CHAPTER 1

CAPITAL PUNISHMENT AND THE BIBLE[1]

Recent years have witnessed a strong tendency away from the death penalty in the United States. In 1958 Delaware abolished the legislative provisions for capital punishment; with the statehood of Alaska, the Union now has eight states whose judicial systems operate without recourse to the ultimate sanction. But, in addition, nine states, though possessing enabling legislation, have executed no one in the last five years, and six have had no executions for ten or more years. Thus, in effect, seventeen states are now administerin g civil order without taking the lives of the guilty. Similarly, Great Britain took action in 1958

---

1. [Editor's note: This essay was previously published as "Capital Punishment and the Bible" in *Christianity Today* 4 (February 1960): 3-6. The *CT* editors prefaced it with the following remarks: "During the past 28 years 3,616 persons have been executed in the United States—3,136 for murder, 418 for rape, and 62 for other offenses such as treason, espionage, kidnapping, and bank robbery. Nine states (Alaska, Delaware, Hawaii, Maine, Michigan, Minnesota, North Dakota, Rhode Island, and Wisconsin) have set aside capital punishment, but all the others along with the District of Columbia impose the death penalty (including eight states that in time past abolished capital punishment only to reinstate it).

   "Churchmen have become increasingly vocal over the issue. One group contends that capital punishment is immoral, another argues that the death penalty for murder is not only permissible but mandatory because civil government is under divine obligation.

   "When *Christianity Today* published Jacob J. Vellenga's article 'Is Capital Punishment Wrong?' (see Oct. 12, 1959, issue for his that practically abolishes the death penalty, and similar action has received serious study by a Royal Commission in Canada.

These facts must be kept in mind if we attempt an accurate evaluation of growing American opinion—both the expert opinion of penologists and the human interest opinion of the general public—in extending legal abolition of the death penalty. These are not philosophically motivated idealists attempting to impose on society an unrealistic renunciation of legal sanctions and thereby lower the standards of justice, excuse crime, or gloss over the wrongness of wrong. Rather, the concern of a few Christians for the sacredness of life has coincided with the realism of prison administrators, criminal lawyers, and sociologists who desire, in the interest of the "common good," a more efficient way of dealing with criminals. The existence of the death penalty makes for a far more expensive administration of justice, since it involves unending chains of appeals on behalf even of the most patently

---

answer: an emphatic no!), streams of letters pro and con poured into our editorial offices from high places and low. Limitations of space precluded publication of all but representative letters in this spirited exchange. Much of this subsequent debate turned on modern sociological and penal theories rather than on the biblical witness.

"Along with this flow of correspondence came a goodly number of essays. Two of these have been selected for publication in *Christianity Today* because in dissenting from Dr. Vellenga's view they propose a biblical basis for opposition to capital punishment. Ranged against Dr. Vellenga (from 1948-54 a member of the National Board of Administration of the United Presbyterian Church) are Dr. Charles S. Milligan of the Department of Christian Ethics, Iliff School of Theology in Denver, and Dr. John Howard Yoder who, since completion of doctoral studies at the University of Basel, has been instructor in theology at Associated Mennonite Biblical Seminaries at Elkhart, Indiana. In closing this discussion for the time being, except perhaps for brief letters to the editor, *Christianity Today* has requested one of its contributing editors, Dr. Gordon H. Clark, head of the Department of Philosophy at Butler University, to comment on the series and to reply with an eye alert to the biblical witness to which the various participants in this dialogue appeal."]

guilty who hope to "squeeze through" on a technicality. It makes for greater inequality in the administration of justice, since anyone with enough friends or money can "beat the rap" one way or another. Warden Lewis E. Lawes, longtime administrator of Sing Sing prison, estimates that only two percent of those convicted of capital crimes are actually executed—and these are not the most guilty, not the most willful and wanton, but the poor, the friendless, who are without means of making an insanity plea, without enough "inside" knowledge of the underworld to save their lives by turning state's evidence. The statistically unequivocal experience of states and nations without the death penalty, and also our growing contemporary psychological understanding of the motivation of murderers, further make it clear that the death penalty has no deterrent effect on potential murderers.

Some of the moral aspects of the practice of killing criminals have also contributed to the current reappraisal. Capital punishment presupposes an *infallible* judicial procedure, lest it kill the innocent rather than the guilty. Yet no judicial procedure is flawless. The number of condemnations of innocent persons—being the result of mistaken identification, misinterpreted circumstantial evidence, emotional susceptibilities of juries, and other understandable "human factors"—is estimated to run as high as five percent. We should not condemn our judicial systems for the fact that errors happen, but the moral justification of the death penalty is singularly weakened if the factor of human error is faced. Similarly, our growing understanding of psychological processes discloses that the problem of "accountability" is much more complex than was once supposed when one or two questions were thought adequate to establish a culprit's "sanity" and thereby his or her responsibility. Likewise, we are now less self-righteous about society's share of the "blame" for crime. If society—family, neighborhood, and nation—deprives a child of affection, teaches him or her vice through the world's largest pornographic industry, glorifies violence through the entertainment industry, glorifies crime through the wealth it gives its gangster kings, and shuts off legitimate avenues of growth and self-expression through substandard schooling and ethnic segregation, and then this child becomes a teenager armed with a knife and excited by alcohol and other narcotics, which society permits to be sold, is not society's casting the blame on the teenager a disgraceful search for a scapegoat? Such insistence on "personal responsibility" may well be a mere screen for society's refusal to face its moral decadence in repentant honesty.

These observations are not humanistic theories or vague utopian philosophies; they are realities to which God's Word speaks. The evangelical battle cry, *sola scriptura*, does not mean that the Bible is a substitute for the facts but rather that it is the only authoritative source of light to throw on the facts. To turn piously to "the Bible alone" before having faced the problems for which answers from Scripture are needed is to make oneself blind to one's own extra-scriptural assumptions. Understandably but regrettably, some conservative evangelicals are tempted toward this kind of obscurantism and go on treating the issue of capital punishment as if the advocates of abolition were challenging civil government, whitewashing crime, and tearing the sixth commandment from its context.

As we seek the light of God's Word, the first issue we must face is one of hermeneutics: how are we to understand the relationship between the Old and New Testaments? Does Christ simply complete the Old Testament so that a proper Christian understanding of any problem begins with Moses? Or does he tell us how to read the Old Testament so that a proper approach to the Bible begins with Christ himself? In spite of theoretical affirmations of the centrality of Christ and the finality of the New Covenant, the history of Protestant and Catholic thought on the question of civil order has been overwhelmingly dominated by approaches that consider the Old Testament, not the New Testament, to be fundamental. In effect, this does not mean even that the two Testaments are placed on the same level; for the Old speaks directly to the issue of civil order, and the New speaks to it only obliquely, with the result that in applica-

tion the Old is placed above the New. This is the real hermeneutic significance of the position of most of those who try to
justify the death penalty by "what Scripture actually teaches."

The first shortcoming of this approach is that none of those
who advocate it are interested in following it consistently. It is
cited where it favors the argument and dropped where incon-
venient. To apply consistently this approach to Old Testament
prescriptions concerning the social order would mean that the
death penalty should also apply to animals (Gen 9:5, Exod
21:28), to witches, and to adulterers. When it is exacted for
manslaughter, the executioner should be the victim's next of
kin and there need be no due process of law, but there should
be cities of refuge for the innocent and those guilty of unintentional killing (Num 35:11). And while trying in this way to
"take the Bible seriously," the disputant can offer no logical
reason for respecting less its prescriptions on the sabbath, the
cure for leprosy, slavery, and the economic order.

The manifest impossibility of honestly applying such a hermeneutic is not the primary argument against it. The fact is that
at two significant points the New Testament directly modifies the
teaching of the Old. One of these points is the spiritual understanding of what it means to be God's people. In the Old Testament, at least in the period to which the civil regulations of
the Pentateuch relate, the ethnic, civil, geographic, and religious
communities were one. The New Covenant changed this. Being
a son of Abraham is a matter of faith, not of linear descent (Matt
3:9; John 8:39-42; Gal 3:9), and the civil order is in the hands of
pagan authorities. All of this so shifts the context of social-ethical
thought that a simple transposition of Old Testament prescriptions would be illegitimate even if it were possible.

There is, nonetheless, a stronger reason for challenging the
finality of Israelite law. The ultimate basis of the death penalty
in Genesis 9 was not civil, that is, in the narrow modern sense
of serving the maintenance of order in society or the punishment of the guilty. It was expiatory. Killing men and consuming
the blood of animals are forbidden in the same sentence, for

creaturely life belongs in the realm of the "holy" (in the original cultic sense of the term). Life is God's peculiar possession, which man may not profane with impunity. Thus, the function of capital punishment in Genesis 9 is not the defense of society but the expiation of an offense against the image of God. If this be the case—and both exegetical and anthropological studies confirm strongly that it is—then the central events of the New Testament, the cross and the resurrection, are overwhelmingly relevant to this issue. The sacrifice of Christ is the end of all expiatory killing; only an unbiblical compartmentalization can argue that the event of the cross, itself a typical phenomenon of miscarried civil justice issuing in the execution of an innocent, has nothing to do with the civil order.

The Law of Love

If Judaism is not an adequate key to understanding the Bible's teaching on human life, then what is the key? Is it not to be found in the frequent New Testament teaching—especially clear in Matthew 25:31-46 and in 1 John 3:18; 4:12 and 20—that we are to see and serve God in our neighbor? Countless other New Testament admonitions tell us to love our neighbor and to keep God's commandments. Furthermore, they define what loving our neighbor means. The idea that we could kill his body while loving his soul is excluded. Love considers the total well-being of the beloved: "love worketh no ill" (Rom 13:10 KJV). This divinely sanctioned worth, which my neighbor should have in my eyes, is due not to some philosophical idea of inherent human dignity but to the grace of creation, to the impartation of the divine image, and to the reaffirmation of this grace in the incarnation, teaching, and behavior of our Lord. Bodily life is not simply a carnal vehicle for the immortal soul; it is part and parcel of the unity of human personality through which the divine Word condescended to reveal himself.

The only direct New Testament reference to capital punishment is in John 8, a passage generally recognized to be authentic Gospel tradition even by those who deny its belonging in the original canonic text of John. Romans 13 deals with the principle that Christians should submit to the established pagan civil authorities. It affirms that even they are instituted to serve the "good" (v. 4). This text alone, however, does not spell out what "good" is. The "sword" of which Paul writes is the symbol of judicial authority; it is not the instrument used by the Romans for executing criminals. Even if it were, the passage would say nothing of the tempering effect that the leaven of Christian witness within society should have on its institutions. Neither the passage in Romans nor comparable ones in the epistles of Timothy or Peter speak to the issue of the state's taking life; the incident from the life of Jesus remains our first orientation point.

The striking thing about the attitude Jesus takes to the woman, patently guilty of a capital offense, is not what he says about capital punishment but the new context into which he places the problem. He does not deny that such prescriptions were part of the Mosaic code, but he raises two other considerations that profoundly modify the significance of that code for his day and for ours. First, he raises the issue of the moral authority of judge and executioner: "Let him that is without sin cast the first stone" (John 8:7 RSV). Second, he applies to this woman's offense, which is a civil offense, his authority to forgive sin. There is no differentiation between the religious and the civil which says that God may forgive the sinner but justice must still be done. Once again we see that the expiation wrought by Christ is politically relevant. Like divorce (Matt 19:8), like the distortions of the law, which Jesus corrects in Matthew 5:17-48, and like the institution of slavery, capital punishment is one of those infringements on the divine will that takes place in society, sometimes with a certain formal legitimacy, and which the gospel does not immediately eliminate from secular society even though it declares that "from the beginning it was not so." The new level of brotherhood in which the redeemed community is to live cannot be directly enforced upon the larger society; but if it be of the gospel, it must work as a leaven, as salt, and as light, especially if, as in the case in the Anglo-Saxon world, the larger society claims some kind of Christian sanction for its existence and social pattern. If Christ is not only prophet and priest but also king, the line between church and world cannot be impermeable to moral truth. Something of the cross-bearing, forgiving ethics of the kingdom must be made relevant to the civil order.

This relevance will not be direct and immediate. The state is not and should not be the church, and therefore it cannot apply New Testament ethics in an unqualified way. Yet to have made this point does not mean that the state may operate according to standards that *contradict* those of the gospel. There is a difference between diluting, adapting, and qualifying standards, which the state must do, and denying them altogether, which the state has no right to do. To dispose of the life of fellow humans—who share with us the image of God and for whom Christ, being made in the likeness of men, died—oversteps the limits of the case that any government within "Christendom" can make for ethical compromise. The state is not made Christian by the presence of the church in its population or by the presence of pious phrases on its postage stamps and coins. It has at least been made aware of and has partially committed itself to certain divine standards that it cannot ignore. If a given society permits slavery, divorce, and vengeance against criminals (most of the biblical arguments for capital punishment can be closely paralleled by similar ones for the institution of slavery), the church cannot legally abolish these practices; but she can call the state to a closer approximation to true standards of human community.

The sanctity of human life is not a dogma of speculation, but part of the divine work of creation and redemption. We call for the legal abolition of capital punishment not because we think the criminal is innocent but because we share his guilt before God who has borne the punishment we all merited. Certainly we are not saying that he is a nice person worthy of another chance. It is God that gives another chance to the unworthy. We expect to do away with civil order, but redemption has shown us what purpose that order serves and by what yardstick it should be measured. "I am come that they may have life" (John 10:10 KJV) was not spoken only of men's "souls."

CHAPTER 2

THE CHRISTIAN AND CAPITAL PUNISHMENT[1]

On July 18, 1957, nineteen-year-old Cleo Eugene Peters shot and fatally wounded Paul Coblentz, a young Holmes County, Ohio, farmer. This happened in the course of a celebration following the release from prison of a friend whom Peters had met while he himself was serving a prison sentence. There was never any doubt that Peters would be found guilty of the murder, and after all the possibilities of appeal to higher courts were exhausted, the date for his

---

1. [Editor's note: This essay was previously published as a pamphlet, prefaced with the following remarks by Cornelius J. Dyck, who at the time was Director of the Institute of Mennonite Studies, Elkhart, Indiana:

    "Going to press in a time of great national interest in the question of capital punishment, this pamphlet has its origin in the conviction that social and moral reform comes about only through the devoted efforts of those who really care. Many share the concern of the author that on the question of capital punishment Christians are 'letting their silence speak for them.' For this reason the following pages are presented primarily as a contribution to the biblical and theological aspect of the debate rather than to philosophical or sociological considerations, though these likewise carry validity in their own right.

    "The Christian and Capital Punishment is the first of a series planned and sponsored by the Institute of Mennonite Studies on issues vital to the life and witness of the church. Its author has been a vigorous participant in the conversation about the nature and mission of the church during the past several years both in Europe and in the United States through conferences, lectures, pamphlets, and numerous articles in *Concern*, the *Mennonite Quarterly Review*, and other journals."]

death in the electric chair was set for November 7, 1958. Peters faced a death like that of the forty-eight other men and women who were gassed, hanged, or electrocuted in the United States in 1958.

But there was a difference. Paul Coblentz was an Old Order Amish Mennonite, and his death stirred Holmes County, one of the nation's major centers of Amish population, in a surprising way. Their reaction to the brutal deed of this intruder from the outside world was not one of hostility but of forgiveness. Twenty-eight persons, most of them Amish, were refused for jury duty because of their conscientious unwillingness to inflict the death penalty. During the trial numerous Amish families invited Peters' parents into their homes. After the conviction was final, the Amish signed petitions and wrote to Governor C. William O'Neill requesting a commutation of the sentence in such numbers as to surprise those who thought the Amish cared nothing for the outside world.

The commutation was granted by Governor O'Neill seven hours before the time scheduled for the execution. Meanwhile, a few Amish Mennonites had been attempting to draw a spiritual lesson from the event that had so deeply shaken their community. "God has been speaking to many of us Amish people through this act," some of them concluded. "We believe that God allowed this, especially to call us back to him in the work of winning souls to his kingdom." Soon after the commutation, two ministers visited Peters in the Ohio penitentiary bearing a letter from which the above words were quoted. There they learned that Peters had become a Christian a few months earlier and was deeply appreciative of letters he had received from Amish people, some of them as far away as Iowa, among them the widow of his victim.

What does it signify that the Amish, who in the minds of many are the classic example of religiously motivated withdrawal, caring nothing for the outside world, thus contributed to Peters' pardon? In effect, they interfered with the execution of a legitimate ruling of the courts. Though they did not object to or interfere with the proceedings of the court, they asked that the guilty should not be punished, at least not with the death penalty. Was this proper for Christians? Was it proper behavior for nonresistant Christians who themselves take no further responsibility for the affairs of the state?

These lines were written because of a conviction that it is not only right for Christians to ask mercy for particular criminals, but that Christians should, in fact, support efforts to abolish the death penalty as a legal way of dealing with offenders.

The Basic Christian Testimony About Human Life

It should hardly need to be argued that the whole teaching and work of Christ leads Christians to challenge the rightness of taking life under any circumstances, even where secular justice might seem to permit killing. When Jesus himself was asked to rule on an offense that by the laws of the time called for the death penalty, his answer was clearly such as to abolish it; not directly by declaring it a wrong institution, but indirectly by demanding that the judges and executioners must first be sinless (John 8). This is in line with everything he taught about the worth of every life before God (Matt 6) and our responsibility to see Christ himself in the needy neighbor (Matt 25). The reason for this respect for life is not a literal interpretation of the sixth commandment, but a deep spiritual principle: the life (the soul or the personality) of the neighbor is sacred because humans are made "in the image of God" (Gen 9 NIV). If we love God "whom no one has seen" (1 Tim 6:16 NIV), it must show in our love for fellow humans, and this love always includes a concern for their bodily welfare. Far from being purely otherworldly, Christian faith is more "this-worldly," more materialistic in one sense than any other religion; it knows of no way to love others without also caring for their bodily life. If there were no Ten Commandments and no Sermon on the Mount, what we know about Christ, how he lived and why he died, would still suffice to sanctify human life. To sanctify means to set apart as belonging to God alone, and that is just what the Bible says about human life: it is not ours to take.

What does it mean that humans are made in the image of God? Why is his human life sacred? To be made in God's image means to be capable of fellowship; we know of no other basis for our fellowship with one another and with God than our bodily existence. A person's destiny beyond death is dependent on the deeds and choices "done in the body" (2 Cor 5:10 RSV). In the Old Testament, life was sacred—except for that of the murderer and the enemy. By trading places with the guilty and with his enemies, by dying in a murderer's stead (Barabbas), and by teaching us that there is no moral difference between friend and enemy as far as their claim on our love is concerned, Jesus closed the loophole. The lifeblood of *every* man belongs to God alone. Life is sacred not only because Christ, in becoming a human among humans, made us see him in every needy human (Matt 25:40, 45); life is also, in the fallen world, a chance for repentance. To take someone's life is to deprive them of their future and thereby of all possibility of being reconciled with God and fellow humans. Only in this life can we repent; only while they live can our neighbors be benefited by our love. This is why Menno Simons argued

> that it would hardly become a true Christian ruler to shed blood. For this reason, if a transgressor should truly repent before God and be reborn of him, he would then also be a chosen saint and child of God, a fellow partaker of grace . . . and for such an one to be hanged on the gallows . . . or in any manner be hurt in body or goods by another Christian, who is of one heart, spirit, and soul with him, would look somewhat strange and unbecoming in the light of the compassionate, merciful, and kind nature, disposition, spirit, and example of Christ, the meek Lamb. . . .
>
> Again, if he remain impenitent, and his life be taken, one would unmercifully rob him of the time of repentance of which, in case his life were spared, he might yet avail himself . . . the Son of Man says: Learn of me, I have given you an example; Follow me, I am not come to destroy souls but to save them.[2]

---

2.   J. C. Wenger, ed., *The Complete Writings of Menno Simons: Circa 1496-1561*, 920-21.

It would, therefore, be a too shallow ethical approach to be satisfied with legal considerations. The Christian concern is redemptive; redemption means Christ giving himself for his enemies. Concern for the lives of those who are socially desirable is no virtue; a redemptive view of man comes into play only if God's own attitude to the unworthy is taken as guide.

This is all very well for Christians, but can we ask of an unbelieving society and of the state that they have this kind of respect for life? Did not God ordain the state to restrain evil and to punish evildoers? There are serious arguments raised at this point, and we must now turn our attention to them. But we must not do so without being clear where we begin. We begin with the certainty that death is not God's highest will for any man. If lives may be taken, even by the state, this must be proved in the face of what the gospel says to the contrary. The advocates, not the opponents, of capital punishment have the burden of the proof.

Killing and the Moral Order

One set of arguments in favor of the death penalty is of the kind that holds it to be God's will or the demand of the moral order that life should be paid for with life. We can best approach this problem by referring to the origins of the death penalty in human society. The Genesis story, especially chapter 9, will serve as an excellent case in point (if we were to study the secular science of anthropology it would actually tell us about the same thing). "Whoever sheds the blood of man, by man shall his blood be shed" (Gen 9:6 RSV) seems clearly to be speaking of some kind of death penalty. Just what is meant?

A closer study of these earlier chapters of the Bible is that the death penalty, as stated there, is clearly not so much a *requirement* as a *limitation*. It is spoken against the background of a story of corruption (Gen 4–6) in which vengeance was the general pattern. In the line of Cain, who slew his brother, Abel, for a paltry offense, soon we read of Lamech's vicious boast, "I have slain a man for wounding me, a young man for striking me. If Cain is avenged sevenfold, truly Lamech seventy-seven-fold" (Gen 4:23 RSV). Vengeance, this example shows, was all out of proportion to the offense.

Let us, therefore, begin realistically as the Bible does. Vengeance does not need to be commanded; it happens. It is the normal response of fallen humanity to any situation that calls forth hostility. And normally such vengeance is unlimited. Primitive peoples show the same pattern as Lamech from the intertribal wars of Borneo, through the bloody gang justice of the Sicilian hills and the American underworld, to the proverbial "feudin' hill-billies" of the Appalachians. It is the normal thing for vengeance and counter-vengeance to raise the toll of suffering brought about by any one offense far beyond any proportion to the original damage done.

Thus, if we ask what end was served by the institution of civil order, either in primitive societies in general or in the form we have reported in Genesis 9, it is an error to think that the emphasis is on the necessity for vengeance. Vengeance is happening; the necessity is that it be controlled. The significance of civil order is that it *limits* vengeance to a level equivalent to the offense. In this sense it is one way in which God's grace works against sin. The first murder recorded in Genesis was followed by an act of God protecting the murderer's life against those who could be expected to threaten him (Gen 4:15). This same purpose issues in the setting up of rules for precisely how such equivalents are to be measured: "Eye for eye, tooth for tooth, hand for hand, foot for foot, burn for burn, wound for wound, stripe for stripe" (Exod 21:24, 25 RSV). These rules are supplemented by rules defining acceptable substitutions, which continued to be elaborated down through Jewish history so that by the time of Jesus most of these penalties could be absolved through payments of money. Just as the law of Moses in Deuteronomy 24 does not mean to approve of divorce, but only as a concession to the hardness of men's hearts (Matt 19:8), to regulate the separations which were already taking place, so the law of *talion* does not command, but rather limits vengeance as a concession. The provision for cities of refuge even added a further limitation of vengeance, so that for certain kinds of killing (e.g., unintentional manslaughter) there should be a chance of escaping the avenger.

Thus, when in the Sermon on the Mount or in Romans 12 *all* vengeance is declared illegitimate for the Christian, or when Jesus' own death is seen in the New Testament as a proclamation of forgiveness, this is another step in the direction already taken by Genesis 9 and Exodus 21. Vengeance was never God's highest intent for men's and women's relations with one another; permitting it within the limits of justice (i.e., of equivalent injury) was never really his purpose. What God always wanted to do with evil and what he wants us today to do with it is to swallow it up and drown it in the bottomless sea of his crucified love. There is no such thing as a divine moral order demanding that one evil be somehow paid for by another evil. True though, in a sinful world this does happen; the sinner brings down vengeance upon his own head, and God somehow can use this process within his providential purpose. But from the beginning it was not so (Matt 19:8).

Often Christians, in attempting to describe how the laws of the Old Testament are to be understood since Christ, divide them into civil, ceremonial, and moral laws. One can then explain that the moral law continues to apply to Christians, the ceremonial law is abrogated by its fulfillment in Christ as the final sacrifice and the final high priest, and the civil law ceased with the end of the Jewish state, though it might have some indirect application to other states. This division is helpful for the purposes of classification, but careful study of Genesis 9 and similar passages makes clear that in the earliest parts of the Bible the distinction does not fit. Just as Christ is prophet, priest, and king all at once, so the covenant established by God with Noah is moral, ceremonial, and civil all at once. It speaks of the blood of man and beast as belonging to God, certainly a sacrificial concept. Likewise, the provision that an animal guilty of murder shall pay with its life (Gen 9:5; Exod 21:28-32) is hardly what we would call a moral or civil provision. The passage is not only sacrificial; it is clearly moral and civil as well in its intent. Yet its basis is the religious understanding that all animate life, not only that of man, is sacred, belonging to God alone. Not killing humans thus comes under the same heading as not consuming the blood of sacrificed animals.

This means that we can never make the question of the death penalty a purely legal, nonreligious matter; it is a sacrificial act. The blood, i.e., the life of every man and beast, belongs to God. To respect this divine ownership means, in the case of animals, that the blood shall not be consumed; for humans it means that there shall be no killing. If there is killing, the offense is not simply a civil offense; it is also a ritual, religious evil, and it demands ceremonial compensation. If we must make a distinction at all between ceremonial and other considerations, it is not so much a legal or an ethical consideration as a ceremonial requirement that blood must be paid for with blood. If we would understand Genesis 9, we must think not of a moral order decreeing that one injury can be righted by another—there is nothing moral about that—but a deeply religious reverence for life as sacred, belonging to God alone, so that he who robs God by shedding his brother's blood forfeits his own blood in expiation.

It is the clear witness of the New Testament, especially of the epistle to the Hebrews, that the ceremonial requirements of the Old Testament find their fulfillment and their end in the high-priestly sacrifice of Christ. "Once for all" is the triumphant proclamation of the epistle (Heb 10:10). Henceforth no more blood is needed to testify to the sacredness of life, and no more sacrifices are called for to expiate for humanity's usurping the power to kill. With the cross of Christ, the moral and ceremonial basis of capital punishment is wiped away.

Often such biblical texts as Genesis 9:6, Exodus 21:12, and Deuteronomy 19:19-21 are understood as teaching a view of justice that is primarily legal and which dictates that one offense can be righted by another. Once this idea has been argued or taken for granted, it is possible to understand the work of Christ who "bore our sins" and took upon himself "the chastisement of our peace" (Isa 53:5 KJV) as his being legally punished in the place of guilty men. It has even been argued by some that to challenge capital punishment undermines the orthodoxy of one's view of the atonement. Although persons of unimpeachably evangelical convictions sometimes hold this view, it is a serious modernization of the Bible. The church was a thousand years old before it occurred to Christian theologians that, in order to communicate and illustrate the gospel to persons of a legal turn of mind, Christ's sufferings could be spoken of in terms of legal punishment. This was not a bad idea, since every generation must find new ways to testify to its faith, but at the time it was a new idea and not orthodox. The large place such penal conceptions have had in western civilization does not change the fact that the Bible does not see the killing of murderers as dictated by the demand of an impersonal moral order for justice.

We have clearly seen that authorized killing in the Old Testament has a sacral, not a legal character. Even the holy wars of early Israel were more like sacrifices than like political campaigns. It cannot be said of a law that called for the death penalty for oxen (Gen 9:5; Exod 21:29), discussed murder in the same breath with the eating of blood (Gen 9:4-6), and explained the treatment of offenders as "putting the evil away from your midst" (Num 35:33), that its major concern is for objective, retributive legal justice. Its concern is sacrificial, not social; the order it seeks to restore is sacral, not moral. In fact, the well-known passage speaking of "life shall go for life, eye for eye, tooth for tooth" (Deut 19:19-21 KJV) is discussing the punishment of only one offense, namely, the bearing of false witness. The punishment of the perjured person depends on that which would have been meted out to the accused if the testimony against him had been true. "Life for life" in this passage prescribes death not for murder, but for testifying falsely on a matter worthy of the death penalty.

Since the death penalty in the Old Testament is expiation rather than penalty, its antitype in the New Testament is not the sword of the magistrate, but the cross.

Killing and the Function of the State

The only direct New Testament reference to capital punishment is in John 8, a passage generally recognized to be authentic gospel tradition even by those who deny its belonging in the original canonical text of John. Romans 13 deals with the principle that Christians should submit to the established pagan civil authorities. It affirms that even they are instituted to serve the "good" (v. 4). This text alone, however, does not spell out what the "good" is. The sword of which Paul writes, the *machaira*, is the symbol of judicial authority; it is not the instrument used by the Romans for executing criminals. Even if it were, the passage would say nothing of the tempering effect that the indirect effect of the Christian witness within society should have on its institutions. Neither the passage in Romans nor comparable ones in the epistles of Timothy or Peter speak to this issue of the state taking life. Thus, the incident from the life of Jesus remains our first orientation point.

The striking thing about the attitude Jesus takes toward the woman, patently guilty of a capital offense, is not what he says about capital punishment but the new context into which he places the problem. He does not deny that such prescriptions were part of the Mosaic code, but he raises two other considerations that profoundly modify the significance of that code for his day and for ours. First, he raises the issue of the moral authority of judge and executioner: "Let him that is without sin cast the first stone" (John 8:7 RSV). Second, he applies to this woman's offense, which is a civil offense, his authority to forgive sin. There is no differentiation between the religious and the civil, which says that God may forgive the sinner, but justice must still be done. Once again we see that the expiation wrought by Christ is politically relevant. Like divorce, like the distortions of the Law, which Jesus corrects in Matthew 5, and like war and the institution of slavery, capital punishment is one of those infringements on the divine will that take place in society, sometimes with a certain formal legitimacy, and which the gospel does not immediately eliminate from secular society even though it declares that "from the beginning it was not so" (Matt 19:8 RSV). The new level of kinship on which the redeemed community is to live cannot be directly enforced upon the larger society; but if it be of the gospel, it must work as a ferment, as salt, and as light, especially if, as in the case of the Anglo-Saxon world, the larger society claims some kind of Christian sanction for its existence and its social pattern. If Christ is not only prophet and priest but also king, the border between the church and the world cannot be impermeable to moral truth. Something of the cross-bearing, forgiving ethics of the kingdom must be made relevant to the civil order.

One frequently hears the charge that to challenge capital punishment is essentially to advocate anarchy, especially if this is done in the name of Christ and with reference to his action as reported in John 8. If we claim that the state should forgive or that only the innocent may "throw the first stone," where will we stop? Does this not destroy all government? Although its intention is often only rhetorical, this question deserves further serious attention, for it illustrates a basic problem in the relation of Christian ethics to non-Christian society.

One error involved in this question is its assumption that in the application of a Christian social critique it is possible to "carry things to their logical conclusion." This assumption distorts everything. Christian social criticism speaks to a fallen world. Since the critique finds its standards in the kingdom of God—for there are no other standards with ultimate theological validity—the logical consequence of the consistent application of those standards would be the full realization of God's kingdom; but to apply these standards consistently lies beyond the capacities and the intentions of the fallen world and is not what the Christian asks or expects of unregenerate society. Thus, to undercut Christ's claims on the secular order by asking "Where would this lead?" is to distort the whole problem. The world, by the very fact of its rebellion, has guaranteed that the Christian social critique will not lead too far; at most, the world can be challenged, one point at a time, to take one step in the right direction, to move one more notch in approximation of the righteousness of love.

The state is a fact; that it might be done away with by the criticism of love is inconceivable. Just as Genesis 9, parallel to every primitive state, does not command vengeance, which is already present, but limits it, so the Christian (and the believer in democracy) will attempt to limit the state. The state *is*; it does not need to be defended.

We may observe the symbolic demonstration of this point in the fact that anarchy is only a word, a grammatical invention, an imaginary concept. There is no such thing as anarchy. There are varying forms of government, from tyranny to the constitutional democracy; and there are varying degrees of centralization of power, from the world empire through the nation to the independent tribe. There may even be government through the interaction of rival powers as in a guerrilla war or where the criminal underworld is highly organized. There may be variation in the effectiveness of control, from total regimentation to a weak power barely able to pursue the least criminals. Authority may be delegated or seized; it may be exercised wisely or stupidly, efficiently or clumsily, overtly or undercover. But there is always authority, and where it seems to function too little for the welfare and stability of society, the reason is never that the critique coming from the direction of Christian love has been too effective. The concept of anarchy does not arise from the study of states and government; it is an abstract creature of the urge to carry things to their logical conclusions—an urge which is out of place considering God's rule over the fallen world.

The second error in this question is the assumption that there exists some clear concept of justice consisting in the exact equivalence of offense and retribution and that this justice is either wholly respected or fundamentally rejected. In reality there is no one sure yardstick by which to measure the "justness" of a penalty; every culture and every age have different conceptions of what is fair retribution. Opinions change as to how much it matters whether the offender was human, adult, and of a sound mind, and whether he was aware of the demands of the law. They vary equally in their judgments of what equivalent means. "Eye for eye" is measurable when we are dealing with bodily wounds or "ox for ox" in the economic realm, but what equation shall be used for adultery or for covetousness?

Justice is, therefore, a relative, not an absolute concept. It is a direction, not a level. Moral acts may be more just or less just, but we know of no ideal justice, distinct from love, which "too much emphasis on love and forgiveness" would jeopardize. Justice may well be endangered by idealistic schemes for reformation, by social criticism that does not propose a relevant alternative action, by a sentimental misunderstanding of the nature of love, or by failing to recognize how much order and mutual respect have already been achieved by the society one criticizes; but justice is not endangered by love.

Killing and the Christian Influence upon Society

We have thus far seen two reasons for rejecting, on Christian grounds, the idea that the will of God demands the death penalty. First, we have observed that biblical references to equivalent punishment should be understood not as *requiring* but as *limiting* vengeance; the same is true of pagan concepts of justice. They do not, therefore, mean that vengeance is good or necessary. Second, we have seen that the idea of expiation grows from the truth that life is sacred, that is, it belongs to God. Christians do not deny the reality of a spiritual need for expiation when blood has been shed, but they confess that Jesus Christ has met this need for all humans. The fact that modern secular society has abandoned the idea of expiation in its interpretation of the death penalty is a result not only of secularization and loss of faith, but also of the indirect influence of Christ on modern culture.

There is yet another set of facts that also weakens the "moral order" view. One of the indirect influences of Christianity on modern society has been the progressive limitation of killing by the state (apart from the problem of war). Distinctions are now made between the insane and the legally responsible; between accidental manslaughter, self-defense, and premeditated murder. It has come to be recognized that all of society bears some of the blame for the situations of conflict, the temptations, and the weaknesses of personality that result in killing. Faced with this development, the friends of the "moral order" theory of capital punishment must, it would seem, choose one of two answers: either they may stand by the claim that "a life is a life," rejecting such considerations; or they must claim that there is one clear and sure way of calculating the exact degree of blameworthiness, so that what the moral order calls for by way of punishment is always definite and easy to agree upon. But in the latter case it must be admitted that today capital punishment in law and in practice cannot be any nearer to this ideal moral order than its abolition would be, for no two states or nations are alike in the use and severity of punishment. Those who use the "moral order" theory should first prove their sincerity by working for a far greater uniformity, clarity, and conformity to moral order in all criminal law. They would further need to explain the retention of the ultimate penalty for crimes other than murder.

But someone may well ask, What does this have to do with secular society? Are these arguments not primarily religious, unconnected with law and politics? Can we claim that something that only Christians affirm to believe in, namely, the work of Christ, should really have given us new light on the nature of secular society, even for non-Christians? Does not the claim that the cross has something to do with the death penalty confuse two completely unrelated matters?

This question must be faced seriously, but the answer of the Bible seems clear. Christians call Jesus not only priest, prophet, and teacher, but lord and king; these are political names. The unfaithfulness of Christians begins where they admit that in certain realms of their life it would be confusing to bring Christ and the meaning of his teaching and life to bear on our problems. Certainly, non-Christians will insist that our *religion* and our *politics* should not be *mixed*. But their reason for this insistence is not that Jesus has nothing to do with civil society, but rather that they are not Christian. If we confess that it is the Lamb that was slain who is "worthy . . . to receive power and wealth and wisdom and might and honor and glory and blessing!" (Rev 5:12 RSV), we are relating the cross to politics. Whatever we believe about Christ we must apply to all our behavior, no matter how many of our neighbors remain unconvinced. Of course, the fact of humanity's unbelief will mean that society will not fully keep the law of God and, when it thus falls short of righteousness, God will nonetheless know how to use that disobedience to his glory; but this is no reason for Christians to justify and defend the lower level of behavior that results from unbelief, whether it be in the political realm or elsewhere.

The words of Paul in Romans 13:1-7, which affirm that the "powers that be" are divinely ordained, have often been further interpreted to say that, therefore, Christians have no grounds for criticizing what any given state does or no standards to guide such a criticism unless the state were to go so far as to prevent Christians from meeting and preaching. Paul does not say this. He says the state is to serve "the good" (v. 4) and that it is God's servant when (or insofar as) it "perseveres attentively toward this very end" (v. 6). Both these expressions, as well as the very similar statements in 1 Peter 2:13-17, indicate that there are standards of good and right order, not dependent on the arbitrary judgment of individual rulers, by which every government is judged. This does not authorize Christians to rebel against an unjust state, using against it the same kind of violence with which it expresses its injustice. It does, however, give us standards for identifying that unrighteousness and grounds for denouncing it.

Actually, the passage in Romans is simply one application of a New Testament truth that is stated more frequently: the confession that "Christ is Lord" (e.g., Phil 2:11; 1 Cor 12:3). This *lordship* does not apply only over the church; Christ has been exalted "far above every principality and power, and might, and dominion, and every name that is named" (Eph 1:21; Phil 2:10; 1 Cor 15:27; Matt 28:18). This lordship is not acknowledged by the world but is nonetheless real; it is what Protestant tradition, using a nonbiblical term, has sometimes referred to as God's overruling providence. The state, like any other rebellious power, can attempt to be independent, can claim to be its own master, but Christians know the claim is false and the attempt doomed to failure. Actually, the state does rebel; but ultimately it cannot do so and the certainty of the accomplishment of God's purposes is what Christians proclaim even to the principalities and powers already in the present age (Eph 3:19). It is not the purpose of this essay to discuss the Christian view of the state; from the fact of Christ's dominion we can, however, draw conclusions sufficient for our present purpose. If it is Jesus Christ, and not some other god or some other lord, who rules at the right hand of God, then the purpose, goals, and standards of that rule can be no other than this same Jesus revealed to us while in the flesh, seeking not to destroy, but to save. It cannot, therefore, be argued that under his dominion the state has the right or the duty to destroy life.

We have seen that the existence of the death penalty in early human societies is due not to the fact that God or society demands punishment, but rather to the action taken by God or society through the establishment of civil order to *limit* the exercise of vengeance. The normal process in a healthy society subject to the *salting* and *illuminating* effect of the Christian witness should be for this limitation to be pulled tighter and tighter. This is what has actually happened in the development of Western civilization. The courts have defended the right of the accused to defend themselves; the rules of evidence have been defined; a second jeopardy for the same offense has been forbidden and extenuating circumstances have been weighed. It is in line with this development that the number of offenses for which the death penalty can be inflicted has dwindled rapidly.

Two centuries ago the death penalty was required by English law for over three hundred different offenses, including counterfeiting, forgery, and petty thefts of as little as two pounds. Today only four crimes are capital offenses in England, and in practice only murder is thus punished. In 1776 the North American colonies had from ten to eighteen capital crimes; today, with great variations from state to state, there are in the United States only eight such offenses, and of the eight only murder (and in the South rape by African-Americans) is actually punished with death. Likewise, the number of executions in proportion to the number of convictions for murder has decreased markedly.

It would be logical to conclude that the next step should be to abolish the death penalty completely. This would be in line not only with Christian conviction, but also with the purpose of civil order, namely, to keep violence to a minimum. Eight states in the United States—Rhode Island, Michigan, Minnesota, North Dakota, Wisconsin, Maine (for forty years or more), Alaska (since 1957), and Delaware (since 1958)—and numerous other nations have done this; England suspended executions in 1958, though the legal provision for it has not been completely abolished. Yet when Christians and others request that this same step be taken elsewhere, numerous arguments are raised against it. Most of them no longer avow social vengeance as a justifiable motive, and thus they argue the retention of capital punishment for reasons different from those that originally caused its institution. Yet these arguments must be faced.

The Death Penalty as a Deterrent

The most serious of the social arguments for the death penalty is the theory of deterrence. It is claimed that if persons who are tempted to commit a crime know what the punishment will be, they will turn away from crime. At first glance, this seems sensible. That it is basically an error can be seen, however, upon closer attention. The major source of error is the assumption that murder is like speeding, in that a normal person, if sure of being caught, will refrain from it out of consideration for the consequences. Murderers are, however, not normal people. Most of them are driven by forces of emotion or outright insanity such that no reasoning, no weighing of consequences takes place as they decide to kill. Numerous psychological studies have made this clear. Some cases are, in fact, on record where unbalanced persons, lacking the strength of will to kill themselves, have committed murder as an indirect means of suicide. A small minority are professional criminals for whom the "hot seat" is simply one of the risks of the game; they are also reasonably sure of avoiding capture, or if captured of avoiding conviction, or if convicted of avoiding execution.

The error of deterrence theory can also be shown statistically. Now that several states have had no death penalty for a number of years, it is possible to compare neighboring states, with similar populations and educational and economic levels, some with and some without capital punishment. Rhode Island (without capital punishment) has a consistently lower murder rate in proportion to the total population than its neighbors, Connecticut and Massachusetts (with); likewise Michigan (without) has a better record than Indiana and Ohio (with); and Wisconsin (without) than Iowa and Minnesota (with). If all the states are compared, the murder rate is from two to three times greater in states that have and enforce the death penalty than in those that do not. This by no means proves that abolishing the death penalty will reduce the crime rate by one half; but it does prove that other considerations—social, economic, educational, racial—have far more to do with deterring or favoring crime than does the kind of punishment the law calls for.

Even though the deterrence argument seems logical and is most often used, it is not actually a true description of the motivation behind present legal practice. For if the purpose of executing murderers was to frighten prospective murderers into better behavior, the executions should be public as they used to be, the means of execution should be as painful as possible, and the certainty that every murderer will be executed should be absolute. Yet the trend is away from this. Executions are made painless and are poorly publicized or even forbidden to the public. Lewis E. Lawes, longtime warden of Sing Sing prison, estimates that only one person out of fifty convicted of murder is actually executed. The argument for deterrence can hardly be reasonably appealed to as a reason for retaining capital punishment, since it is not what determines its application in actual practice; and the effect of such punishment is not deterrence, even if this was its intention.

The Fallibility of Penal Institutions

One of the great values of the democratic conception of government is the control it exercises over the misuse of authority. If a tyrant were perfectly wise and good, then one could argue that tyranny would be the most efficient form of government; but men being what they are, it is better to have constitutions, elections, and checks and balances in order to keep the possibilities of error and of the misuse of authority under control.

In the courts this control is exercised by means of the possibility of appeal to higher courts, with the further possibility of a new trial if new evidence is found. In both of these ways, judicial errors are frequently made right. But there is one kind of judicial error that can never be made right, and that is an erroneous sentence of death. In effect, the death penalty assumes that the courts are infallible and that they have all the evidence. Unless this infallibility and omniscience are assumed, the inflicting of an irrevocable punishment is unjustifiable; yet this assumption is one that is made in no other realm of government or judicial practice. The advocates of the retention of capital punishment have never yet answered Lafayette's challenge: "I shall ask for the abolition of the penalty of death until I have the infallibility of human judgment demonstrated to me."[3]

---

3. [Editor's note: Yoder does not provide the reference but, in "The Case Against the Death Penalty," Hugo Adam Bedau introduces this quote saying, "Speaking to the French Chamber of Deputies in 1830, years after the excesses of the French Revolution, which he had witnessed, the Marquis de Lafayette said, 'I shall ask for the abolition of the punishment of death until I have the infallibility of human judgment demonstrated to me'" (American Civil Liberties Union, 1992, avail-

In practice it is impossible to know just how many innocent persons have been murdered by order of the court because of false testimony, mistaken identification, a biased jury, or misinterpreted circumstantial evidence. By the very nature of the case, it is seldom possible or useful to review judicially such a case once the victim has been executed. Thus, if such an error is to come to light, it must be through the disinterested curiosity of some journalist or lawyer, or through a subsequent confession by the guilty person. Such rehabilitations are therefore rare, and it is impossible to know how many other cases of innocent persons executed remain undetected. Known cases are still frequent enough to fill numerous articles and books, the most recent of which is *Not Guilty* by Jerome and Barbara Frank. Responsible estimates of the proportion of innocent persons among those executed run as high as five percent.

The friends of the death penalty can continue to argue strongly that the danger of such miscarriages of justice is very slight. It may well be true that the actual number of such cases is well under five percent. But the Christian attitude to this question should not be to quibble about whether the proportion is five percent or five-tenths of one percent, as if the desirability of the death penalty were to depend on whether a certain minimum percentage of error was overstepped. How often such unjust executions occur is not the question. That they occur at all, even if only rarely, is proof enough that society, as long as it is fallible, should never lay claim to *absolute* authority over life and never make decisions about men's fates that cannot be reviewed. The courts should do the best they can, without interrupting the normal course of justice out of the fear of making mistakes; but this can be done confidently only if a door is always left open for review and for new evidence. Only the abolition of the death penalty can keep this door open.

---

able online at http://users.rcn.com/mwood/deathpen.html, accessed Jan 1, 2011). Bedau cites as his source for this quote Charles Lucas, *Recueil des Débats des Assemblées Législatives de la France sur la Question de la Peine de Mort* (Paris: 1831) pt. II, 32.]

The fact that capital punishment closes and locks a door that must be kept open has numerous undesirable accessory effects on the administration of justice itself, beyond the obvious fact we have already dwelt on, namely, that errors of justice cannot be corrected. The prosecution of murder cases is much more lengthy and thereby more costly to society in a death penalty state than in an abolition state, because the defense will leave no stone unturned and no legal technicality untried. If the accused is wealthy enough to hire qualified lawyers, there is almost no limit to the possible delaying tactics. One case in California has cost the state over half a million dollars and took over ten years. Trials in abolition states are far shorter and cheaper, to say nothing of the economics involved in not maintaining a special death row in the prisons and in reducing the number of appeals.

Furthermore, it has been seen that under certain circumstances the existence of the death penalty can actually interfere with the execution of justice. Jury members sometimes have acquitted persons known to be guilty simply because they felt the penalty too great for the offense. For centuries British law demanded hanging for forgery, counterfeiting, and stealing two pounds or more. As a result, almost no one was convicted of these crimes, and their repression was made almost impossible. Forgers and petty thieves feared no punishment, since no jury would have the heart to hang them for such a crime. When the penalties were reduced, it again became possible to enforce the law. It is not sure how much these considerations apply to the punishment of murder, where the disproportion between the offense and the punishment is not so great, but in any case, it cannot be argued that the existence of the supreme penalty on the law books increases the chances that juries will judge a case on its merits.

We have noted in passing that the ability of the convicted to delay or even avoid execution depends on his wealth. Warden Lewis E. Lawes says that those who are executed are always poor and friendless.[4] Whoever has either money or friends to

---

4.   [Editor's note: Yoder does not cite his source here, but Lawes makes similar statements in *Man's Judgment of Death*, 9-10.]

assure that their case will be kept in the courts or before the governor has excellent chances of avoiding the electric chair. This is why only one of fifty convicted persons is executed (according to Lawes; others estimate one of one hundred). Not only are the time and the taxpayer's money wasted, which the prosecution spent attempting to convict the other forty-nine persons, the end result is discrimination in favor of the economically and socially powerful. In a similar way, the death penalty is used in the southern states as an instrument of racial discrimination. White men convicted of rape are practically never sentenced to death, whereas African-Americans often are.

The Christian Response

We have examined the Christian reasons for considering capital punishment to be unjustified not only for Christians, but even for the state. We have further seen the inadequacy of the only serious argument in favor of retaining the death penalty and have seen both that this argument is refuted by the facts and that it is not the real reason for the continued existence of the practice for which it argues. What do these facts mean for Christians? What do they mean specifically in the United States where, besides eight states that have abolished the death penalty, there are still forty-four jurisdictions (forty-two states, the Federal Government, and the District of Columbia, to say nothing of military courts) where capital punishment is still in the law? This question becomes even more significant for Christians when the problem comes to a matter of public concern; in 1957 abolition was obtained in Alaska and in 1958 in Delaware. In 1959 a dozen states or more had attempts made, none of them successful. In Ohio the attempted abolition law had the support of the governor; in other states (e.g., Indiana), it had the support of the legislative committee though insufficient support from the public. This means that Christians, especially Christians who at other times and places have testified to their high respect for the sacredness of human life, are letting their silence speak for them, permitting their indifference to testify that as far as they are concerned this matter is one about which the Lord they profess to represent has no opinion.

Is this silent testimony of nonconformity the one we want to give? It is the conviction of this writer that such a testimony is one for which we cannot conscientiously take the responsibility before our Lord. If we confess his lordship over every knee and every tongue, we must believe, and if we believe we must proclaim that the killing of criminals is not God's will even for a sub-Christian society. We must make this testimony real to those who make and who execute the laws, not leaving it to an occasional request for mercy as in the Peters or the Chessman case.

It might be argued that legislation is not needed. Every year there are fewer executions. A number of states have not used for five, ten, or more years the capital punishment provisions they have in their law. Might we not just hope for this trend to continue without making so much of an issue of it? There are good answers to this question. For one thing, as long as the law is on the books, all that is needed is the hysteria of a war or major political crisis or a wave of resentment against some particularly brutal murderer for the dormant law to come back into effect. Furthermore, we are not interested only in the lives that might be saved by abolition. (In 1958, forty-eight were executed; perhaps a similar expenditure of funds and efforts would save more lives if invested in cancer research if our only interest were the saving of a certain number of lives.) As Christians we are also interested in testifying to Christ's lordship as a matter of principle and, therefore, to the insistence that the taking of life is not part of the state's divine mission. If no one were executed (which is still far from being the case, especially in the South, New York, and California), we should still protest against the presence of such laws on the books.

Prison experts add a further reason for formal abolition. They tell us that seriously needed improvement of methods of prison administration and rehabilitation is hampered by the symbolic presence of the death penalty, which distorts the public understanding of and the legislators' concern for problems of prison reform.

There is actually one weighty argument for *not* campaigning intensively to obtain at all costs the abolition of the death penalty. This reason is not that the retention of capital punishment is desirable, but that by concentrating their attack on the one issue of the death penalty, abolitionists are tempted to forget the host of other crying needs in penal institutions. Housing facilities, education of prisoners, methods of psychological therapy, and procedures of parole and rehabilitation all need serious attention from the public and from experts and will not necessarily be helped by changing some death sentences to life imprisonment, which might in fact be for some a suffering worse than death. Only deeper changes in the treatment of offenders can give its full worth to the preservation of their lives. What for the humanist is only the mending of a set of reflexes is for the Christian, who sees the criminal's sickness as a moral and not only a mental one, a part of Christ's total redemptive work.

Some Christians have argued that to speak of the treatment of criminals in terms of therapy and rehabilitation rather than punishment is to deny the moral character of their offense, to excuse their guilt as only an illness. This is not the point. The issue is not whether there is moral guilt. There is. The issue is what the Christian attitude toward the guilty should be. If the preoccupation is more with defending an abstract moral order, and thereby punishing, than with the redemption of persons, this will of course show in one's attitude to open sinners.

The whole penal system needs to be changed; yet it is the retention of the gas chamber, the gallows, and the chair, with their enshrinement of the retributive mentality and of the state's claim to absolute competence that warps our view of all these problems. Many European and even Soviet prisons are ahead of many American prisons in their living conditions and their effectiveness in rehabilitation because of the vengeful conception of the treatment of offenders, of which capital punishment is the extreme expression and which abolition would symbolically undermine.

What should Christians do? First of all, we should become informed. Our convictions on this matter should be as well thought through as those concerning military service. We should contribute to the awakening of public opinion by speaking to our neighbors and writing to newspapers. We should witness to legislators, especially if and when abolition legislation is being considered. We should assure our church leadership, locally and on a state-wide and denomination-wide level, of our support in any approaches they might make through legislative committees, conference resolutions, or other channels of testimony. Underlying all of this effort, justifying it, and enabling it, we should remind ourselves that when we are instructed to "pray for kings and all who are in high places" (1 Tim 2:1-2 RSV), it is concrete things like this that we are to have in mind. "That we may lead a quiet and peaceable life" (v. 2) does not mean that Christians are to be interested primarily in their own tranquility; it means that the purpose of government is to keep all violence within society at a minimum. In our land and in our day, one of the best ways to testify to this divine imperative is to proclaim to the state the inviolability of human life.[5]

---

5. The study of the issue of capital punishment, in the broader context of the Christian witness to the social order, was made possible by a part-time assignment under the Institute of Mennonite Studies of the Associated Mennonite Biblical Seminaries of Elkhart, Indiana. Additional assistance was received through the criticism and comment of J. Lawrence Burkholder, Guy F. Hershberger, Cornelius J. Dyck, Otto Driedger, J. Maynard Hoover, and Maynard Shetler, for which the writer is sincerely grateful.

    [Editor's Note: Yoder recommended the following works for further reading: *Capital Punishment*, a scientific study contained in a special issue of Philadelphia's *Prison Journal* (Oct 1958); Arthur Koestler, *Reflections on Hanging* (New York: Macmillan, 1957); *Murder and the Penalty of Death*, a scientific study in Philadelphia's *Annals of the American Academy of Political and Social Science* (Nov 1952); Giles Playfair and Derrick Sington, *The Offenders: The Case Against Legal Vengeance*; and the San Francisco Friends Committee on Legislation's popular level piece, *This Life We Take* (1965).]

CHAPTER 3

CAPITAL PUNISHMENT AND OUR WITNESS TO GOVERNMENT

The following is a slightly condensed transcript of a discussion that students and faculty of Bethel College had with John Howard Yoder.[1]

With this kind of a group it would be out of place simply to try to reproduce off-the-cuff what I already put in a pamphlet, which you could read if you want to.[2] I would only make two background points. One of them is the fundamental question whether it is the Christian's business to speak at all to the government on anything of which, of course, capital punishment would be one example. The other question is of more narrow biblical nature.

The State in God's Plan

Because of our nonresistance, people have told us, "You can't participate in government," and we said "OK." Basically the position has been that our discipleship was not consistent with major responsibilities at least in the police arm of government. Assuming that that's right, what business is it of ours to speak to the people who are where we can't be about how they do what we can't do?

Assuming that the Christian church can do nothing in this realm as Christians and that all the people who are doing this

---

1. [Editor's note: This prescript was part of the original article published in *The Mennonite* 78, no. 24 (June 1963): 390-94.]
2. Chapter 2 of this volume.

63

are pagans, have we anything to say? Of course, both of those assumptions are questionable. There are Christians in positions of political responsibility, and we are not necessarily now completely out of the realm. But I'm trying to pose the problem in the sharpest form. Assuming that we are a tiny Christian minority in the Roman Empire of AD 60 or in the Soviet Union in 1960, what business have we to speak to a pagan government?

The answer in the New Testament, I think, is quite clearly the proclamation that even though the powers that be don't know it, they have a place in God's plan for the salvation of the world through the church. We know about it. This place is to keep the peace and defend humankind. Nobody will tell them if we don't. Telling them is part of the gospel, because we are proclaiming that God's purpose in this world is to save the world through the church, within the *framework* of the interplay of violences that we call the political order. Christ is Lord not only over the church but also over the world. The Christian proclamation is the proclamation that Christ is Lord. This not only qualifies us but orders us to speak to anyone about divine righteousness and the place of the social order in God's ultimate purposes.

Expiation and Vengeance in the Old Testament

Expiation in Genesis 9:6

The second question [as to whether the Old Testament commands capital punishment] is a much narrower one but similar in a way. The earliest Anabaptist confessional document, the Schleitheim Confession of 1527, says that the sword is ordained of God for the punishment of evildoers "outside of the perfection of Christ." [This suggests that] in the world in general and under the law of the Old Testament, [the sword] is proper.[3] This, we have taken it to mean, authorizes certain kinds of violence in the fallen world (not in the church, of course). It includes at least punishment—

---

3.   [Editor's note: Yoder is quoting here from his translation of *The Schleitheim Confession*, 14.]

eye for eye and tooth for tooth—and perhaps the entire military operation, but *at least* the police function and the punitive function. This has seemed to be supported by the way in which the Old Testament legislation for a whole people of Israel—the Mosaic Laws or even the earlier very brief text in Genesis 9 in the form of God's orders to Noah—seemed to be orders for ethics for the whole world. These provided for some kind of death penalty and so it seemed to be said that we have two levels.

The death penalty is certainly not the way to deal with sinners in church, but it is someone's responsibility thus to deal with offenders in the social order, for the text says, literally, "Whoever sheds the blood of a human, by a human shall that person's blood be shed" (Gen 9:6 NRSV)." And this is the one point at which textual debate—understanding of the meaning of the biblical passage—actually does contribute to the present conversation.

The closer we come to that Genesis passage, which I think is the basis of all [else] the Old Testament [says on this topic], the clearer it becomes that the reason humans should not shed blood, and the reason that if humans shed blood their blood shall be shed is not a moral or a political reason; it is not on the level of defending the social order or on the level of right and wrong, because we know that in primitive cultures the taking of human life doesn't have that kind of moral opprobrium. It's a ritual concern, a "cultic" concern if we use the terminology of the anthropologist.

The blood of a human being is sacral—sacred. It is God's because it's used in the sacrificial rite. It is only God who owns this blood and only he can shed it. If an animal is killed, it can be killed only in a sacrifice. There was no secular slaughtering done among primitive peoples or in early Israel. When an animal was killed, it was first of all a sacrifice and the blood belonged to God, and then some of the meat belonged to the person who brought the beast.

We see this in a number of ways, and the closer we look at the text the more we see it. But it's striking especially in the fact that if a person is gored to death by a bull, then the bull shall be killed. That's not a moral problem, not a political problem; this is a ritual concern. Where blood has flowed, regardless of the reason, the guilty party's blood must flow.

We sometimes think we have simply risen above this kind of ritual sense of what is proper and improper, what is holy and what is profane. Maybe we have. But if we have, it's only because there was something to it. And that valid meaning of ritual has somehow fit into the gospel. The valid meaning of ritual is that humanity does offend against the divine order of things, and something like propitiation or expiation (to use technical terms)—something like setting the moral order right again through sacrifice—is called for. Why? I can't explain it—speaking as a philosopher, historian of religion, anything else that I'm not—but at least it seems to be the presupposition of Old Testament faith that it is the case that when you interfere with the order that God has established by taking a life only God has a right to take, then the order of creation is warped, and to set it right calls for a sacrifice, namely, the sacrifice of the life of the murderer. But murderers are not punished because they have been entitled to punishment. They sacrifice themselves because they are interfering with the divine order of things.

This was also the meaning of the holy wars of the Old Testament. They were not wars; they were sacrifices, they were cultic acts, they were ritual. We shouldn't relate them to the problem of whether or not you should have wars.

Well, what does it mean if I'm saying that the Old Testament has something to say to us? How does that relate to what we now do about the death penalty? The statement of the New Testament is that this entire ritual order of sacrifice and expiation was meaningful, was proper, was revealed, was required by God; but Christ has done away with it. His sacrifice of himself at the cross ends all sacrifice and is the end of all ritual. So if we can rise above ritual, it's because whatever happened in Christ—and this is of course ritual language—has freed us from the older way of dealing with this same problem. We deal with each human as a human, each neighbor as a neighbor in whom God dwells and whom we have to deal with as if Christ were in him.

Vengeance in Mosaic Law

This means the end of dealing with moral offense through expiation or, for that matter, through vengeance. Most of the rest of the death penalty held in the Old Testament was rather vengeance than expiation. When we read that the punishment shall be eye for eye, tooth for tooth, burning for burning, dagger wound for dagger wound—this is not prescribing vengeance nor is it the ritual that we have just been talking about, but it's a limiting of vengeance—for one eye, no more than one eye. If a man steals you don't cut off his hand. The punishment shall be no greater than the crime.

From the very start, the Mosaic Law was limiting vengeance rather than calling for vengeance. The normal extension of this process is that in Christian times, times when the Christian gospel has an effect on a larger society, the vengeance that is capital punishment and the expiation that is capital punishment have come to the end of the recognition we had given them. Therefore, we don't simply say, "The Old Testament is one level and that is still right for government; the New Testament is on another level that is right for us." We say, "The validity of Christ's lordship applies in such a way that the Old Testament rite in its place, in its time, in the process of God's working with humankind, is not the standard now not even for government."

These two questions—the Old Testament demand for vengeance or for expiation, and the general question of whether or not Christian people can speak to the government—are the only general questions we need to look at by way of introduction. But they are really central in a sense, because all of the sociological and criminological arguments are against the death penalty. It has pretty well been demonstrated that it does nothing to decrease the crime rate and it does a lot to interfere with the prosecution of justice. There are long lists of common sense and sociological arguments against the death penalty. So your problem is dealing with the reasons why we have thought in the past that we shouldn't speak on the subject or that God wanted the death penalty.

Q&A

You say that "an eye for an eye and tooth for tooth" was to limit vengeance. Do you think the Jews would have permitted the violation of one of their members without retaliation?

No, that's just my point. Retaliation is built in, not only to human nature but also to primitive societies. In fact, the "institution" that carried this out was the *avenger of blood*—that's the way it's sometimes translated. It's actually the same Hebrew word as "redeemer"—the person who sets the moral order right after somebody is offended. It's the responsibility of the avenger of blood, usually the next of kin or the uncle, when there has been a murder, to go out and murder the other person. That was the normal procedure. But this was subject to abuse because usually to make one murder right it takes two. So the Mosaic Law was really setting a stake here, limiting it to punishment fitting the crime.

Then over the years there were rabbinical developments. For instance, there was more and more concern for being sure that the punishment wasn't too much, and by the time of Jesus most of these penalties were replaced by financial payments for damage, which is a sign of the way in which the prophetic impact upon vengeance is always to limit it; and Jesus just did this to the end. It is a matter of vengeance and not of justice in the sense that the "moral order" calls for another death or another piece of suffering. There is nothing just and nothing moral about that.

Now how was an excess of vengeance handled? Who then administered justice?

Then the other party started. If the correction was greater than the crime then there was more correction, which was still greater—a snowballing of corrections—which is precisely what happens in certain societies. These feuds go on for generations. So then the Mosaic Law came along and said, "No, we're going to have judges and the punishment is going to be no more than the offense." This was a terrible wallop in the face of this normal drive. There is special significance to the story of Cain's descendants, which is the first tableau we have of what sin means. They built the first cities, made the first metal instruments and the like. His line ends with Lamech who boasted about the fact that he always avenged himself sevenfold. This is the epitome of fallen society. In the New Testament, it's precisely this figure, "sevenfold," that comes up in the description of Christian forgiveness. These are the extremes and justice is somewhere in between. There is no pure justice, but there are ways of limiting drives to vengeance and the ritual that motivated the drive to expiation.

If the sociological and empirical evidence is as convincing as you imply, then why is it so hard for us to convince society?
There are two explanations. The one is, in North America, a kind of fundamentalism which misunderstands the Old Testament—and it is especially strong in the West and Middle West—and actually believes that there is some kind of divine imperative for vengeance. On the other hand, there is a deep-down emotional feeling that's just the same as in the time of Lamech. And when there has been this kind of offense, "this guy's just got to get it!" It is an emotional, subrational—not irrational—but just a visceral response to an offense against our security to think that the only thing we can do is get that person out of the way.

There is one further reason that we need to respect, and that is that there is one point at which the death penalty might have a deterrent effect. That is when somebody who is already in prison for life is trying to escape and shoots his guard because he has nothing more to lose by being caught and everything to gain by getting free. And so prison guards and policemen sometimes press for what they think is the protection of the death penalty. At least one state abolished the death penalty *except* for crimes against prison guards and policemen. Now that's understandable. I wouldn't agree, because I don't think evidence proves even there, but at least you understand those people. They have a messy job given them by society, and they feel especially threatened. Anything that reassures them is a help.

I've heard that the justice of God demands that this capital punishment be carried out. Would you say that this doesn't hold because Christ was the final sacrifice?

There are different ways of saying it. We can begin with the history and say "the justice of God" is another word for the ritual need for restoring the order of the universe. But then we also have to believe the New Testament when it says this ritual need has been satisfied. The other more abstractly theological approach would be to say that it is Christ—and no philosophy or legal order—who defines for us the justice of God. What does the Bible say when it talks about the justice of God? It says he "is faithful and just to *forgive.*" Justice isn't a matter of recompense. Human justice is a matter of recompense. But the justice of God is precisely not that. It's a mistranslation, partly. The Greek and Hebrew words that are translated "justice" are more properly translated "righteousness" in the traditional ring that those words have for us. And they don't mean really anything about "eye for eye" or the impartiality or neutrality that we ask of a just person; it's rather faithfulness, reliability. Very close to the word "justice" is "steadfast mercy," another Hebrew term that bears similar meaning.

There wasn't always a need to fulfill this ritual basis of vengeance, was there? It seems to me they also had cities of refuge where the slayer was taken.

Yes, there was this one exception for unintentional killing. There were certain places where a person could be protected from the avenger. But the fact that these certain places were centers of sacrifice where there was a Levite operating again demonstrates that this too was a ritual matter. The men came in under the ritual protection of the altar and the priests in that place. But there is one qualification that needs to be added. There began then to be consideration for whether the killing was intentional.

How much can we expect the government to provide a society to live up to our expectations?

The issue of the death penalty is an excellent example because it is a point at which the connection is quite clear. In other questions, like whether we tell the government that persecuting minorities or enforcing racial segregation is wrong, the connection between what we ask of the state and Christian morality is not always quite as clear.

Traditionally, we've felt that we were imprisoned between two possibilities. We could be puritans—using this word with a small "p" for a type—referring to the traditions of the churches that told the world how to operate. You set up a pattern: this is the way it must be in the city of Geneva and the nation of the Netherlands or the province of Cape Cod, and the government's responsibility is to make the whole society live on a Christian standard. This we're convinced is wrong. Wrong, partly because in order to do it you then have to lower the Christian standard, but wrong also because it gives people a misinterpretation of the foundation of Christian behavior. It gives people the idea that you behave like a Christian because you have to. This gets people "all screwed up" for generations later.

The other alternative is that we work clearly with a dualism— on one level church ethics, discipleship, nonresistance, forgiving; and on the other level world ethics, eye for eye, tooth for tooth, capital punishment, war—and claim that there is no way to speak between the two. Traditionally, Mennonites have thought you must choose one or the other. And since we can't be puritans, then we must pull out of the whole thing.

My conviction is that both of those possibilities are wrong. The New Testament simply says we can speak to the authorities about what it means to be decent, what it means to be human, what it means to be honest, *case by case*. We can never really say what an ideal Kansas government would look like—that's a contradiction in terms, at least in Kansas. It's a contradiction in terms because the only ideal we know is the kingdom of God. We can't have that where men are in rebellion. But what we can do is tell the statesman what he can do better. And here we can speak to him on any issue if we know enough to be able to be sure that what we're saying is on the subject and that it's a live option. If he's hanging all the criminals, we can say "Don't do that!" We can even explain it in his language—not only our language. And if he's poisoning the atmosphere with nuclear tests we can say "Don't do that!"—not because a Christian disciple wouldn't, but because an intelligent statesman would not.

So case by case we speak to a definable offense by suggesting to the statesman the way he could be more just, more intelligent. We are under no obligation to have a total pattern for society that would work according to our convictions. That would be the church. We take into account the fact that the state is one of the expressions of unbelief and violence and hatred. We know that God is using that expression of unbelief and violence and hatred to hold things together. At certain points it could be a little less violent, little less unbelieving, little less hateful.

To what extent do you think the government is the arm of God or God-ordained?

To what extent? I don't think it's a matter of extent. That is, it isn't that we know that God can use certain things the government does and that there are other things he can't use. So whatever government does, God can use it, but that never makes it right. God can use Hitler, God can use Stalin, God can use George Washington, and God can use Assyria. Isaiah 10 is one of the clearest passages on this sense of how God makes meaningful the brutality of pagan nations. But that never means that what they are doing is right. If we come at this thing like puritans, we say we must have a proper pattern, and then you measure any government by whether it lives up to the proper pattern. Romans 13 doesn't do that. It doesn't say that because Caesar is

a relatively good guy or because the Romans at least had a constitution that therefore the powers that be are ordained of God.
No, it just says, "whatever rulers are there, you are to accept
and not rebel against them. You're to believe that somehow God
uses pagan rulers in his purposes." So it's not a statement on how
good or bad the government is. It is on our attitude toward any
government.

*This whole Romans 13 passage is sometimes used to preserve
a separationist attitude—that things are okay the way they are.
Is there some way that this can be a little more constructive?*

Romans 13 explains why it's not the Christian's business
to attempt to set up a counter-government—to rebel against
the state on its own terms and with its own methods. But the
broader proclamation that Christ is Lord gives us not only reasons, not only an excuse, but a mandate to speak to anything
that's wrong with our society, saying that it must be better, saying also, "We as Christian disciples are aiming still higher; but
as a statesman you should at least do this much better."

I think one of the best examples is one that was cited once
for me by a French friend who was trying to work in Algeria.
The French police could stop anybody on the street without any
restrictions, without any kind of a warrant, and subject them
to all kinds of physical mistreatment in order to get secrets out
of them about what the rebels were doing. Most of the people
probably did know something, but this is not due process of
law and is extremely inhumane and illegal according to any
courts, including the French. Now he didn't say to the policeman, "How can you do that and be a disciple of Jesus?" The
policeman wasn't interested in being a disciple of Jesus. But he
said, "How can you do that in the name of liberty, equality,
and fraternity?"—which was on the policeman's letterhead, of
course, as an agent of the French state.

Now this doesn't mean that liberty, equality, and fraternity
are discipleship. They don't even exist; they're mythology. But
it means that we speak to the authorities in terms of the ideals

to which they commit themselves. We say, "At least live up to that. At least be a human. At least be decent." We don't tell them that if they decide to be a human and be decent that we'll be satisfied. No, we still wish they'd be a disciple. And if they get as decent as we ask them to be now, we'll find new places where we'll ask them to be still more decent. There is no level of decency with which we would be satisfied in the pagan world. We are always asking for more. And really we're never asking for decency, but we're asking for discipleship, which is way up there somewhere on the scale of degrees of unselfishness. And yet we have a mandate at every level to tell people that the only way they can move and be human, be moral—is up.

We can look at our own government and say we have certain qualities here that we want to preserve and we can see places where it is not very good, but in communism it is hard to see any good in that. How can we look at this as an arm of God?

Paul's willingness to accept the Roman government had nothing to do with his looking at it and finding some things he could like. It was a government that had crucified Christ and was probably going to crucify him. The very next year after he wrote, they made living torches out of the Christians in Rome. It has nothing to do with our approval of the thing. It's just the way it is and God's using it. God doesn't want us to spend our time getting that dictator out.

Obviously, we have some preferences; although it's only in North America that the difference between communism and what we have looks this important. The common folk in Brazil would rather have Khrushchev, from what they know about Kennedy. Maybe that's because they don't know the right things about Kennedy. In any case, the difference is not as black and white to most people as it seems to be to us. But even if it were, the responsibility of Christians in the Soviet Union is to pray for their government and be subject to it and do the best they can. And our responsibility to Christians in Soviet Russia is to encourage them to do that and not try to make fifth columnists out of them.

Would you say then that our Mennonite ancestors were wrong when they left Russia and other countries because of the condition of the state?

What I think is clearly wrong is rebellion against the state. I don't think emigration is the same issue. It's still an issue but, of course, some stayed as well. If you say they were running away from military service in Russia in 1870, then that might sound irresponsible. If you say they were going to evangelize the American plains, then that sounds good. But if they had risen up and said, "We're going to resist this thing," I wouldn't have seen the grounds for that. And certainly there are some places where the Christian's duty is to stay. I think the Christian's duty in East Germany now is not to emigrate. And those who do are falling down on their responsibility. Not only that, but they are getting the gospel mixed up with Western military power.

CHAPTER 4

AGAINST THE DEATH PENALTY: A DEBATE WITH WAYNE HOUSE[1]

PREFACE: THE SHAPE OF MY TASK AND THE SHAPE OF MY PRESENTATION

I was first personally introduced to the theme of capital punishment more than thirty years ago, as part of a larger research assignment from the then newly created Institute of Mennonite Studies in Elkhart, Indiana. This was only a fraction of a study of the warrants and criteria that would tell Christians why we should care and what we should think about the doings of the state. Since then it has not been my privilege to be vocationally involved in ministries or witness related to "corrections," nor in the social sciences that study these matters, but my conviction as to the importance of the matter has not diminished.

I respond therefore with gratitude to the occasion, provided by the invitation of Word Publishing and of series editor Vernon Grounds, to return to a subject that in thirty years has lost none of its urgency. I must alert the reader that in the space available I cannot undertake the encyclopedic review, which might be needed, of what has changed in law and criminology

---

1. [Editor's note: This "debate" should not be confused with the vituperative back and forth dialogue one might find in a town hall meeting. These authors were invited to set forth their position on this topic—House *for* the death penalty and Yoder *against* it—and then respond once to the other. In the present volume, we have only included the nine brief chapters of Yoder's position. None of House's material is presented, nor is Yoder's critique of House's specific position.]

since I first wrote *The Christian and Capital Punishment*.[2] Laws have changed and changed back again, as have the arguments for them. Social science studies have become more complex in ways I can do no more than cite.

One thing that the years of watching this debate have taught me is that there is no one right place to begin. There is no "scratch" where we might start. The argument is in full swing, with claims of different kinds flowing past each other often without meeting. People who think their view is nothing but "biblical" make unavowed assumptions about facts that the social sciences would need to test. Other people who think their view is purely "scientific" or humanistic make unavowed philosophical or religious assumptions about what is "true" or "good."

It would therefore be a mistake to begin this work of Christian witness, as one might begin a textbook, with the attempt to go back to a nonpartisan beginning and neutral definition of terms. I must rather accept the fact that the debate is already under way and must myself enter it in the form it has already taken, in midstream.

These pages can, therefore, not simply state one "side" of a simple pro/con debate. They must take account of how the other side of the argument has been promoted, sometimes deceptively, though often sincerely. In so doing, I am of course an advocate. I was asked to be that; the book is laid out as a dialogue, guided by the recognition of the very conflictual shape of the conflict of which I have been writing. Yet this bipolar structure may mislead the reader in several ways:

1. There are more than two positions. There are many not specifically Christian arguments against capital punishment, which I shall underplay not because (especially in our secular democratic context) they are not valuable, but because their theological foundation is not clear. There are refined "yes, but . . ." or "no, but . . ." positions all along the scale between the

---

2.   [Editor's note: Yoder refers here to his 1961 pamphlet that has been published as chapter 2 of this volume.]

poles; by no means do only extreme stances have integrity. So the bipolar "debate" format may partly mislead. Those who wish the death penalty retained in the law do not all want it to apply to all possible capital crimes or to all perpetrators of such crimes.

2. Although I am an advocate, much that I shall report is not the product of bias. Much of the time I shall be having to refer to the literature, to report the "lay of the land," to review the history of the debate, and to survey the views of others in a relatively objective reportorial mode. I shall be providing background that is not all part of my own argument.

3. Some of the time I shall be selecting for special attention a few specific points, especially in biblical interpretation, to which tradition has given a wrong interpretation. At such points I shall be debating not in the first instance with Professor House, but with the broad stream of our culture's tradition and its multiple ways of arguing.[3] More than once I shall seek to clarify the course of the conversation by listing the varieties of different meanings that a given word can have, while often its users are unaware of the problems of semantics. Debate has come down to us in legal and institutional terms. Capital punishment is something that governments do, although that was not always the case in history or in the Bible. Our debate must therefore have a legal edge to it. But it should not be only or primarily legal. Christian revulsion at the notion of legal killing is rooted in spiritual experience and in grateful response to the love of God before it takes shape in critiquing the civil laws. It would be out of order to discuss society's dealing with the offender without asking first how (and why!) God has dealt with our offenses. A Wanda Rempel or a Marietta Yeager, driven by Christian compassion to forgive the murderer of her child

---

3. Of the numerous contributions to the debate in scholarly biblical terms, that of Lloyd R. Bailey (*Capital Punishment: What that Bible Says*) is the strongest recent scholarly case for retention of the penalty of death. When I can allude to it, I shall dispense with other older references.

and then to reject the death penalty as an institution, incarnates the order of insight and involvement that befits the gospel. It is, therefore, with apologies and under some protest that in much of what I shall be writing I shall be meeting the retentionist argument on the legal level.

There is a widely accepted picture of the shape of the debate that is, if anything, still more misleading than the notion of being able to begin from scratch. This picture is widely held and, therefore, I must openly identify it and set it aside. It is that support for the death penalty is directly correlated with respecting the Bible or with historic Christianity, and that support for abolition is therefore a part of unbelief, of disrespect for tradition, or of "humanism" or "liberalism." Obviously, there are some people on both "sides" of that stereotyped dualism; but it does not fairly describe the history of the question nor the position advocated here.

This study does not survey with any fullness the "human" and social science considerations that count against the death penalty. This is not because I consider them invalid; in a pluralistic society such arguments must be respected. Arguments based on the nature of things or on documented experience cannot ultimately be contrary to arguments derived from revelation. Nonetheless, I underplay them here. I do this because they are already adequately represented in the literature, because some of those who *believe* their advocacy of the death penalty to be "biblical" are not open to such general humane arguments, *and* because I mean to accentuate the specifically Christian foundation of my most fundamental witness.

It must follow that with no apology I must attend to some matters of detail concerning the language of the Bible and the right way to read ancient texts that are generally not looked at so closely in the popular literature. I shall seek to do this in an understandable way, but without disrespect for the expertise of those who study such matters in detail.[4]

---

4.   [Editor's note: At this point in the original piece, Yoder thanks without naming names those who assisted the publication of his earlier writings on capital punishment, which are also included in

PART 1: WHERE DOES THE DEBATE STAND?

I have already pointed out that there is no one proper place at which to begin the treatment of a topic like the social institution of capital punishment. This is not a topic into which one can enter "from scratch," by defining the terms as if they were not already laden with prejudice and adducing arguments as if all minds were objectively open.

By saying we cannot begin at some neutral beginning I do not mean merely to draw attention to the obvious fact that in any realm involving laws and institutions there is a long history and a large literature. That is certainly also true for the subject of this study. The debate has been going on for centuries. No attempt can be made to survey the vast debate; the texts of McCafferty, Bedau, and van den Haag all do that quite well.[5]

---

this volume, and then explains his continued use of predominantly masculine pronouns. We have not included the latter explanation in the main text of this volume because we have brought all of Yoder's essays into conformity with the sort of gender-inclusive language that he began using with increased frequency later in his life. The original text reads as follows: "Moral thinkers are not exempt from the change in language usage brought about by growing awareness of the sexism built into our language. As far as possible I shall attempt here to decrease the gender tilt of ordinary usage: yet the clumsiness of always needing to say 'his or her,' or resorting to the ungrammatical singular 'they,' has not always seemed necessary. Neither for the offenders nor for those who take their lives does reality demand that we routinely say 'he or she.' After all, this is not a realm where gender-free approaches are pertinent. Executioners are men, almost all of those they execute are men, and the power structure they perpetuate is macho. A feminist critique of the entire correctional enterprise would have enriched our study considerably, but would also have expanded it beyond the scope of the stated project and the competence of the authors."]

5. Hugo A. Bedau, ed. *The Death Penalty in America*, 3d ed., and *Death Is Different: Studies in the Morality, Law, and Politics of Capital Punishment*; James M. McCafferty, ed., *Capital Punishment* (New York: Aldine, 1972; Lieber-Atherton, 1973); and Ernest van den Haag and John P. Conrad, *The Death Penalty: A Debate*.

Any serious reader should not be satisfied with what this book can say. It deals with civil law, with cultural history, and with the diverse legal traditions of different nations or even of various states within the United States.

More is meant than that, when I refer to the impossibility of finding a place for the conversation to start. Our subject is by its nature almost sure to mislead. When a society is organized in such a way that certain people are killed—with a good conscience, in the name of the society—that state of things creates a very special kind of institution. By the nature of the case, such an institution does not operate according to ordinary rules. Even if we try to imagine a very simple society, or if anthropologists or archaeologists should be able to dig one up, what it means for the social organism to make standard institutional arrangements to destroy certain of its members is an extremely complex and basic matter, quite difficult to come to grips with.

Stated Rationale Versus Real Reasons

It is not clear on the surface of things what the reasons are for the process of killing offenders. Why people *say* they do things—especially when the things they do are exceptional activities, such as killing some people—is not necessarily the real reason they do it. As we shall see later, the anthropological philosopher René Girard claims to have discovered that there is, in fact, a special set of forces at work, which leads society to hide from itself the real causes for the bloodshed on which people believe the survival of their culture depends. A society deceives itself—through its bards and playwrights, priests and sages—about the primeval vengefulness lying at the base of social order. Girard may be challenged in his reading of the history, but he is certainly right that we give ourselves deceptive and contradictory explanations for why social killing goes on. We properly need to begin with a broad overview of those reasons, religious and otherwise.

There will always be, in anyone's reading of what they think is said by a text of the Bible, a set of presuppositions of which even the people who hold them are not critically aware.

Some of these presuppositions are what we call "common sense": they are the unexamined "glasses" through which we experience our life and read a text. Some of the persons most sincerely convinced that they are listening only to the Bible may be the most naïvely self-deceived about the cultural spectacles they wear. This may happen on both sides of any issue, and it does happen on both sides of this one.

Some would speak of these unquestioned assumptions as "myths" needing to be debunked. But sometimes a "myth" is a figurative way of saying something true, whereas here we are dealing with wrong readings as to matters of fact or debatable readings as to logic.

One set of these presuppositions are amateur ideas about matters of fact which the social sciences can test. The simplest example of this is the widespread assumption that punishments prevent crime and that more stringent punishments prevent crime more effectively. Arthur Koestler reports how in England in 1800 a ten-year-old boy was hanged for stealing mail. The judge justified it on the grounds of "the infinite danger of its going abroad into the world that a child might commit such a crime with impunity."[6]

That judge was taking for granted as self-evident fact that the penalty of death deters: it keeps others from doing the same thing out of fear of the same punishment.[7] People first assume

---

6. Arthur Koestler, *Reflections on Hanging*, 14. Lord Ellenborough, Chief Justice of England, spoke against the death penalty for shoplifting in the House of Lords in 1810, saying, "Repeal this law and I am certain depredations to an unlimited extent would immediately be committed. Repeal this law, and see the contrast—no man can trust himself for an hour out of doors without the most alarming apprehensions that, on his return, every vestige of his property will be swept off by the hardened robber." Cited in Byron E. Eshelman, *Death Row Chaplain*, 31.

7. To deter is literally to "frighten off," to prevent by fear. The word is used in this proper sense in the following pages. It is the effect that capital punishment is supposed to have on other actors. There are those, however, for whom "deter" means simply "prevent."

that *they* interpret the Bible to be saying the same thing. Before we move on to test that idea in other ways, we must begin by clearing away the most basic misunderstandings.

If we want correctly to understand an ancient text, we need to surface its unstated assumptions and test them. We should be even more critical of our modern "glasses" if the text we are reading is our "Scripture"; i.e., if its account has authority for us. Our culture is far from that of the ancient near east. If we do not understand the distance, our very effort to take the text "straight" can lead to misunderstanding. What killing a killer is supposed to achieve, according to the thought of the ancient culture underlying some text of Genesis or Deuteronomy, is not the same as what that English judge quoted above was assuming about the way violence works.[8]

We cannot fairly let the text of the Bible speak for itself without looking at the screen that our modern or medieval presuppositions have put in its way. This "looking at the screen" or "clearing the thicket" will have several parts. We may properly begin with the issue, as I propose to do here, on the level of the uncritical "taken for grantedness" of the idea that future crimes are prevented by punishing those accused of previous ones. Such "deterrence" is the root reason in the minds of most of those who think the matter already settled. If we look closer, we find that the error of that assumption has several dimensions:

1. *Deterrence was not the basis for the blood-for-blood demand of primitive cultures.* We may argue about whether what those cultures called for was vengeance or expiation or something else. With René Girard we might call it "mimetic desire." When we come to look closer at a few Old Testament texts, we shall come to grips with the specific difference between "ritual" and "law." Numerous angles of approach may be helpful; we

---

Obviously, if a guilty person is killed, *that* person will not kill again. But the word for that should be "prevention."

8.   Lloyd R. Bailey, *Capital Punishment*, 31 and 52, argues, I think rightly, that deterrence was not the motivation for the Mosaic jurisprudence.

need not choose only one. But what does not fit the ancient facts, or the ancient texts, is the kind of modern, pragmatic rationalism that claims that if we threaten people with death for committing X, people will be reasonable and will not commit X.

What was really going on culturally in the ancient origins of the death penalty was something markedly different. What was decisive then was the notion that to kill a killer restored some kind of cosmic moral order. If we today believe in that kind of cosmic order, we may have a logical right to appeal to the ancient examples. In that connection, we shall give close attention to the question of how to read the books of Moses. But one thing ancient worldviews cannot sustain is the theory of deterrence.

2. Deterrence does not work. Even when the threat was irrationally disproportionate, as in the bloodthirsty England of which Arthur Koestler wrote, the threat did not deter. When in England around 1800 petty thefts were sanctioned by hanging, there was no lack of people who continued to commit petty thefts and to be hanged for it. Many representative humans, like ourselves—including petty thieves in England in 1800 and cocaine dealers in the USA in 1991—do not order their lives by rationally maximizing predictable cost-benefit trade-offs in such a way that laws, which increase the pain threatened to those who commit harmful actions, will prevent those actions from happening. Most of our decisions—especially wrongdoing—are not guided by computer-like calculations of cost and benefit.[9]

Even less does deterrence "work" in the case of modern capital crimes. Murder is not a normal, rational, goal-oriented, cost-effective human behavior, even if stealing money or selling drugs might be. Many persons who kill are driven by forces of emotion or outright insanity such that no reasoning process, no calculation of the price to pay, takes place when they decide to kill. Some cases are, in fact, on record where unbalanced

---

9.   "After all these years on Death Row, I have come to believe that the only persons the death penalty deters are those who would not be likely to kill anyway," Eshelman, *Death Row Chaplain*, 220.

persons, lacking the strength of will to kill themselves, have committed murder *because of the death penalty* as an indirect means of suicide.[10]

The other major category of killers are persons at home in the world of crime, for whom the risk of punishment is one of the hazards that add spice to the game. In our society they stand a good chance of not being caught, and if caught, of not being convicted, and if convicted, of not being executed.

Thus far, we have been looking in a common-sense way at whether deterrence "works." Another way to test the theory is statistics. Sociologist Thorsten Sellin pioneered this kind of study, comparing the records of states with similar populations, with and without the death penalty. Rhode Island (without) then had a lower crime rate than Connecticut and Massachusetts (with), Wisconsin (without) lower than Iowa and Minnesota (with). If all the states are compared, the murder rate is over twice as great in states that have (and regularly enforce) the death penalty than in those that do not.[11]

---

10. "[Robert] decided he did not want to live, but knew he did not have the courage to kill himself. The thought came to him, after reading about an execution, that if he killed someone else, the state would take his life in return. This particular side effect of the death penalty . . . is revealed in every careful study. . . . Consciously, but more often subconsciously, the mentally adrift use the state as an instrument for suicide," Eshelman, 127. "I began to trace their criminal deeds as symptoms that began to take form in childhood. . . . Did they have the chance to lead normal lives? Only if it is assumed that such criminals have complete free will to counteract their early conditioning and emotional stunting can a rational case be put forward for vindictive punishment and the death penalty. If this cannot be assumed, then the foundation crumbles under every argument in favor of capital punishment," Eshelman, 62.

11. Sellin's state-by-state comparison studies were done in the 1950s and updated in 1980. The evidence keeps changing, as the laws and practices of state courts change (some states have capital punishment laws on the books but execute no one). Likewise, the tools of statistical analysis get much more complex (cf. the fuller statistical work of Klein, et al., in Hugo A. Bedau, ed., *The Death Penalty in*

This by no means proves that to abolish the death penalty would of itself reduce the crime rate. It does mean, though, that other considerations—cultural, social, economic, racial—have more to do with determining how much crime will occur than does the presence of a death penalty on the law books. The same cultural values that make life cheap in the eyes of the courts make it cheap in the eyes of the killers.

The punishments thought to be deterrent may, in fact, have the opposite effect. There is statistical evidence that the wide attention given to executions by the public media may incite others to violence or even killing. The potential killer may see himself as represented in the public drama not by the offender who is destroyed but by the authorities whose violence is acted out with approval.[12]

3. *Deterrence, if it did work, would be immoral.* The fundamental moral axiom of Western civilization, as stated in nonsectarian language, is that I should deal with each person—her or

---

America, 3d ed. The strongest argument on one side is the claim of Isaac Ehrlich, "The Deterrent Effect of Capital Punishment: A Question of Life and Death," 397-417, according to whose complex argument every time a killer is killed several lives are saved. It provoked responses in the *Yale Law Journal* 85 (1975-76), 164-227 and 359-69, as well as Hugo A. Bedau and Chester M. Pierce, eds., *Capital Punishment in the United States*, 372-95. Despite the extended attention the deterrent argument is given on both sides, it is a distraction from the profound levels of the debate. A person who believes on profound religious or philosophical grounds that the death penalty is immoral would not admit that the possibility of deterring other killings would suffice to justify it. A person who believes on religious or philosophical grounds that every killer must in turn be killed will not be dissuaded by evidence to the effect that it does not deter. On both sides of the debate, the theme of deterrence is a second-order or ancillary argument.

12. Cf. William J. Bowers, "The Effect of Executions Is Brutalization, Not Deterrence," in *Challenging Capital Punishment: Legal and Social Science Approaches*, Sage Criminal Justice System Annuals, eds. Kenneth C. Haas and James A. Inciardi, no. 24 (Beverly Hills, Calif.: Sage Publications, 1988), 49-89.

his rights, values, needs—as an end in herself or himself, not as a means to some other end. To inflict pain or death on one person *for the sake of* the interests of other persons, interests, which it is claimed that that threat will protect, is to sin against that basic rule. Even more, of course, is this the case when the penalty is disproportionate, as when petty thieving, even by children, is punishable by death.

> [I]t is a grave moral wrong to treat one person in a way justified solely by the needs of others. To inflict harm on one person in order to serve the purposes of others is to use that person in an immoral and inhumane way, treating him or her not as a person with rights and responsibilities but as a means to other ends. The most serious flaw in the deterrence argument, therefore, is that it is the wrong *kind* of argument.[13]

Immanuel Kant stated this rule most abstractly in the language of Enlightenment philosophy. As cited above, he stated that a person must be treated as an end and not as a means. Yet, it is not a merely "philosophical" rule. Its substance is a paraphrase of the biblical doctrine of the divine image. It *may* be arguable—although hardly in all cases—that in terms of secular social contract philosophy, a killer can be claimed to have forfeited his right to have his life protected, but in the biblical vision that right is inalienable. The offender cannot give it away because it is not his to give; it belongs to God.

Though perhaps sincerely appealed to by the unthinking, the deterrence rationale is thus not really the reason for present practice. If the purpose of killing killers is to frighten others, the executions should be public, as they used to be, and the means of execution should be as painful and disgusting as possible. Yet, the trend is away from this. Executions in the U.S. are not public. There is general embarrassment when, due to

---

13.   David Hoekema, "Capital Punishment: The Question of Justification," 339.

clumsy administration of gas or electrocution, the victim is cruelly tortured before dying.

Likewise, if the deterrent theory were to "work," the certainty that every killer will be killed would have to be nearly absolute. Yet, in fact, most killers are not killed; not even most persons convicted of capital offenses are in fact executed.

We thus have to conclude that the language of deterrence is being used by our society, when it is under attack from a moral perspective, to justify action that, in fact, is caused by a different motivation: namely, vengeance or expiation. This is not a conclusion; it is a restatement of our starting point. We need to pursue our study further in order to understand the deep cultural drivers behind retribution as an established social institution.

PART 2: NOAH'S COVENANT AND THE PURPOSE OF PUNISHMENT

The case for the death penalty as an institution in modern societies has several quite different roots. Different advocates appeal to quite different reasons in its favor. We have already noted in our beginning pages the need to look at them one by one, each in its own terms. The first reason, as most people read it, is the notion of prevention by threat, or "deterrence," which we have already looked at and seen to be deceptive.

The first religiously based argument, on the other hand, for most Christians, comes from the story of Noah. As we range around the argument, seeking the most solid ground, this is one obviously right place to begin. It appears literally to be a direct divine command:

> Whoever sheds the blood of Man
> In Man shall his blood be shed
> For in the image of God
> He made Man (Gen 9:6).[14]

Does This Text Prove What It Has Been Assumed To?

The first task of the biblical interpreter, as I already said, is not to read a text as if "from scratch" or as if its meanings were self-evident to every well-intentioned reader, but rather to protect the text from misuse, even to "liberate" its original meaning from the deposit of interpretations that have already been

---

14. The noun translated "Man" (Hebrew *adam*) here is generic; it means humankind. The Hebrew reader's mind is thrown back to the beginning of Genesis 2, where *adam* meant the human race, without gender division or individuation. That creation narrative was the only place where God's "image" had previously been referred to. [Editor's note: This scriptural quotation does not match any of the most common translations, so Yoder is either supplying his own translation or citing this passage from memory. Whenever Yoder does this below, we simply omit any reference to a known translation.]

laid over it by centuries of readers. To say this is not to suggest that earlier readers were dishonest or insincere. It is merely to take seriously the fact that they were prisoners of their cultures, as we are of ours, even as the text we are seeking to read was the product of its own culture.

We need to make a self-conscious effort to understand the focus of the worldview implicit in the culture from which any ancient text comes to us. Some tend to read a text like this as if it were legislation, providing, prehistorically, at no particular time but with validity for all times, that there should be a particular institution, equivalent to what we call the state, the basis for civil law, to protect threatened social values.

God's covenant with Noah was not that. We need to step back from such modernizing assumptions if we are to have any hope of understanding how the sanctity of life was really understood in the ancient Israelite setting where these words were first recited.

"Recited" is the right description of how this ancient text was originally used. This rhythmic quatrain (further rhythmic in that in Hebrew the words "blood" and "man" rhyme) is not part of a code of laws, though such codes did exist at that time in the ancient near east. It was formulated as oral lore, recited by sages and priests, repeated by the old, and remembered by the young. It is part of the deep symmetry of things, fitting in with the seasonal, rhythmic reliability of nature:

> As long as earth lasts,
> sowing and reaping,
> cold and heat,
> summer and winter,
> day and night
> shall cease no more (Gen 8:22 JB).

This is not legislation for a government to apply. It is wisdom, a prediction, a description, of how things are, in fact, in primitive and ancient societies. The nature of things did not come to be this way only because God said these words, as if without the words, or before God spoke them, matters would have been different. That is true of some kinds of human laws, nonexistent before, which come into being only when voted by a legislature or promulgated by a king or other authority.

We also err when we tend to read this text as if the defense of life through the threat to life were a new arrangement, established only after the flood. It hardly can be taken that way as the text of Genesis now stands.[15] Things were already that way before the covenant with Noah; in fact, that was the way it was as soon as the first murder was reported. That arrangement is already presupposed in the account of Cain, in Genesis 4. There the first murderer, called to account for the life of the brother he had killed, said,

> My punishment is greater than I can bear;
> behold: you drive me from this ground.[16]
> I must hide from you and be a fugitive and wanderer
>   over the earth.
> Whoever comes across me will kill me (Gen 4:13-14
>   JB, slightly adapted).

What Cain feared was, as it were, a defensive reflex of society as a whole, of "everyone who sees me." There is no account of there having been a previous divine command demanding blood for blood. The response of Yahweh to the jeopardy under which Cain saw himself was to intervene, to protect his life by

---

15. Expert Scripture scholarship has projected diverse hypotheses as to the original dates and original authorship of the several strands of the Mosaic literature. That speculation would call into question some simple arguments based on the assumption that a text like that of Genesis was originally a literary unity. There is, however, no serious scholarly claim according to which Genesis 9 would be older than Genesis 4.

16. The ground is personified: "The voice of your brother's blood cries to me from the ground" (Gen 4:10 RSV). The metaphor of "blood" for life is the same as in chapter 9. Yet the "cry" of the blood is not to be satisfied. God intervenes to save the murderer.

a "mark,"[17] and to announce the threat of retaliation. Thus, the first intervention of God in Genesis, counter to the ordinary reading, is not to demand that murder be sanctioned by sacrificial killing, but to protect the life of the first murderer. Far from demanding the death penalty for murder, Yahweh saved Cain from it. That is the first and the most characteristic action of the God of the Bible with regard to our subject.[18]

Yet, the pattern of violence continued and escalated out of all proportion. Cain's descendant Lamech boasted,

> I have slain a man for wounding me,
> a young man for striking me.
> If Cain is avenged sevenfold,[19]
> truly Lamech seventy-seven-fold! (Gen 4:23-24 RSV)

---

17. Patristic symbolic theology speculated that the "sign" given to Cain to protect him was *tau* or the cross. Biblical scholars hypothesize that it may have been the trace of a tattoo worn by metalworkers; in the ancient world smelting was thought of as a secret stolen from the gods of the underworld (Lloyd R. Bailey, *Capital Punishment: What that Bible Says*, 40).

18. JHWH (usually pronounced "Yahweh") is the proper name of God. It is rendered "Lord" in the Authorized Version and in Jewish piety serves as a reverent substitution. Jehovah and Yahweh are hypothetical reconstructions of the name. Bailey suggests that Yahweh made a mistake and that if vengeance against Cain had been permitted, then "violence in the earth" would not have escalated so as to necessitate the Deluge (*Capital Punishment*, 39 and 107). This would take more argument than either Bailey or Genesis provides. Genesis 6:6 says what God regretted was having created mankind, not having protected Cain. Bailey also makes much of the claim that narrative texts should not be taken as bearing moral instruction (40, 70). This is an assertion without an argument. Of course each genre of literature should be read in its own terms. Bailey would have done well to distinguish more than he does between Genesis 9 and the Mosaic civil code, or between "moral" and "civil" texts. But narrative can be the vehicle of moral instruction, especially in settings called *etiological*, i.e., texts that deal with why and how things came to be, or in texts exhibiting God's or Jesus' character.

19. Lamech's reference to Cain should not mislead us to think that he was escalating what had been said before by Yahweh. (a) The

This is the normal pattern: fallen humanity responds to evil with *escalating* vengeance. Primitive peoples show the same pattern as Lamech, from the intertribal wars of Borneo through the bloody gang justice of the Sicilian hills and the American underworld, to the proverbial "feudin' hillbillies" of the Appalachians. Each *particular* act of vengeance is thought of as "setting things right" or as "defending the peace," but, in fact, the spiral escalation of vengeance and counter-vengeance raises the toll of suffering brought about by any one offense, far beyond any proportion to the original damage done.

Having opened our minds to the awareness that the reason for primitive revenge was not the same as our modern arguments, we can and should move on to note what is different about the agents of the action.

The ancient quatrain does not say who the "man" is who shall shed the killer's blood. Certainly, it was not a constitutional government by means of a trial by judge or jury. Historians tell us that it was the next of kin, called "the avenger" (*goel*, the same Hebrew word as "redeemer"), who executed family-based vengeance. The mechanism of retaliation, once unleashed, had to run its course. Later laws spell this out. If a corpse was found with no way to know whom to punish, very special ceremonies were needed on the part of the elders of the nearest town to "cover" them against the blood-vengeance that was due (Deut 21:1-8). A person who killed accidentally could be protected only by taking refuge in one of six designated "cities of refuge" and staying there for the entire life of the high priest (Num 35:11-28, cf. Deut 4:41-42; 19:1-19). No ransom was possible for blood guilt, even when the death was accidental (Num 35:32-33). Nor was bloodshed the only occasion for such sanctions. Death was the penalty as well for dozens of other offenses.[20]

---

vengeance threatened in Genesis 4:15 was to be inflicted by Yahweh, but Lamech avenged himself; (b) the threat of 4:15 was successful in deterring harm to Cain, and was not carried out.

20.   [Editor's note: Yoder lists 26 such offenses after his footnotes in

There are others who read the Noah story as if it belonged in Exodus or Leviticus as part of a body of rules set out to govern the particular nation of Israel, to be established much later in the land of Canaan, in the light of the sovereignty of Yahweh, in whose name Moses was to make of his mixed multitude a nation (Exod 12:38). It was not that. When that civil legislation did arise later, it too was to have provision for the death penalty, as we shall see, but not for the same reasons and for many other kinds of offenses.

The context of Genesis 9 is that of ritual sacrifice. The

---

his response to House (*The Death Penalty Debate*, 206-207). That note is reproduced verbatim here for convenience's sake:

1. Anyone but the priests touching tabernacle furniture (Num 1:51; 3:10, 38; 4:15; 18:7)
2. Priests drunk on duty (Lev 10:8-11)
3. Blaspheming the holy name (Lev 24:16)
4. Sabbath breaking (Exod 31:14; 35:2)
5. False prophecy (Deut 13:1-11; 18:20)
6. Idolatry (Exod 20:1-6; 22:20; Deut 13:1-19; 17:2-7)
7. Sorcery (Exod 22:18; Lev 20:6, 27)
8. Cursing one's father or mother (Exod 21:17; Lev 20:9)
9. Striking one's father or mother (Exod 21:15)
10. An incorrigible son (Deut 21:18-21)
11. Murder (Exod 21:12; Lev 24:17; Num 35:16-34)
12. Kidnapping (Exod 21:16; Deut 24:7)
13. False witness in a capital case (Deut 19:16-21)
14. Adultery (Lev 20:10; Deut 22:22-24)
15. Incest (Lev 20:11, 17-21). There is no word for "incest"—the rules simply list ten different forbidden relationships.
16. Sex of man with man (Lev 20:13)
17. Sex during menstruation (Lev 20:18)
18. Sex with an animal (Exod 22:19; Lev 20:15-16)
19. Prostitution by a priest's daughter (Lev 21:9; Deut 22:13-21)
20. Rape (Deut 22:25)
21. Contemptuous disobedience to a court (Deut 17:8-13)
22. Keeping a dangerous ox (Exod 21:29)
23. Negligence leading to a loss of life (Exod 21:28-36; Deut 22:8)
24. Failing to bring to trial both parties caught in the act of adultery. House (p. 64) claims this was a capital offense, but the texts he cites do not support it. [list continues on p 96.]

anthropologist will call it "cultic" or "sacred." These four rhyming lines about human killing do not stand alone. In the same breath, the text had just been describing animal sacrifice. As contrasted with the vegetarian arrangement implied before the deluge, animal flesh may now be eaten, but only subject to a ceremonial sense of the holiness of animate life as such, which is represented by the blood:

> Every living and crawling thing shall provide food for you
>   no less than the foliage of plants
> I give you everything, with the exception
>   that you must not eat flesh with the life
>   —that is, the blood—in it
> I will demand an account of your life blood
> I will demand an account from every beast and from man
> I will demand an account of every man's life
>   from his fellow man
> he who sheds man's blood (Gen 9:3-5 JB, slightly adapted).

The setting of our text is thus the account, after the flood, of God's authorizing the killing of animals for human consumption. In the context, it is evident that the subject of the passage is sacrifice. The sacredness of human life is described in the same breath with God's exclusive claim on the blood of the sacrificially slaughtered beasts, and as an extension of the same. To kill animals for food is not like picking fruit from a tree, pulling turnips from a garden, or cutting wheat in a field. It is an interference with the dynamics of animate life, represented by the flow

---

25. Sacrificing one's child to Molech (Lev 20:1-5)
26. A wife falsely claiming to be a virgin (Deut 22:13-21)
  There are other commands to kill that are too contextual to be called "legislation," e.g., anyone touching Mount Sinai (Exod 19:12-13). There are also acts of killing guilty persons, which were divinely commanded, or are recounted with the narrator's approbation.
  House (p. 10) designates items 1, 3, and 4 above as "cultural." There is no indication of what that means. The ancient texts recognize no separations among cult, culture, the moral, and the civil.]

of blood through the body, which humans share with the animal world. Every killing is a sacrifice, for the life of the animal, represented by its blood, belongs to God. To kill an animal is a ritual act; the blood belongs not to the killer but to God. There is no "secular" slaughtering of animals in ancient Israel. The blood of the animal is given to God by being sprinkled on the altar or poured out on the ground. The act of eating that meat is an act of communion with God. The provision for shedding the blood of a human killer is part of the same sacrificial worldview.

The closest approximation in the later Mosaic laws to the sense of the sacred, which sanctions killing in Genesis 9, is the prohibition of serving another god (Deut 13:1-16). This text emphasizes the responsibility of any individual to be the agent of retaliation, even against one's closest kin. A whole town could need to be slaughtered and even the property destroyed.

Other ancient societies, primitive or highly developed, used human sacrifice for many other purposes. The God who renews with Noah his life-saving covenant with humanity permits human sacrifice—for that is what is prescribed here—*only* on one specific grounds, namely, to correct for a previous wrongful taking of human life.

Thus, it is not at all the case that in addressing Noah God intervenes to make blood vengeance a duty, when it had not been so before. The pattern was already old. It is then a mistake to read the word to Noah as if it were a command ordering its hearers to do something that they would otherwise not have done. It is not that; it is a simple description of the way things already are, an accurate prediction of what does happen, what will happen, as surely as summer is followed by winter, seedtime by harvest. That killers are killed is the way fallen society works; it is not a new measure that God introduced after the deluge to solve a problem that had not been there before, or for which God had not yet found a solution. It rather restates, as a fact and as a prediction, in the framework of the authorization now being granted to sacrifice and eat animals, that the sacredness of human life, already stated when God saved the life of the murderer Cain, still stands. Spoken just at the place in the story where the killing of animals is for the first time authorized, the point of God's word in Genesis 9 is to reiterate the prohibition of the killing of humans.[21]

Motives and Meanings for Primitive Revenge

The careful cultural historian will have to ask at this point which of several descriptions or explanations best fits the primitive fact of blood revenge. We cannot yet review fully the several answers to this question as they are operative in modern debate,[22] but we must at least recognize the wrongness of leaping past it to too simple an answer. What were the possible meanings for Cain's contemporaries or Noah's descendants of shedding a killer's blood?

1. It might be more precisely described as "eradication," getting rid of the source of trouble. The Old Testament speaks of "purging" evil from the Israelite people.[23] This would be the social equivalent of what white blood cells do to microbes or what exterminators do to vermin. The organism defends itself against a threat by removing whatever threatens. The threatening organism has no rights of its own. It is removed because it is bad, not because of a particular bad behavior.

2. It might be described as "imitation," *mimesis*. I do to you what you did to my friend, not out of some general theory of social hygiene but rather, primitively, reflexively, because it does not occur to me to do anything else.[24] You "have it coming."[25]

---

21.   Some have argued that "by man shall his blood be shed"(Gen 9:6) is a simple future rather than an imperative; a prediction but not an authorization. That is too little. God avows that the retributive process is under his rule: "I will require a reckoning." Yet, what God thus owns is an extant practice; he does not create a new institution nor decree a new duty.

22.   I shall describe the variety of views more fully below.

23.   Bailey, 32.

24.   We shall see below how the ethnologist René Girard uses "mimesis" as a far-reaching interpretation of the origins of violence and of government.

25.   [Editor's note: This phrase anticipates the title of Yoder's later work on Girard, chapter 5 of this volume.]

3. It might be understood as "intimidation." If as a general pattern it is known that those who harm others are harmed in return, this may keep them from doing it. This interpretation has several levels of meaning. One is the more narrow, mental, and therefore more modern sense. The thought is that an individual premeditating an evil deed will "think twice" about the cost and will therefore renounce the evil deed on cost/benefit grounds. "Deterrence" is another modern term for this. Intimidation also has a less mental, more primitive, more "educational" sense. The generalized practice of avenging certain offenses, it is held, tends to be one way a society has of trying to teach people what deeds are offensive, not to be considered, therefore hoping to make it less likely that they will occur.

4. Both of the above concepts, "imitation" and "intimidation," can be understood to be founded in *retaliation*. The root -*tal*- means "such" or "like." One may believe that God or the gods or "the moral order" should be understood in terms of a kind of balancing exercise whereby each harmful act needs to be "paid back" or "set right" by another harmful act of the same kind and dimension. When the "moral order" is thought of in analogy to a courtroom, we may also speak of the *talion* as "vindication," but in the old Semitic setting the courtroom is not the best symbol for that.

5. None of the above is quite what we mean when we use the word *revenge*. Usually the term revenge connotes an element of passion.[26] To do something "with a vengeance" suggests disregard for proportion, or for limits or barriers. It reaches beyond "eye for eye." A vengeful society, or the individual avenger, demands retaliation, claims moral legitimacy for the vindictive act and may draw emotional satisfaction from carrying it out. Some would avow "anger" as a valid description of the motivation that is at work in so punishing the offender, and some would disavow it. Others would say that there is no anger in justice.

---

26. Under "retribution" [see Part 6, 1, A] we shall return later to the question of emotion.

6. None of the above is quite what we mean by "expiation." This term points past the harm done to the social order, to the offense against the will of God or the gods. The divine anger must be placated, or the cosmic moral order must be set back in balance, the offender must "pay." In some religious and cultural settings, the divine wrath is understood very anthropomorphically: God gets "mad." In others, the claim is that the "balance" needing to be restored by punishment is quite dispassionate, objective like a court's judgment, and holy.

Certainly, these several possible characterizations of why killers are killed are not all the same. The differences are significant. We shall come back later to try to disentangle them more abstractly, as part of our review of the modern debate. But now we want merely to understand the Noah story. Which of them most adequately describes the facts? Which of them is morally most or least acceptable?

On the above scale, most of those who today hold the death penalty to be morally justified would hold to a somewhat sanitized, modernized version of "legislation" combined with "intimidation." This is what we previously referred to under the broader heading of "deterrence." It has the least basis in the ancient text.

On the other hand, most historians studying where the legal killing of humans actually came from in ancient society, including ancient Israel, would point to one of the more angry versions of "vengeance" combined with "imitation." Journalists watching in our own times the public outcry after some particularly brutal killing would agree with the historians.

Our debate to this day is skewed by the difference between these two interpretations. Is killing a killer a vengeful action against the evildoer himself? Or is it the restoration of divine moral balance through sacrifice?

For now, this first overview of the spectrum of reason is intended only to provoke the reader's vigilance. We need to be warned against the assumption that we know easily just which of those meanings the Genesis text originally had for its first hearers and against the assumption that the ancient meaning has any direct connection with the reasons for the modern death penalty.

The provision of Genesis 9:6 is thus not a moral demand, saying that for every pain inflicted there must be another pain inflicted to balance the scales of justice. It is not an educational demand, teaching the offender (or destroying the offender in order to teach others) a lesson to the effect that crime does not pay. It is not a political order describing how to administer a healthy city.

The order underlying the words in question is ritual: human life, human blood is sacred—whoever sheds it forfeits his own. The demand for that "forfeiting" is not vengeance on the part of the victim's family, although it easily degenerates into that; it is the organic society living in immediate awareness of the divine quality of human life. The death that sanctions death is ceremonial, celebrative, ritual.

The killing of a killer is not a civil, nonreligious matter. It is a sacrificial act. The blood—i.e., the life—of every man and beast belongs to God. To respect this divine ownership means, in the case of animals, that the blood of a sacrificial victim is not to be consumed. For humans, it means that there shall be no killing. If there is killing, the offense is a cosmic, ritual, religious evil, demanding ceremonial compensation. It is not a moral matter; in morality a second wrong does not make a right. It is not a civil, legislative matter; it is originally stated in a setting where there is no government.

Ritual Worldview and the Cultic Change

One way that the ritual worldview differs from our own is that there is no concern for personal accountability. The death penalty applied to an ox that gored a man. It applied to unintended or accidental killing. If the ritual worldview of Genesis 9:6 alone were to be applied to our culture literally, there would be no provision for exculpating minors or the mentally ill, no separating of degrees of homicide according to intention. We would execute the contractor whose bridge collapses, the engineer whose train is wrecked, and the auto driver whose brakes malfunction, if death results. For every death, blood must flow.

Christians in recent centuries, in order to attempt to understand and describe how the laws of the Old Testament ought to be respected since Christ, have proposed to divide them into civil, ceremonial, and moral laws. They then explain that the "moral" laws continue to apply in all times, but that the ceremonial ones are abrogated when the sacrificial order is fulfilled in Christ as the final sacrifice and the final high priest. Some of the civil laws, it is held, should apply to modern states, and others were intended only for the government of ancient Israel. This threefold (really fourfold) distinction may help to organize our thought, but careful study of the death penalty provisions of the books of Moses makes it clear that the distinction is alien to that world.

The covenant given to Noah involved no such distinction either; the elements we call "moral" and "civil" were not stated, not separated. We saw that Genesis 9 speaks of the blood of animals and of fellow humans as belonging to God—certainly a sacrificial concept. The covenant given through Moses was no less holistic. Just as the Christ who was to come would be prophet, priest, and king all at once, so the covenant established through Moses was moral, ceremonial, and civil all at once, not one of them in distinction from the others. For centuries after Moses, there was in Israel no king, nothing specific to call "civil."

The distinction between different types of law has served, although in an indirect, illogical way, to make room for a valid point. The valid point, which these distinctions allude to, is that there was going to have to be change over time in how the laws would apply and that in those changes the sacrifice of Christ was to make the biggest difference.

It is the clear testimony of the New Testament, especially of the epistle to the Hebrews, that the ceremonial requirements of the Old Covenant find their end—both in the sense of fulfillment and in the sense of termination—in the high-priestly sacrifice of Christ. "Once for all" is the good news. Not only is the sacrifice of bulls and goats, turtledoves and wheatcakes at an end; the fact that Christ died for our sins, once for all, the righteous one for the godless (Heb 9:26-28; 1 Pet 3:18), puts an end to the entire expiatory system, whether it be enforced by priests in Jerusalem or by execution[ers] anywhere else.[27]

Thus, by asking where killing began, and finding in the stories of both Cain and Noah what is said and what is not said there, we have been led to the most precise statement of the specifically Christian reason for the death penalty's being set aside. There are other reasons as well, more widely effective in our world, in which Anglo-Saxon democracy has spelled out the implications of the Hebrew and Christian heritage, but this is the reason closest to the heart of the gospel.

That shedding blood exposes the killer to killing is expiation in the name of the cosmic order. The death of Christ is the end of expiation.

The Ritual Nature of Social Behavior

To kill a killer is a ritual act, we have begun to see, not primordially or only in a political sense. When people gather for the funeral of a public figure, when they build a wall around their house or buy an assault gun, when they fly a flag or take off their hats, the event is not adequately interpreted by asking about a specified moral imperative or about a pragmatic social goal. We have just attempted briefly to explain something of this sense of the sacred as it appears in the Noah story; now let us note that it is still the case today.

When society takes a life, the action is, obviously, not being undertaken for the well-being of that person. Counter to the general moral rule that a person is always to be treated as an end and not as a means, most simply stated in modern times

---

27. Cf. Karl Barth, "The Command of God the Creator," in *Church Dogmatics* 3/4, (Edinburgh: Clark, 1961), 442-43: "Which category of particularly great sinners is exempted from the pardon effected on the basis of the death penalty carried out at Calvary? Now that Jesus Christ has been nailed to the cross for the sins of the world, how can we still use the thought of expiation to establish the death penalty?"

by Immanuel Kant, killing a person cannot be an action in that person's interest. It is a public ritual, celebrated in the interest of others—in the interest of society's controlling elite and those who support them and their vision of the society's well-being.

When a parent or a teacher spanks a child, when an offender is put in prison or fined, it can be *claimed* that it is done in order to "teach" that guilty person something. Even then, the careful psychologist or social scientist will warn us that the real "learning" resulting from that event is probably something else. A child trained by spanking may grow up to become a teenage gangster or an abusive parent. What beating a child teaches most effectively may well be less "don't get into the cookie jar" than "might makes right," or "if you cannot reason, use force." The same may be true of other punishments as well. The petty pilferer sent to prison may learn there the skills of the professional burglar.

So the claim to "teach them a lesson" is often factually wrong. Nevertheless, it may be sincerely so intended. The sincere intention may be that offenders themselves should learn that "crime does not pay," so that they do not repeat the offense. The time behind bars may lead them to think differently.

Rationales for Rehabilitation

This notion of changing the offenders, ordinarily called "rehabilitation," *can* be given as a serious reason for depriving them of their liberty. They are shown how wrong their actions were. They may become convinced that they are under society's control. They may be led to promise (sincerely or not) that they will not repeat the offense. They may be given time to show by their actions that their promise to behave is credible, and they may even be taught a trade or helped to finish school. This is why prisons were once called "penitentiaries," places to repent. Some persons, after a prison term, do not return to crime. As long as the prospect of a future life in freedom is real, there is *some* chance that this may succeed. Yet even in these cases it is not clear that the time in prison or other kind of punishment is what made the most difference in a person's readiness to become a good member of society.

But when the line of life is crossed, the entire "teach-a-lesson" rationale becomes a lie. The only persons who can "learn" from a lethal public ritual are the others.

- The victims of the past crime (if they are alive) or their relatives can take comfort in the fact that the person who hurt them has been hurt in return: "vengeance" is the ordinary word for this. Vengefulness, taking comfort in the pain of others, is not a good moral quality in an individual, but some feel that it becomes right when the killing is done by the authorities.
- Those who stand to lose by a crime are reassured that it may be less likely to happen to them—although this confidence in the "deterrent" effect is, as we have seen, often mistaken.
- Persons who have not committed a crime should be warned that they should not think of doing so out of the fear that they may be caught and punished. Yet, in fact, the limitations of our enforcement system do not make that threat very real in the minds of most potential offenders.
- The civil authorities celebrate and reinforce their posture of social control. In the Aryan feudal roots of our common law, the authority to dispose of the life of one's subjects was what defined a lord's sovereignty. The killers claim to be the instruments of God; they celebrate that their authority to rule is legitimate by having the right to destroy some of their subjects.

Thus far, our purpose for itemizing a few of the diverse modes of motivation has not been to be complete, but only to be broad enough to open for the reader a sense of the complexity of things and of the inadequacy of simple explanations.

PART 3: A SECOND LOOK AT "AN EYE FOR AN EYE"

Before we move from ancient Israel back to modernity, we may be helped by one other close textual study, following up a notion that many think is a timeless and universal principle. It is widely assumed (rather than being argued with self-critical care) that the death penalty is one part of a broader foundational logic of equal retaliation, which God generally demands or commands as the basic meaning of "justice." We shall look later at the notion of equal retribution, tit for tat, as a claimed universal, philosophical truth. Here we may be helped by looking closely at the texts in the Old Testament where many think it is expressed.

Because Jesus referred to it in the Sermon on the Mount (Matt 5:38) as one of the traditional teachings that . . . the righteousness of God's kingdom would transcend, we tend to think that the rhyme-like rule

> an eye for an eye
> a tooth for a tooth

is a very important part of the Hebrew heritage, or even more than that, a part of the definition of divine justice.[28] It is, in fact, not that, and that fact is worth pursuing.

This rule appears only three times in the entire body of Mosaic legislation and never in a context that is textually central. Let us look at each of them carefully. In Exodus 21:24-27, it is cited as background for the special case of a woman's being

---

28.   A striking specimen of this symbolic meaning of the phrase is its use as the title of the book by J. H. Christopher Wright, *An Eye for an Eye: The Place of Old Testament Ethics Today*. Evidently the publishers considered the phrase to be highly representative of the ethical problem posed by the Old Testament (the British original edition was entitled, *Living as the People of God*). Yet in the text of this study Wright does not interpret at all any of the three "eye for an eye" passages. He even refers only fleetingly to the entire notion of retribution, 166.

wounded while two men are fighting. If the woman is pregnant and the injury causes her to miscarry, the compensation shall be fixed by the court. Apparently the life of the fetus can be compensated for as an economic value. But if the woman dies, the penalty shall be

> life for life;
> eye for eye;
> tooth for tooth;
> hand for hand;
> foot for foot;
> burn wound for burn wound;
> knife wound for knife wound;
> whip wound for whip wound.

It is striking that only the first pair of nouns is in any way pertinent to the context. The rest of the dictum was repeated from memory, just because it was part of the oral legal lore of the time. It is recited as a celebration of the poetic fittingness of letting every punishment fit the crime, one more reminder of the ancient near eastern vision of deep cosmic symmetry, even though it is of no use for the present case. We note that *if* the rule is applied literally in this case, the death penalty is here to be imposed for an *accidental* killing. As elsewhere in the sacred worldview, whether the killing was intentional or not is less important than in our time.

In Leviticus 24:17-22, the setting is narrative: an inquiry is being addressed to Yahweh. The people are petitioning for an oracle regarding the punishment they should inflict for a particular act of blasphemy. The answer given them by oracle is that the blasphemer should be stoned by the whole community, but then the statement of that command is followed by a series of others:

> if a man kills any man he must die;
> if a man kills an animal he must make restitution for it;
> a life for a life;
> if a man injures his neighbor,

what he did must be done to him:
broken limb for broken limb
eye for eye
tooth for tooth;
as the injury inflicted,
so must be the injury suffered.

Then the narrative goes on to recount the stoning of the blasphemer by the sons of Israel. The text is again odd, in that the last of offenses and punishments is not pertinent at all to the question put to Yahweh, and further odd in that the one particular offense involved in the framing narrative is not dealt with by the same rule. The penalty for cursing God is not to be cursed by God but to be stoned by people.

The third occurrence of the dictum is, on more careful examination, not on the same subject either. In fact, it formally contradicts the general notion of retaliation. The context of Deuteronomy 19:19-21 is a set of rules for evidence in a court. More than one witness is always needed to find someone guilty.[29] The penalty for the crime of perjury is that he who commits it shall be subjected to whatever the false accuser was asking to have done to the falsely accused. There is an element of symmetry—"deal with him as he would have dealt with his brother"—yet that does not mean that the false accuser should be punished by being falsely accused. It rather means that he is to be treated as if he had been fairly found guilty of what he was unfairly accusing his brother:

life for life,
eye for eye,
tooth for tooth,
hand for hand,
foot for foot.

---

29.   Cf. also Deuteronomy 17:6 and Numbers 35:30. The New Testament refers to this rule of evidence in Matthew 18:16; 1 Timothy 5:19; Hebrews 10:28; and metaphorically in 1 John 5:7. Rabbinic judicial practice, already by the first century, was very reluctant to condemn anyone on circumstantial evidence.

We can summarize: In each of the three occurrences, the list of pairs is drawn in on the edge of the treatment of some other subject. In none of them is it the center of the passage. In none of the three cases is it presented as revelation, an oracle presenting new information (in Leviticus 24 it is alluded to within the text of an oracle, but logically it is not limited to that case nor is it applied to it literally). In none of the three cases does the "eye-for-eye" rule actually dictate what happens. In neither of the two references to "life for life" is the loss of one's own life the penalty for murder.

The lists of pairs are quoted as a reminiscence of a self-evident, already known, easily remembered folk wisdom, a sense of poetic symmetry taken for granted whenever it applies. It never needs to be explained. The *lex talionis*[30] is then best understood not as a new and central revelation of the demands of the covenant, but as a commonsense, natural, pre-Mosaic rule of thumb, a distillation of the mimetic reflex at the root of all social sanctions. There is nothing Mosaic or Hebraic about it.

Those who are concerned to explain how Jesus could in the same discourse say "I have not come to dissolve the Law but to fulfill it," and then go on to set aside "an eye for an eye" as no longer adequate, have usually argued that the provision for symmetry in the Mosaic texts had the concrete meaning of a restraint on vengeance, which, if not thus limited, would naturally escalate (after the model of Yahweh in Genesis 4:15 or Lamech in Genesis 4:24). Then the concrete meaning was "For an eye *no more than* an eye, for a tooth *no more than* a tooth." Thus, the symmetry rule already represented restraint. It was a first step in the direction that Jesus later "fulfilled" by taking the concern for limits to its logical conclusion.

This is a very reasonable argument, especially when we note in how many places elsewhere in the Mosaic laws the penalty of death is, in fact, disproportionate. The consistent appli-

---

30. The very currency of a Latin term for the concept of retaliation confirms that it is part of a general pagan social wisdom, not intended nor received as a new disclosure of revealed righteousness.

cation of the rule of *talion* would thus be less lethal than the Mosaic rules as a whole.

This interpretation also fits with the way in which the other five "but I say to you" antitheses of Matthew 5 seem uniformly to "go farther in the same direction" beyond what is cited from the "law," rather than contradicting it.[31] Yet, the three particular *talion* texts we are here concerned with do not make explicit this *no-more-than-one-eye* argument. The argument has validity, but it must be made on the basis of our general understandings of the place of more-than-equal retaliation in all ancient law.

It is noteworthy that there is in the Mosaic literature nothing of what is called "indirect *talion*." Other laws of that period provided, for example, that if a house collapsed and killed the owner's son, the builder's son should be killed in return. There is in Hebrew law no such interest in symmetry for its own sake.[32] There is no notion of lying to a liar, raping a rapist, or stealing from a thief. In most of the several provisions for the death penalty in the Mosaic laws there is no such symmetry.[33]

The appetite for imposing symmetrical suffering is thus a natural reflex in primitive cultures, poetically apt but not always applicable. It is not a revelation either from an oracle of Yahweh or from universal moral reason. It is more an aesthetic imperative than a moral one. It is a standard cultural reflex rather than a prescriptive guide. Jesus explicitly sets it aside.

---

31.   I myself made the same argument in my *The Original Revolution: Essays on Christian Pacifism*, 44. I do not withdraw the point today, but I did overvalue the extent to which the original use of "eye for eye," etc., was stated as if it were divine law.

32.   Lloyd R. Bailey lists numerous other ways in which the Mosaic rules and practices were conditioned, in ways we might call "humane," in contrast to the rules of the environing societies (*Capital Punishment: What that Bible Says*, 27-30). Similar contrasts are pointed out by Wright, *An Eye for an Eye*, 166.

33.   Bailey's detailed count is seventeen (*Capital Punishment*, 19-22).

PART 4: JESUS AND THE CIVIL ORDER

The only clear New Testament reference to the infliction of death as a penalty is in John's Gospel (8:1-11). A woman was brought to Jesus with the report that she was known to be guilty of adultery:[34] "Moses has ordered us in the Law to condemn women like this to death by stoning. What have you to say?" (v. 5 JB). The intention of the "scribes and Pharisees," we are told, was to put Jesus to a test; i.e., they were not really looking for help with defining or doing God's will. Their primary motivation was not to wipe out adultery. They were, rather, challenging Jesus to continue to exercise the authority he had been claiming while teaching in the temple (ch. 7). Jesus did not evade the challenge. We may, therefore, rightly take his response as bearing on our study.

Jesus could well have pointed out that "Moses" (i.e., the Law, in Leviticus 20 and Deuteronomy 22) does not say that a woman should be condemned without the man with whom she was caught in the act. Why did they bring him the woman without the man? Jesus could have made an important point about male sexism and the victimizing of women. But he chose not to.

Jesus could well have challenged the factual accuracy of their report about the offense, as the law requires and as a judge would have done. He did not. Nor did he deny that the provision for death was in the Law. Nor did he cite in the woman's defense, as a rabbinic court would have, the longstanding hesitancy of Jewish local authorities, for several centuries already, to inflict the death penalty. He did not (explicitly) make the point, which according to the same Gospel "the Jews" later argued before Pontius Pilate (18:31), namely, that under the Roman rules currently in effect Jewish authorities did not have the right to put anyone to death. All of these responses would have been fitting. In a full account,

---

34.   The first narrative in chapter 8 is missing in some of the ancient manuscripts, and some doubt that it was originally part of the Gospel; but even those scholars who doubt that these verses were originally in John's Gospel tend to grant that it nonetheless represents an authentic tradition.

we should need to consider them all. Jesus, however, preferred to make two other points, to which we should also give priority.

"Let him that is without sin cast the first stone" (v. 7).[35] If the death penalty is understood as an act of God (as it certainly was in ancient Israel), then the judge and executioner must be morally above reproach. "When they heard this they went away one by one, beginning with the eldest" (v. 9 JB). Why was it the eldest who first disqualified themselves? The Christian challenge to the death penalty properly begins where Jesus does, by challenging the self-ascribed righteousness of those who claim the authority to kill others.

Secondly, Jesus applied to this woman's offense his authority to forgive. He did not deny her guilt, but he absolved it as far as punishment was concerned and liberated her from its power over her: "Sin no more" (v. 11). He recognized no differentiation between the religious and the civil, according to which the sin could be forgiven, yet punitive justice should still have to be done.

John's concern in telling this story was, of course, not to provide his readers with new information about the legality of capital punishment.[36] His testimony was about the authority of Jesus as the one uniquely sent by the Father. That is just our point. We are not studying law for its own sake; we are learning that the saviorhood of Jesus applies to law and to social punishment for sin, no less than to prayer. Jesus as the forgiver of sin removes not only sin's power over the sinner's behavior but also its power to dictate guiltiness and demand punishment.

Jesus' Good News Condones the Lesser Moral Level of the Civil Order

Like the divorce that Deuteronomy 24 condoned, like the distortions of the law that Jesus corrected in Matthew 5, like the institu-

---

35. That the persons bearing the incriminating witness should cast the first stone is part of the provision of Deuteronomy 17:7.
36. Bailey expresses an exaggerated dislike for seeing moral meaning in narrative texts (*Capital Punishment*, 40, 70).

tion of slavery and the oppressive presence in Judea and Galilee of the Roman Empire, which neither Jesus nor Paul rose up against, capital punishment is one of those infringements on the holy will of God in society that can claim a certain formal legitimacy. The gospel does not immediately eliminate such from secular society, since, being noncoercive, the gospel cannot "rule the world" in that way. Yet to condone the way things stand is not approval: "from the beginning it was not so" (Matt 19:8 RSV). Jesus said that literally about the Mosaic provision for divorce, but the Christians of the apostolic generation thought the same way about the other points where the world was ruled by pagan powers.

The new level of mutual love and forgiveness on which the redeemed community is called (and enabled by the Spirit) to live cannot be directly enforced on the larger society; but since it is the gospel, i.e., since it represents authentically good news for the real world, it will necessarily work as salt and light. This should be true anywhere; even more evidently should it be the case in the Anglo-Saxon world, where a large number of citizens claim some kind of Christian sanction for society's values. If Christ is not only prophet and priest but also king, the border between the church and the world cannot be impermeable to moral truth. Something of the cross-bearing, forgiving love and dignity, which Jesus' life, death, and resurrection revealed to be the normative way to be human, must be the norm for all humans, whether they know it or not. We cannot *expect* of anyone, not even of believers, to live that norm out perfectly. Yet, it is the calling of the followers of Jesus to testify that there is no other norm. The one strategy, which will not serve that calling, which could not be done in the first century, and which cannot be done in our century, is to claim to possess, and to impose on society, a body of civil rules independent of the faith of the persons called to respect them. The alternative is to work within the acceptance of the others' unbelief, which is what I call "condoning" the lesser moral level of the civil order.

Some will claim that to challenge the death penalty in the name of Christ is to advocate anarchy. If sinners should be forgiven, if only the innocent may "throw the first stone," they ask, where will we stop? Does this not destroy all government?[37]

The question is not always meant sincerely. Most who ask it do not themselves propose to follow the Mosaic Law by advocating capital punishment for adultery today. They do not really believe that society will collapse if rebellious sons are not executed by stoning. Nonetheless, the question does merit attention. It illustrates a real problem in relating Christian ethics to non-Christian society.

The first mistake that question makes is to assume that in interpreting a Christian social critique the right question to ask is how to "carry things to their logical conclusion." That assumption distorts everything. Christian social criticism addresses a fallen world. Since that critique derives its ultimate standards from the kingdom of God—for there are no other *ultimate* standards—to "carry them to their logical conclusion" would mean the presence of that kingdom. Yet, such consistent application would demand faith. It lies beyond the capacities and the intentions of the rebellious world as it is in fact.

The Christian cannot expect that of fallen society. Thus, to undercut Christ's call by asking "where would this lead?" is to distort the whole problem. By the fact of its rebellion, the "world" has guaranteed that Christian social critique will not lead "too far." Yet the resurrection and ascension of Christ guarantee that there is no situation in which nothing can be done. The world can be challenged, one point at a time, to take one step in the right direction, to move up one modest notch in approximation of the righteousness of love.[38] To challenge capital punishment no more undermines government than does the rejection of the oath (Matt 5:33-37; James 5:12) undermine

---

37. "The opponents of capital punishment offer no theory of civil government," in Gordon H. Clark, "Capital Punishment and the Bible," 10. As a rationalistic philosopher, Clark felt that to have the right to say anything about human justice you must have a theory covering everything in the field.

38. Cf. Yoder, *Christian Witness to the State*, 60.

truth-telling; no more than does the concept of the consent of the governed destroy the authority of the state.

The civil order is a fact. That it might be done away with by pushing the critique of love "too far" is inconceivable. We saw above that Genesis 9, like every primitive government, does not *demand* vengeance, since it is already present, but rather works to restrain it. Thus the Christian (and any believer in democracy) will be concerned to restrain the violent vengeful potential of the state. That potential for violence does not need our advocacy; it is already there.

"Anarchy," the scare concept quoted above, is a grammatical abstraction, an intellectual construct, an imaginary entity. There is no such reality. There are varying forms of government, from tyranny to constitutional democracy, and there are varying degrees of centralization of power, from the independent tribe through the "nation" to world empire. Where the criminal underground is highly organized, or in the case of civil war, there may be two powers claiming authority over the same territory. There may be great variation in how effectively a power controls its subjects. Authority may be delegated or seized. It may be exercised wisely or wantonly, overtly or undercover, with or without a constitution, with or without the consent of the governed. But despite all these possible variations, there *is* always authority.[39] In the (very rare) cases where it may seem that authority is functioning too little for the welfare and stability of society, the reason is never that the critique coming from the direction of Christian love has been too effective.

The scare concept of "anarchy" does not arise from the study of societies. It is the creature of the mental urge to carry things to their "logical conclusions," an urge that is out of place in a fallen world.

---

39. The above argument has to do with authority in the sense of the state. Sober social science will add that there are also always other kinds of non-state authority holding societies together: the orders of the clan, the marketplace, the school, religion, entertainment, etc.

The second error in the "where will we stop?" argument is the notion that there exists some clear and univocal concept of justice, having the same meaning in all times and places, consisting in an exact logical or mathematical equivalence of offense and retribution, and that such "justice" must (or can) be either wholly respected or fundamentally rejected. In real life—and in clear logic—there is no one sure yardstick by which to measure the "justness" of a penalty. Every culture and every age have different conceptions of what is fair retribution. Opinions have changed enormously from culture to culture as to how much it matters whether offenders were human, adult, free and of a sound mind, and whether they were aware of the laws they broke. They vary enormously as well in judging what "equivalent" means. "Eye for eye" is measurable if there has been bodily injury,[40] and "ox for ox" will work in case of material loss; but what are the equivalent penalties for adultery or for covetousness? We noted before that there is no command to lie to a liar or to rape a rapist.

Justice is a direction, not an achievement. It is a relative, not absolute concept. Moral acts may be more just or less just, but we know of no ideal justice, distinct from love, that "too much emphasis on love" would jeopardize. Justice may well be undermined by lack of wisdom. It may be undermined by idealistic schemes for reformation, by social criticism that does not propose relevant alternatives, by a sentimental misunderstanding of the nature of love, or by failing to recognize to how great an extent order and mutual respect have already been achieved by the society one criticizes; but justice is not endangered by too much love.

Despite Concessions, No Other Lord

The classical Christian confession referred to earlier states that Jesus is not only prophet, priest, and rabbi, but also Lord and

---

40.   But note in Deuteronomy 19:19-21, one of the three texts on "eye for eye," that the offense to be punished "equally" was not wounding an eye but perjury about who had wounded an eye.

King. Those are political names. Even the name "Christ" (the anointed one) was originally a royal designation. Christians begin to deny their Lord when they admit that there are certain realms of life in which it would be inappropriate to bring Christ's rule to bear. Of course, non-Christians will insist that we should keep our *religion* out of the way of their *politics*. But the reason for that is not that Jesus has nothing to do with the public realm; it is that they want nothing to do with Jesus as Lord.

If we confess that it is the Lamb that was slain who is "worthy . . . to receive power and wealth and wisdom and might and honor and glory and blessing" (Rev 5:12 RSV), we are relating the cross to politics. If we ask who crucified Jesus and why, the cross is political at the outset. What we believe about Christ must apply to all our behavior, no matter how many of our neighbors remain unconvinced. Of course, the unbelief and the contrasting beliefs of our neighbors, added to our own disobedience, will mean that no society will fully keep the law of God. When a society falls short of his law, God knows how to use even that disobedience for his glory. "Providence" is the traditional Christian word for the fact that God's being in charge of history includes his power sovereignly and savingly to take into account what the fallen world does against his will. This is not a reason for Christians to justify or to defend the lower level of behavior that results from unbelief, whether it be in the political realm or elsewhere.

The words of Paul in Romans 13:1-7, which affirm that the "powers that be" are subject to God, mean what I have just been saying. They have often been further interpreted to say that, since the powers are under God, Christians have no grounds for criticizing what any given state does or no standards to guide such a criticism. Paul does not say that. He says that government is "for our benefit" (v. 4) and that it is God's servant when (or insofar as) it "perseveres toward this very end" (v. 6).[41]

These expressions, as well as the parallel ones in 1 Peter 2:13-17, indicate that there are standards of good and right

---

41.   Cf. my *Politics of Jesus*, 207-208.

order, not dependent on the arbitrary judgment of individual rulers, by which government is to be judged. The state is not a law unto itself. This does not authorize us to rebel against an unjust state by using against it the same weapons it uses oppressively. It does, however, give us standards for identifying oppression and grounds for denouncing it. No standard is more simply applicable to what governments do than "thou shalt not kill."[42]

The Romans passage is but one application of a New Testament truth that is stated more frequently and more clearly in other texts. The broader claim is that "Christ is Lord" (Phil 2:11; 1 Cor 12:3). His status as "Lord" does not apply only to the church; Christ is exalted "far above every principality and power, and might, and dominion, and every name that is named" (Eph 1:21; Phil 2:10; 1 Cor 15:27; Matt 28:18). Protestant tradition, as we saw, has used the term "providence" to say the same thing.

The world does not acknowledge Christ as Lord; but his being Lord is not dependent on the world's acknowledgment, any more than George Bush's being president in 1989 was dependent on whether all U.S. citizens and resident aliens liked him or on whether they were all informed that he had been elected and inaugurated. A government, like any rebellious power, can attempt to be independent, can claim to be its own master, but Christians know that the claim is false and the attempt doomed to fail.

It is not our theme here to discuss the Christian view of government in general.[43] The mere confession of Christ's dominion generates conclusions sufficient for our present purpose. If it is as the apostles said, that Jesus Christ and not some other lord rules at the right hand of God over the powers of this world, then the purpose, goals, and standards of that rule can be no other than this same Jesus revealed to us when in the flesh; he

---

42.   Jean Lasserre, "The 'Good' in Romans 13," in *On Earth Peace*, ed. Donald F. Durnbaugh, 130-35.

43.   I do offer some of this in *The Christian Witness to the State* and in *The Priestly Kingdom*, 151-71.

came not to destroy but to save. On the grounds of his rule, it cannot be the duty of governments to destroy life.

The Sword in Apostolic Thought

The New Testament epistles are silent about capital punishment. The apostles do instruct their readers that they are to be subject to their rulers. Rulers are supposed to rule "for your benefit" (Rom 13:4). Those who chose to break the law called down punishment upon themselves, but there is no reference in the epistles to specific penalties. Rulers should enable us to "lead religious and reverent lives in peace and quiet" (1 Tim 2:2). Governors should "punish criminals and encourage good citizenship" (1 Pet 2:14), but there is no specification of the content either of the citizenship or the "punishment."

The "sword" (*machaira*), of which Paul writes to the Romans that rulers do not "bear it in vain" (Rom 13:4), is the symbol of judicial authority, not the weapon of either war or the death penalty. In imperial Rome the *machaira* was the arm neither of the solider in combat nor of the executioner. The civil order as such is the theme of the passage. The state's taking of life is not.

There is in the epistles no allusion to the provision for animal sacrifice or for killing killers in the covenant with Noah, and none of the apostles—Jews that they all were—would have thought of the Roman courts as applying the Mosaic penal provisions.

The epistles say even less than the Gospels about urging society to move toward the kingdom; that should be no surprise. The epistles are addressed to believers who constitute an infinitesimal minority within Roman/Mediterranean culture. There was no place for them to contemplate immediately effective social critique. The Gospels, on the other hand, recount Jesus' impact in a setting where Hebraic notions of divine justice were less alien. Jesus' gracious demands (or rather, offers) were not accepted by all who heard him, but they were not inconceivable for his Jewish hearers. The notions of a personal, caring, intervening, righteous, demanding, chastising God—

notions that underlay Jesus' message and his forgiving practice—had been understandable to Jesus' Jewish hearers, but
they would not have been to the polytheistic Romans.

It is thus formally wrong to look in the New Testament for
specific guidelines for a good civil society. If such prescriptions
had been given, they would embarrass us, as they would have
had to be written to fit first-century Mediterranean conditions.
We should rather look there for a general orientation toward
ultimate human values and the nature of redemption, and then
ask what *those meanings* have to say for our time. This is what
happens when we remember that the foundational level of the
Hebraic vision with which we began was not about civil penalties but about ritual expiation.

PART 5: CHRIST TRANSFORMING CULTURE

Among the differences between the biblical age and our own of which we must take account, many new political institutions and cultural insights have been developed, especially in recent centuries, particularly in our Anglo-Saxon world. We cannot study these matters here with the care they deserve, but failing to name them would mean unconsciously making untested assumptions—favorable or unfavorable—about them. None of these developments is directly or uniquely Christian, but in general it could be shown that they have been derived—whether by a sequence of rational arguments or by historical experience—from the impact upon society of biblically derived understandings.

1. Our culture has developed the notion of "rights" belonging to individuals by virtue of their being human, vested in each one by creation, not needing to be earned by some special performance or capable of being awarded only to a few as special privilege. This philosophical notion was stated at the foundation of our republic. Philosophically, this idea can be challenged. It is individualistic and it is hard to define just what all the "rights" are in a way that convinces everyone. The people who first stated the theory did not believe that it applied to women or to people of other races.

Nonetheless, this notion of "rights" borne by each person is the best way we have yet found to interpret in our time, and to defend against encroachment by the authorities, the dignity of every person as created by God in his image. To say that every human being is endowed at birth with an inalienable right to life is our analogy to the Bible's speaking of the sacredness of blood. That this right is inalienable means that it cannot be transferred, even by the bearer himself. One cannot sell oneself into slavery; one cannot forfeit the right to live by misbehaving.

2. Constitutional democracy—in the special American form that provides for an independent judiciary; freedom of speech, press, and assembly; *habeas corpus*; and the rights of due process (speedy and fair trial, the presumption of innocence, no

self-incrimination)—provides a wholesome way to discipline the innate tendency of the bearers of power to abuse the prerogatives of their office.[44] In some special circumstances, when due process rights serve to defend the accused, they are sometimes decried as "protecting criminals." This is to forget that for the founding fathers of the U.S. as for the early Christians and for morally concerned persons in the nondemocratically governed majority of the world's societies even today, the primary threat to human dignity is not the impunity of individual offenders not proven guilty, but the absolute power of the state itself to punish.

Yet, because—in the Anglo-American system—the courts rather than the legislatures defend certain values, especially the rights of the accused, a regrettable arbitrariness is imposed on our society. If a case comes to the United States Supreme Court for review from Massachusetts or California it may enhance personal rights; if it comes from Georgia or Florida, it may not. The fact that government itself does not defend victims in general, to say nothing of the victims of wrongs done by the courts, has largely left significant social change to the initiative of tiny volunteer agencies, which fight seemingly hopeless issues through the courts. Values won in the courts can be struck down again by legislatures, where demagoguery or the impact of a rare atrocity can sway votes more easily than fairness or compassion. Nonetheless, this system of checks and balances represents more adequately than does any modern alternative the biblical vision for a government that acknowledges its limits and provides to its subjects the instruments whereby it may itself be held in line.

3. One large change, which has gradually taken place during the last century and a half, is consideration of the reduced accountability of the very young and the mentally incompetent. Even the strong retentionist van den Haag does not call

---

44. The phrasing above is not legally precise or exhaustive. Some of these values are defined or safeguarded in particular articles of the Bill of Rights, some by custom, some of stature.

for reinstating death for children or the insane.[45] Certainly, this change is part of the long-range impact of Jewish and Christian humane sentiments. [This impact is already evident in] the Mosaic provision of cities of refuge for the innocent and the demand for multiple witnesses.

4. All modern societies have seen over the past two centuries a striking diminution of use of the death penalty. Laws provided for death as the penalty for many crimes have been taken off the books.[46] Death sentences still possible in the law have been inflicted less frequently on those found guilty; they have more often been overruled on appeal. The quality of justice has been tempered with mercy *on the average*, even though the extent to which this has happened has been most uneven. As Chief Justice Wright of California wrote in 1972, even persons who want death penalty laws on the books apply them less and less: "[A]mong those persons called upon to actually impose or carry out the death penalty it is being repudiated with ever increasing frequency. . . . What our society does in actuality belies what it says [in the lawbooks] with regard to its acceptance of capital punishment."[47]

Wright is not describing here the work of "liberal" lobbies or public defenders, but that of the main line of prosecutors, juries, and courts of appeal. This growing humanization (quoting a 1958 Supreme Court decision, *Trop v. Dulles*, Wright called it "evolving standards of decency that mark the progress of a maturing society") is due, of course, to many factors within our society, but most of them are derived from the Hebraic and Christian value of compassion, the conviction that the sacredness of human life is a gift of God rather than something to be

---

45. Ernest van den Haag does argue, as I would, that insanity would best be considered as a factor in determining proper punishment, rather than as grounds for a "not guilty" finding (in *The Death Penalty: A Debate*).

46. There were over 220 capital crimes in England around 1800; cf. Arthur Koestler, *Reflections on Hanging*, 7.

47. *People* [California] versus *Anderson*, 1972.

earned or easily forfeited, and the post-Christian sense of fairness, which the democratic experience nurtures.

5. Most democratic societies tend over the years to grow in their recognition that discrimination based on race or class is unjust. Already two generations ago, Warden Lewis E. Lawes of Sing Sing noted that no one was put to death who was not poor.[48] The system of public defenders for the indigent and the thin network of private-sector agencies that defend some individuals are still a far cry from fairness, but at least our society at large recognizes the problem of unequal access to justice, and the courts will in some cases take account of it.

This kind of gradual "humanizing" change, however, is at the root of a new kind of injustice. The less frequently the maximum penalty is applied (as seen in the previous paragraph), the greater is the likelihood that the victims to whom it is still applied are chosen arbitrarily. It was this evident "capricious and arbitrary" unfairness that led to the 1972 Furman decision (Furman vs. Georgia), which struck down the extant death penalty laws until the laws were rewritten. To let live most persons found guilty of capital offenses and then to execute only a few, and to have those few chosen not on the grounds of the special nature of the crime but on the basis of their race, their means, or the state in which they were tried made those executions, it could be argued, a "cruel and unusual punishment," forbidden by the Eighth Amendment, or it identified them as "arbitrary and capricious," a denial of the "equal protection" provided by the Fourteenth Amendment.

6. The constitutional guarantees of the free exercise of religion and the prohibition of governmental action regarding "the establishment of religion" have been developed into the notion

---

48. It is noteworthy that several highly respected professionals in corrections have come to reject the death penalty *in the name of* their concern for the effective implementation of the laws; e.g., Clinton Duffy of Alcatraz and Lawrence Wilson of San Quentin. Wilson reported that most wardens agree with him against the death penalty (Ian Gray and Moira Stanley, *A Punishment in Search of a Crime*, 123).

of "separation of church and state." The growing religious plu-
ralism of our society makes it harder to connect faith-based moral convictions to public life. It opens complex debates about the
framers' intent and how to read the Bill of Rights. The fathers of
the Republic certainly did not intend to "establish" some kind of
religious neutrality as preferable to religious commitment. That
does leave a vacuum, or room for complex negotiation, among
the religious perspectives that ought to count in public matters.

Some Protestant fundamentalists and some Roman Catholics deny that such "separation" can exempt the civil government from the jurisdiction of what they hold to be the revealed
will of God, since the sacredness of human life, as distinct from
some other social values, is a matter of natural moral law, not of
denominational diversity. This is not a matter concerning *directly*
only the death penalty; its most immediate contested relevance in
practical politics today is, in fact, to the abortion debate. Yet, *if
taken consistently*, this argument would have to apply as well to
the death penalty. For American Catholics today, it does apply
against the death penalty, as quite parallel to the wrongness of
abortion. For some fundamentalists, on the other hand, it may
apply in favor of capital punishment, although not many "right
to life" advocates have argued openly, as logically it would seem
they should have to, that death should be the penalty for abortion.
Conflicts of that kind—between those who agree that "nature" or
"the law of God" teaches just one thing, regardless of denomina-
tion—weaken logically their claim that the natural moral law is
evident to everyone. If it really were evident to all, there would be
no argument. That should invite to greater modesty anyone making the claim to interpret revelation with final authority. It tends
to mean that when Christians converse with their fellow citizens
in the public arena, they properly should express their values in
terms the neighbors can follow. Thus, it does not count against the
Christian opponent of the death penalty that others—"liberals,"
humanists, Jews—may support the sacredness of life in terms other than references to creation and cross, which are most clear for
the Christian, and which I have been using here.

Let us look back at these developments taken all together; we may speak of them as cultural transformation under the pressure of the gospel, or as humanization. Some socially conservative Christians, for reasons which they have not yet thought through carefully, have come to speak as if "humanism" were opposed to Christian commitment. It is true that there are ways, as there are a few people choosing those ways, to seek to separate the value of the "human" from God's concern as Creator and Redeemer. True: one can be "humanist" in an atheistic or "secularistic" frame of reference.

Yet we must refuse to concede "ownership" of the "human" to those who deny creation and redemption. The God of creation, making humankind in his image, was the first humanist. The story of the "humanization" of Western culture—limping, imperfect as it is, but real—is part of the work of the God of Abraham, Father of Jesus, partly done through his body, the church. That humanization of cultures is not the same as the salvation of individual souls, nor is it the same as the praise of God in gatherings for worship, nor is it the same as the coming of the ultimate kingdom of God, but it is a fruit of the gospel for which we should be grateful, and for whose furtherance we are responsible. The fact that persons believing in other value systems share in the humanization process, and that some of them may overvalue it as if it could do away with evil, is no reason for followers of Jesus to disavow it or leave it to unbelievers to carry out.[49]

---

49. As I have stated above and repeat below, numerous "humane" or "liberal" arguments, which this study does not survey, are nonetheless valid.

PART 6: THE CLASH OF RATIONALES

We began in the middle of the debate, and our attention has ranged thus far across some of the main themes in biblical backgrounds. We have tested the assumptions of those who *assumed* their views to be biblically founded. We have looked at how Christian concern moves on from biblical times to our own. We can now proceed toward a sort of synthesis of the state of the question.

That offenses must be punished, all societies agree. Yet why this should be is not agreed. A great variety of reasons are given for punishment. Even when the same words are used, the meanings differ. Several scholars have sought to spread these reasons out along a logical spectrum. Gerber and McAnany, for instance, list four: retribution, rehabilitation, deterrence, and "social defense." Conrad lists the same four but calls them retribution, reform, intimidation, and incapacitation.[50]

This possibility of a neat listing may give the first impression that the debate is more orderly than it is. Ernest van den Haag, one of the shrewdest debaters, denies that "retribution" standing alone is a meaningful concept, but thinks that "justice" is. What he means by "justice" is, after all, what others call "retribution." In any case, we must seek to make some kind of order, in the awareness that word usage varies:

1. Retribution is the first category of justification we now must turn to interpreting. A careful observer must distinguish within the realm of "retribution" at last three quite different strands of justification for repaying evil for evil:

A. The victim of any crime, or in the case of murder the next of kin and the neighbors, may desire emotionally that there be pain inflicted on the guilty person. The simplest and more accu-

---

50.   Rudolf J. Gerber and Patrick D. McAnany, eds., *Contemporary Punishment: Views, Explanations, and Justifications* (Notre Dame, Ind.: University of Notre Dame Press, 1972). [Editor's note: Yoder is likely referring to John P. Conrad co-author with Ernest van den Haag of *The Death Penalty Debate: A Debate*.]

rate name for this is "revenge." The sentiment that demands it is anger. Van den Haag calls it "an emotion universally felt . . . which all societies must gratify." Yet certainly there are deeply and widely felt emotions that should not be gratified. Racism and xenophobia are deeply and widely felt emotions, too. The near-universal experience of history, as van den Haag also recounts, until recent centuries called as well for elaborate torture, making immediate death a form of mercy. Today, however, we do not gratify legally that appetite, and van den Haag does not suggest that we should.[51]

B. It may be held that God (B/1), or the gods (B/2), or "the moral order" (B/3) demands retribution. The classical image is that of a balance, where evil done on one side can be compensated for by pain inflicted on the other. Yet, why a second wrong should right the first one is not easily explained. It cannot count as a universal moral demand without more argument.

C. It may be held that the dignity of offenders themselves demands that they should pay the price of their offenses. Part of being human is taking responsibility for the results of one's actions. To be adult in the economy is to be able to make promises and to be held to keeping them. The same should apply to paying the price of one's offenses. Sometimes (C/1) it is society that tells offenders that taking their "deserved" punishment is the price of their readmission into society. Sometimes (C/2) it is the individual who knows his or her guilt and wants to pay for it. C. S. Lewis, the well-known Anglican apologist of the mid-twentieth century, argued strongly for the notion of deserved punishment as a part of the human dignity of the offender, over against "humanistic" notions of punishment as rehabilitation (3 below), or of excusing the crime as socially caused.[52]

---

51.   Van den Haag and Conrad, *The Death Penalty: A Debate*, 13.
52.   C. S. Lewis's special concern was that if some social elite takes over deciding what makes us worthy of returning to society independently of consideration of just desert, that could become tyrannical. He had been provoked to write this test by the British debate about capital punishment. Yet he did not stretch his argument to

Some criminals do want to be executed. Some psychotherapeutic theories see "guilt" as the person's having so thoroughly internalized the value system of the surrounding power structure as to want to be punished. But the fact that offenders think they should be killed does not prove that they should.

Which of these three—in fact, at least five or six—different arguments is the "real" meaning of retribution? Our point is precisely that there is no right answer to that question; the debate is far more complex. To boil them all down to one or the other is to be deceived and to deceive. Beneath them, i.e., deeper in cultural history, there are yet two other levels, somewhat like B above (God or the gods) yet not the same.

D. The literal sense of Genesis 9:6, when taken alone, does not refer to crime in general, or to moral offenses against God's commands, but specifically and only to the shedding of blood. It does not cover the *lex talionis* as a general rule for retribution or the penal provisions of the Mosaic laws. In the covenant with Noah, a sacrificial view of our link to the animal world and to God as its Creator makes killing a sacrilege. The blood, which is the life, belongs to God its giver; killers forfeit their life by that act of desecration. "Retribution" is a possible term here, but "expiation" might be more adequate. Its frame of reference is the sacral cosmos, not the social contract. The "balance" it restores is cosmic and ceremonial, not moral or legal.

E. According to René Girard, literary critic turned cultural anthropologist, the reality underlying both B and D above is a prehistoric cultural transaction, an event whereby the primitive vengefulness that sufficed to maintain order in prehistoric societies was replaced by killing a substitute. In order for this primeval, vicarious, ritual killing to "work," i.e., to have the effect of pacifying society, its meaning must be covered over with the cultural artifice of myth and poetry. It can be unearthed only,

---

the claim that every killer's human dignity does or should make him want to die. Cf. "The Humanitarian Theory of Punishment" and "On Punishment: A Reply to Criticism," in *God in the Dock*, 287-94 and 295-300, respectively.

as Girard has done it, by dint of careful archaeological and anthropological sleuthing. To interpret and evaluate Girard's hypothesis would take us much too far,[53] yet he represents the most serious effort in contemporary cultural studies to make sense of a basic social fact: namely, the way in which society's viability is thought to demand that the quasi-universal appetite for violent retaliation must be at the same time both validated and buffered, both satisfied and diverted, both acknowledged and denied.

2. Under the heading "incapacitation," "prevention," or "social defense," we find the varieties of justification given for incarceration as well as for execution. The action is based not on "setting right" a past offense but on preventing what one holds is a likely future one. Certainly there are offenders who if freed might offend again, although the recidivism rate for persons who have killed is less than for other crimes. It is doubtful that this justification calls for killing someone who has already been made harmless by incarceration. Many who have killed in the past will not do so again. This consideration would call for discrimination on the basis not of past guilt but of future prospects.

3. Under "rehabilitation" or "reform," we find those views that would make incarceration a positive service to offenders by helping them become better persons. Some prisons have been called "reformatories" or "penitentiaries" with this understanding. Society has a right to demand that people become good before setting them free. For some, this is a subcategory of the "social defense" notion; for others, it expresses a more optimistic view of human nature. We have noted C. S. Lewis's claim that it insults the personal dignity of offenders to manipulate

---

53.   I offered a very brief résumé of Girard's thought in *Religion and Literature* 19, no. 3 (Autumn 1987): 89-92. The importance of Girard for Christian thinking about atonement and capital punishment is summarized by Raymund Schwager, *Must There Be Scapegoats?* [Editor's note: Yoder's most extensive treatment of Girard's thought with reference to capital punishment is included as chapter 5 of this volume.]

their character and condition their liberties by criteria other than desert. Lewis links this mentality with another issue, namely his polemic against the "liberal" idea that people are not to blame for their crimes and should not be called to retribution because of their lack of opportunity, lack of good parental models, or other exonerating considerations.[54] So this category, too, is complex rather than univocal; yet *for our purposes* this is not very important, since this is the one of the four standard reasons, applicable to punishments in general, that can never be used to justify the death penalty.

4. There remains deterrence, or intimidation, with which we began. The arguments against it were surveyed before. As we have gone along it has become increasingly evident that the generally assumed equation of deterrence with the Mosaic or the "cosmic order" warrants for retribution is incorrect.

Which View Is Right?

In the face of such a complex spectrum of views, our normal intellectual defense mechanism is to oversimplify and to excommunicate. We would like to be told why one view is clearly right and to overrule the others. Yet, the discussion rules of a free society will not permit that, nor will the gospel. The several modes are all socially operative. They are all part of the discussion, whether we deem them worthy or not. The most powerful are sometimes the least morally worthy (e.g., vengeance) or the most tied to a bygone worldview (the retaliatory world order, where a second wrong makes a right). What we here properly should retain, both from the Old Testament and from the universal presence of retribution in human societies, is not one right general theory about the background "reasons" for the death penalty, but the fact of its universality. The various

---

54. It is not clear whether Lewis would on these grounds oppose all exonerating arguments based on insanity, retardation, or duress. He would accept exonerating children, which already weakens the rigor of his case.

"reasons" are all relevant, all meaningful to someone, and all questionable when examined morally more closely.

Our interest should rather be to discern, *in the midst* of this complexity, what the Christian gospel has to say. We have already seen that the constant theme of the Hebrew story is God's intervening to save the guilty. This begins by his saving Cain, the prototypical murderer, from the lethal workings of the *talion*. It continued in the covenant with Noah in that although [God let] stand the concept of blood vengeance, [he restricted it to] the setting of sacrifice, parallel to God's jealous ownership of the blood of every victim, [thereby halting] the escalation threatened by Lamech. It continued in the age of national Israel in that, although legislation [was observed] like that of the neighboring peoples, its harshness was mitigated. There was no indirect *talion*, there were refuges for the accidental killer (at the places of worship, continuing the sacral connection of Genesis 9), and more than one witness was needed to condemn.[55]

The Bible's witness on these matters is a long story, not a timeless, unchanging corpus of laws or of truths. What matters for us is not the cultural substance of where the story started (with its racism, its superstition, its slavery, its holy warfare, its polygamy, and its abuse of women), but where it was being led. That direction is toward Jesus; toward validating the dignity of every underdog and outsider, of the slave and foreigner, the woman and the child, the poor and the offender. This is done not on the grounds that this or that outsider is an especially virtuous person, but on the grounds of God's grace.

The culmination of the story for our purposes is that the cross of Christ puts an end to sacrifice for sin. The sacrificial worldview of Genesis 9 is not abandoned by the New Testament as culturally obsolete, as we are tempted to do. It is rather assumed and fulfilled when the epistle to the Hebrews takes as its

---

55.   Lloyd R. Bailey, in *Capital Punishment*, lists further ways in which the general retributive drive was mitigated, 27-31.

central theme that the death of Christ is the end of all sacrifice. The most primitive, the culturally most basic rootage of violence against the violent is freely faced and nonviolently accepted by Jesus, the innocent, reluctant, but ultimately willing victim of an unjust execution.[56]

> The love of Christ leaves us no choice,
> when once we have reached the conclusion
> that one man has died for all
> and therefore all mankind has died (2 Cor 5:14 NEB).

To say it in the most orthodox theological terms, the end of expiation for bloodshed, the end—not as abrogation but as fulfillment—of the arrangement announced in Genesis 9:6, is the innocent death of the Son, wrongly denounced by a righteous religious establishment and wrongfully executed by a legitimate government.

By unjustly condemning the Righteous One in the name of the *Pax Romana* and the welfare of the people (John 11:50; 18:14), the claimants to human righteousness refuted their claim for the rightness of the death penalty in the very act of imposing it.

That is the specifically Christian way to say it—although as Gandhi and Girard show us, one need not be Christian to see it. The power bearers of this world will not understand it in these terms, so we shall need to find ways to translate. We may speak of the unity of all humanity under the indiscriminate providence of God; of inalienable rights endowed by the Creator; of crime being partly the result of a local social situation; of the right to life being inalienable and therefore not something which a person can lose by doing evil.

All of these translations or parables are inadequate. Yet they are all valid parts of the argument in a multicultural democracy. They are not true in themselves as secular philosophical dicta, but for what they point to, namely, to the grand reversal

---

56. Oddly, yet profoundly, René Girard makes the same point in the terms of his new synthesis of cultural anthropology and literary history.

of world history when the Maker and Model became willingly the victim, bearing all human retribution, whether merited or not, and dying the death earned not only by the murderer but by all of us.

PART 7: THE TEST OF CONSISTENCY

This is not the first time in the course of our pilgrimage through our problem that I have needed to show how the public debate about legal death has become so clouded that what I most need to argue is not whether life, even guilty life, is sacred, but rather the inconsistencies of the case usually made for the death penalty.

Do You Really Mean It?

Probably the most strongly believed claim of those who advocate the retention of the supreme sanction is that the death penalty as currently practiced is the same as what God once commanded—whether in the very broad terms of the covenant given Noah or in the more rational argument. This is the conviction held to the most self-confidently by those who are most sure that their views are biblically warranted.

It is that unquestioning self-confidence that we here must proceed to test, approaching so to speak, "from the inside." We shall bring to light that people who think this is what they believe are not in fact consistent. Most of those who *claim* to be using the ancient biblical argument in favor of the death penalty have not faced the challenge of what it would mean to apply it consistently. There is no evidence—even in the most strongly argued books on the subject—that the costs of such consistency have been weighed. There is a great distance between saying "the death penalty cannot be wrong because the Bible commands it" and saying, "the death penalty laws of my state and nation are what God commands." For example,

- Most persons found guilty of capital crimes by our courts are not sentenced to death, but to some lesser punishment. Christians authentically taking Genesis 9:6 literally as the last word of God would have to be aggressively active in getting all of those sentences made harsher, not only in those cases where the murder was particularly atrocious.

- Many persons sentenced to death are not executed after all. A rare few are still alive to be released when new evidence shows them to have been innocent. Some make deals with the prosecution, some benefit from executive clemency, some are saved on appeal because of procedural errors made by police or prosecutors, some die or are killed in prison, etc. Christians concerned to defend Genesis 9:6 as legislation would have to be especially concerned for saving those in the first category and for assuring the execution of all the others.

- The Mosaic legislation in general made (as we observed) no reference to mitigating consideration and no provision for lack of premeditation. For every death in an automobile accident or in medical malpractice, someone should die. Insanity should be no defense, nor youth. In the conservative Christian literature arguing in favor of the death penalty, one finds little precision about whether these defenses or mitigating pleas should be swept away or respected.

- Those who claim divine revelation as grounds for modern jurisprudence are not usually clear about *which* revelation they mean. The laws of Moses are clear in demanding death for rebellious adolescents, for a bride's deceiving her husband concerning her virginity, for adultery, for sabbath-breaking, for homosexuality, and for false prophecy.[57] If this is truly what our pro-death contemporaries mean, they should say so and somehow deal honestly with the fact that in the U.S., in particular, the direct application of provisions from the Scriptures of one religious community would constitute the establishment of (one particular) religion, contrary to the First Amendment. Do they mean to obtain this legislation through democratic due process? If democratic due process does not work, will they take the law into their hands?

---

57.   Cf. Lloyd R. Bailey, *Capital Punishment*, 17-22.

If, on the other hand, what they mean to appeal to in favor of the death penalty is not the entire Mosaic Law, and if they mean to speak only of death as the penalty for murder, in line with Genesis 9:6, that would be intellectually understandable on the grounds that the covenant with Noah applies to all humanity as the laws of Moses do not. Yet, it would be a very different claim, since the Genesis report on God's words to Noah is not a legislative text. Most of the capital provisions of the books of Moses would have to be dropped. The very point of the word to Noah is that *only* murder is grounds for bloodshed to return.

When I point out that my fellow Christians who *think* they are in favor of retaining death penalty laws on biblical grounds are, in fact, inconsistent, my concern is not that they ought to become more consistent by working for a much more lethal government. Consistency is not a virtue if it applies to the hilt an inadequate rule or insight. Inconsistency is not a sin but it may be a flag, a marker indicating the possibility of self-deception or self-contradiction. It signals that one may not be doing what one does for the reason immediately avowed.

My concern is rather that those who have been led to think that the retentionist stance is obviously Christian should recognize that what they really want is not more killing after all. What they really want is compassion for the victims of crime, or security in an increasingly violent society, or a dramatic statement about the sanctity of life, or reassurance that the values of their faith have some standing in society. I want those things too, but asking our civil order to be more bloodthirsty is not the way to work toward them. These fellow citizens *have been led to believe* that this is what God has called for and that more vengeful laws would provide it; but they do not really deeply believe that. If they did, there would have to be a pro-death counterpart to the American Civil Liberties Union, dedicated to increasing a thousandfold the number of offenders our society legally kills.

As a matter of fact, however ("fact" both in verifiable social experience and in facing all the issues in rational argument), those same goals—compassion for victims, security, affirming the sanctity of *all* life, addressing public values from a faith stance—would be better served by a thorough anti-death witness, continuing the "humanization" process in which Christians have been leading for centuries.

PART 8: WHEN THE DEATH PENALTY ITSELF IS MURDER

The previous point at which the advocates of retention needed to be challenged was their conviction—more an assumption taken for granted than an argument they would recognize the need to support—that the modern legal practice of capital punishment is in some important way like the biblical precedents they claim.

Now we move to another dimension of our challenge to the integrity of the retentionist tradition: namely, its failure to avow the fallibility of human instruments of justice and, therefore, its failure to recognize that in a small but real percentage of cases the innocent are killed *by the state*, *in our name*, in the defense of our society's power system.

All human institutions are fallible. They are capable of errors of fact or of interpretation. According to Christian convictions, all humans are sinful, using power, including sometimes the power of the law, for purposes less than purely honest and unselfish.

One of the great values of the democratic vision of civil government is its realism about human fallibility. If a tyrant were perfectly wise and good, tyranny would be the most efficient form of government. We need freedom of speech and assembly and the press, we need constitutions, guaranteed rights of majorities and individuals, elections, and checks and balances to keep under control the real possibilities of error and of misused authority.

In the courts this kind of corrective control is exercised by higher courts through the right of appeal. But there is one kind of judicial error that can never be made right: a wrongful sentence of death. The death penalty assumes that the judicial process is infallible and has all the evidence; yet we do not assume infallibility and omniscience in any other branch of government.

Marquis de Lafayette is credited with saying, "Until the infallibility of human judgment shall have been proved to me,

I shall demand the abolition of the penalty of death."[58] His friend Thomas Jefferson is quoted as saying practically the same thing. No matter who said it first, should not persons seeking a biblically oriented view of things have even more profound reasons than the noble French general or the deist Federalist had to believe both in the sacredness of every human life and in the fallibility of every human institution?

Christian sobriety calls us to mistrust any social practice whose mistakes are irrevocable. Even the lesser penalties of unjust incarceration are irrevocable, in that they steal years from a person's life that cannot be returned. It is one of the institutionalized injustices of our society that in most jurisdictions there is no standard provision for compensation to those subjected wrongfully to lesser penalties of conviction and punishment.[59] Yet death imposed on an innocent person is the absolutely incorrigible error. It is murder, committed in the name of the people.

The works of Borchard, Frank, Stanford, and Bedau detail some *known* cases of the innocent being convicted.[60] There are

---

58.   [Editor's note: Yoder does not provide the reference but, in "The Case Against the Death Penalty," Hugo Adam Bedau introduces this quote saying, "Speaking to the French Chamber of Deputies in 1830, years after the excesses of the French Revolution, which he had witnessed, the Marquis de Lafayette said, 'I shall ask for the abolition of the punishment of death until I have the infallibility of human judgment demonstrated to me'" (American Civil Liberties Union, 1992, available online at http://users.rcn.com/mwood/deathpen.html, accessed Jan 1, 2011). Bedau cites as his source for this quote Charles Lucas, *Recueil des Débats des Assemblées Législatives de la France sur la Question de la Peine de Mort* (Paris: 1831), pt. II, 32.]

59.   Eugene B. Block, *And May God Have Mercy: The Case Against Capital Punishment*, 1. Sometimes a state legislature will make amends for wrongful incarceration by a private law if there is a public outcry, but our legal system does not acknowledge a *right* to compensation for miscarriage of justice.

60.   Edwin M. Borchard, *Convicting the Innocent: Errors in Criminal Justice*, 374, 415; Barbara and Jerome Frank, *Not Guilty*; Hugo A. Bedau and Michael L. Radelet, "Miscarriages of Justice in Poten-

scores of them. They happen because of (innocently or malevolently) false testimony, mistaken identity, or misinterpreted circumstantial evidence. By the nature of the case, it is a matter of chance that these particular examples have come to light.[61]

Likewise, by the nature of the case, it is seldom possible or useful to review such a case judicially after execution. The American legal system has no agency responsible for keeping track of miscarriages of justice. When such errors come to light, it is through the disinterested curiosity of some journalist, the persistent pleading of the victim's family, or a later confession by the truly guilty person. There must be more cases than we can know in which no one brought forward the facts that would have exonerated the accused. Warden Lewis Lawes (of Sing Sing) spoke for his colleagues in estimating that one in fifty of the persons executed by the state is innocent. Others estimate five percent.

Retentionists can continue to argue that the danger of such miscarriages of justice is slight, though the testimony of those who monitor current penal practice is not reassuring. But the Christian attitude should not be to quibble about whether the rate of judicially sanctioned murders is five percent or two percent. That such killings can occur *at all* is the question. A *fallible* civil order should never lay claim to *absolute* authority over life. It should *in the name of its own honor* deny itself the right to make irrevocable decisions.[62] The courts should do the best they can, without interrupting the normal course of justice out

---

tially Capital Cases," *Stanford Law Review* 40.1: 21-180; cf. also Charles Black, *Capital Punishment: The Inevitability of Caprice and Mistake.*

61. Cf. Bedau and Radelet, "Miscarriages of Justice."
62. "It belongs to its nature as an orderly society that its measures can have only a provisional, relative and limited character, that they must always be in a position to be transcended and corrected. But in punishing by death it does something unlimited, irrevocable and irreparable." Karl Barth, *Church Dogmatics* 3/4 (Edinburgh: Clark, 1961), 444.

of fear of making mistakes,[63] but this can be done confidently only if the door is left open for review and for new evidence.

The point at which we began to consider the need for Christian sobriety about the fallibility of social institutions was the jeopardy of the innocent; yet there are other instances of sinfulness in the system. Our courts are routinely discriminatory in terms of race and class. Despite the theoretical right of all to counsel, only the wealthy (and a few individuals whose peculiarly promising cases are taken on by voluntary agencies) are assured adequate legal assistance. Especially in Texas, Louisiana, and Florida, where executions are the most numerous, a Caucasian convicted of the same crime will not receive the same sentence as a black; the same crime committed against a Caucasian will be punished more harshly than against a black; and in proportion to the number of crimes committed, the Caucasian is less likely to be convicted.[64] Any retentionist claiming to be motivated not by fear or vengeance, but by the honor of an impartially gracious God, would have to actively militate against these injustices.

---

63. We honor the fact that in our society certain due process rights are respected. The defense of constitutional rights in the U.S. Supreme Court suspended executions for awhile in the 1970s and has made some kinds of convictions more complicated. These rights make the prosecution of capital cases through the various levels of appeal enormously time-consuming and expensive. Prosecutors costing the government over half a million dollars are not rare. If the accused is wealthy, there is practically no end to the possible delays. Removing capital punishment would greatly alleviate the burdens on some courts.

64. The evidence of this bias has been recognized by the courts, and the growing complexity of the sentencing process takes some account of it. Cf. Michael Meltsner's account of the backgrounds to Furman vs. Georgia, in *Cruel and Unusual: The Supreme Court and Capital Punishment*. Yet, the courts are a weak remedy for a deep injustice in our culture, especially when the moral elites appealing to the courts do not have strength at the polls. The effect of the corrective measures partly achieved through the events in the 1970s has begun to be largely eroded both by new legislation and by the rulings of the Reagan Supreme Court.

The fact that execution closes and locks a door, which morally should be kept open, has numerous other undesirable accessory effects upon the administration of justice, beyond the obvious evil of making an error of a court irreparable. The prosecution of murder cases in states with the death penalty is much slower and is a greater burden on the courts and taxpayers because the defense will leave no stone unturned, no costly appeal untried. One case in California took over ten years and cost the state more than half a million dollars. Abolition states need not maintain a separate death row.

Penologists tell us, in addition, that the very presence of the death penalty on the books is a symbolic block preventing direct attention to the other unsolved problems of prison administration and reform. Overcrowding of prisons, education, recreation, work and rehabilitation, and procedures of parole and resocialization are catastrophically in need of new measures. To take the death penalty off the books will solve none of them. In terms of human pain, lifetime incarceration without prison reform might be, in fact, a fate as unpleasant as death. Yet the cultural defensiveness and vengefulness that keep the absolute sanction on the books are barriers to their being addressed adequately. The retention of the gas chambers, the gallows, and the chair, enshrining as they do the retributive mentality and the state's claim to absolute competence, warp our view of all the other problems. Prisons in other countries are ahead of those in the U.S. in the humaneness of their living conditions and their effectiveness in rehabilitation. Some think that our entire corrections enterprise is vitiated by the notion of vengeance as the underlying goal of the system, of which capital punishment is the extreme symbol even when seldom inflicted. Its abolition in the other Western democracies symbolically undermines that barrier to creativity.

Some Christians have argued that to speak of the treatment of criminals in terms of therapy and rehabilitation rather than punishment, as "liberal" or "humanistic" penologists do, would be to deny the moral nature of the offense, or to excuse guilt as only an illness. This is not the point. The issue is not whether there is moral guilt;

of course there is.[65] The issue is what the Christian attitude to the guilty should be. If our priority social preoccupation is with defending an abstract moral order by means of punishment rather than with the redemption of persons, public offenders will, of course, continue to be the most accessible victims of our self-righteousness.

65. Cf. George N. Boyd, "Capital Punishment: Deserved and Wrong," 162-65.

PART 9: FROM SURVEY TO SYNTHESIS

DENYING THE LEGITIMACY OF THE DEATH PENALTY

Thus far I have been faithful to the initially stated method. I have responded to one issue at a time, from the middle of the current social debate, picking up the themes and slogans that already dominate that debate. This has meant questioning some of the simplest and least self-critical assumptions of those who hitherto have carried on the discussion on both sides.

I have not repeated the naïve claim that "thou shalt not kill" in the Decalogue is a direct prohibition of judicial killing. That argument is made, too simply, by some of those who call for the death penalty to be abolished or radically restricted. The meaning of "thou shalt not kill" certainly did not, in the original setting, literally exclude all killing, since the Ten Words stand side by side in the Mosaic texts with others that provide for legal killing.

That does not, however, justify the simple way some declare this text irrelevant by saying that it means merely "do not murder." Logically, the distinction between "murder" and other killing is not that clear. Our society's laws distinguish a number of different degrees of murder and culpable manslaughter. The Hebrew language has a number of different words for taking human life, but the Hebrew usage is too infrequent to permit saying that *rsh* (also spelled *ratsach*)—the Hebrew verb in the Sixth Commandment—means only "murder" in some narrow modern sense. It can include killing in legal retribution (Num 35:27). Several respected recent Hebrew scholars have suggested that the original meaning was "do not take the law into your own hands."[66] Then this wording in the Decalogue would testify to the transition from the primitive form to which Genesis 4 and 9 testify, with the "blood avenger" being the next of kin, to the jurisdiction of some tribunal (such as the "judges" of

---

66. Cf. Yoder, "Exodus 20:13—'Thou Shalt Not Kill,'" 394-99 [Editor's note: also available in Yoder's *To Hear the Word*, 2d ed., 38-46]. Walther Koehler and Brevard Childs are the scholars using this phrase.

the time before Saul or the "elders in the gates" of an Israelite town). It would then in its original import have been a measure of restraint, a check on the arbitrariness and escalation that marked that primitive arrangement.

Thus, without being literalistic about "thou shalt not kill," we should still affirm with confidence that the sacredness of human life is rooted in the Law. We do not relativize the call to sexual integrity with the argument that for the ancient Hebrews "thou shalt not commit adultery" did not forbid polygamy, harem slavery, and concubinage. We do not relativize "do not give false witness" by limiting it to lying before a court of law. In Christian moral instruction, we typically expand, not contract, the meaning of the other commands of the Decalogue.

We may now be in a position to state, with more care and clarity than would have been possible at the outset, how we then *should* take the total witness of the Scripture story, including the place of legal killing in the Hebrew heritage. That legislation cannot be taken as a simple, institutional imperative—timeless, placeless, demanded by God of all societies regardless of culture or creed. The Hebrew Bible is not and does not claim to be that kind of civil law. If there was a time and place where some of those texts applied as civil law, it would *at most* have been thinkable between the time of Joshua and that of Josiah. Nothing in the teaching of the prophets or the later rabbis or the New Testament indicates that ancient Israelite civil legislation, with its score of capital offenses, was meant to be universal. It was abandoned in the sixth century BC, together with Israelite statehood, not only by the Jews but by God, even in its own land.

Before there were those civil rules, there was the different witness of Genesis, in the previous covenant, the one with Noah. As we saw, there exists only one occasion for shedding blood, namely prior bloodshed. The rootage for this was not a practical view of protecting the civil order but a sacral view of restoring the cosmic order. This demand for mimetic vengeance was present before history began (Gen 4); God's first action was to limit it, whereas Cain's lineage escalated it. Even less than can obtain for the case rules of Exodus through Deuteronomy, we have no way to make the Genesis 9 arrangement a basis for civil law. Our American practice of capital punishment at its most rigorous falls far short of expiating every death with another death.

How then should we take this Hebrew heritage? Many Jews, Christians, and other contemporaries take for granted that it is obsolete, irrelevant, and that we should build our society on newer insights. Then they have numerous other good reasons, reasonable in our time, to oppose capital punishment. Most of those "other good reasons" are, in fact, very strong, although I have not made much of them:

- the general dehumanizing effect it has on a society to assume that it is up to us to dispose of human life;
- the general human vision according to which every human life, even the unwanted and the morally unworthy, is sacred. Persons who abandon the details of ancient Israelite social norms still understand the notion of divine image in every person;
- modesty about the inaccuracy and fallibility of human power structures: without making a statement about the value of any particular individual's life, a low view of government's righteousness will militate against granting the government absolute sovereignty over life and death;
- sobriety about how the presence of the death penalty on the books makes all the administration of justice slower, costlier, and less fair;
- sobriety about the number of innocent individuals statistically sure to be killed due to the fallibility of the police and the courts;
- a psychological understanding according to which anger and revenge are drives unworthy of mature persons and destructive to social civility.

These arguments . . . suffice to compel most citizens who think about it . . . on general human grounds, to favor the general trend of recent centuries in the West away from the use of death as a civil penalty. For our present assignment, however, they do not suffice to set aside what is really present, both in the Hebrew Scriptures and in popular culture, by way of demand for retaliation.

This demand for retribution may be called "vengeance," "expiation," "mimesis," or something else, depending on the fine-tuning of your social science; but it is always there. It is still there in the strongest pro-death arguments, those of Berns and van den Haag.[67] These two contemporary authors most openly renounce arguing from any specified critical, moral, or philosophical commitment of their own (except for showing the weakness of others' too simple reliance on rehabilitation models). They argue only from the brute fact of vengeful anger as a universal (and, they believe, salutary) human phenomenon.[68] Neither Berns nor van den Haag follows his argument to its logical conclusions which, in historical perspective until very recently, called for torturing offenders before killing them or including the offender's family members in the scope of vengeance. Berns does not even ask that all killers be killed—only the most vile.[69] Thus, they too have been somewhat swept up in the general influence of Jewish and Christian humanism since the Renaissance. They affirm retribution as a political imperative in the worst cases, not as a moral imperative in all cases.

That deep demand for death as redemption for death will not go away under the criticism of modern reasonableness.[70] But neither would a world be livable in which it would have the last word. Since Yahweh's intervention in Genesis 4, it is no longer

---

67.   Walter Berns, *For Capital Punishment*; and Ernest van den Haag, *The Death Penalty*.

68.   A collection of quotations in favor of the validity of retribution, as "instinctive" or as socially useful, is presented by Raoul Berger, *Death Penalties: The Supreme Court's Obstacle Course*, 135.

69.   Ibid., 183.

70.   Therefore I agree with the excellent work of the philosopher Stephen Nathanson (*An Eye for an Eye? The Morality of Punishing by Death*) that the argument against the death penalty must begin by acknowledging the parcel of truth in the popular demand for it.

the last word; another story has begun. It is the story of restraint, of sacrifice to defend and restore the cosmic order. That story comes to its first culmination in the cross of Christ, in which utter innocence died for universal guilt, satisfying and thereby putting to an end the mechanisms of mimetic vengeance.[71] From then on, the story that is needed is ours. Christ's followers, for whom his cross has ended all sacrifice for sin, are to be, if we believe in him as the last word, the instruments of the pardon and the new style of response to evil which he enabled and enjoined.

Love of enemy is the gospel theme where the linkage between Christ himself and the believer's stance and calling in the world is closest. Forgiveness is the response to evil dictated by God's own nature and by Jesus' example and command.[72] We should seek to save the life even of the murderer fully culpable of the act for which society wants to kill him. The death penalty is wrong, not because it is not merited by some, but because merit is not the basis on which, since Jesus, we should decide who has a right to belong to the human race.

If the Bible were to be read fundamentally as a source of timeless, changeless rules for civil societies, it would document God's failure, since the narrative moved farther and farther from any such vision of a stable national theocracy, ever since the death of Solomon. If, on the other hand, the Bible is the story of God's unceasing interventions to move humankind in the direction of

---

71. I have used here the broadest language in order to demonstrate openness to the anthropologist's agenda. The Christian is enabled and commanded to take such sacrificial love as life's law on the grounds of Jesus; yet that does not make it an esoteric notion nor a mystery for others.

72. Concerning the centrality of forgiveness, cf. William Klassen, *The Forgiving Community*; on the importance of the offender or enemy in locating the meaning of forgiveness, cf. William Klassen, *Love of Enemy: The Way to Peace.* "Forgive us as we forgive" is the only petition in the Lord's Prayer to be conditional. It is the task for which Jesus empowers his disciples with the gift of the Holy Spirit (John 20:21), the activity for which he himself has been most criticized by the authorities (Matt 9:2).

righteousness and well-being, then we must read the early chapters of Genesis as the point of departure of that story, rather than as definitive legislation. We can likewise read the documents of the early Israelite nation as a beginning movement, from which the unfolding that did in fact happen properly needed to happen, away from death as sanction threatened for a score of offenses (we do not know how long or how consistently any of these rules were in fact enforced) and toward a society that can live at peace, without having to kill anyone.

God's identity (i.e., God's being authentically and faithfully who God is and not something or somebody else) does not consist in timelessness that resists all change, so that his first word in Genesis would be also his last. His identity consists in his moving and working always in the same direction, through all of these centuries. That "same direction" we know best, most clearly in Jesus; but when we avow that fact, then in its light we can understand the ancient Israelite events and documents as already constituting part of that work, moving in that direction.

We have read with more care than is usual the Old Testament passages that some think demand the civil penalty of death, and it has regularly come to light that they do not mean that. We have learned to discern with more care the difference between civil law, affirmations of a sacred cosmic order, and other ways of knowing about God's will. Each in its place, when read in the way that belongs to its kind and style of language, shows God at work, moving in the same way toward what Jesus ultimately did, toward ending blood vengeance by sacrificing himself.

It is that movement, broadening over the centuries into the derived forms of democracy, humanism, *habeas corpus*, and the other rights of the accused, which since Beccaria has spread out into nonreligious parallels. [In our day this same movement] seeks—not yet very successfully—positive responses to the offender that will link respect for his human dignity with the protection of the innocent and restoration for victims.[73]

---

73. Cesare Beccaria, *On Crimes and Punishments.*

The standard accounts in the literature indicate that challenges to the death penalty began to be raised in western Europe in the eighteenth century with the secular legal philosopher Beccaria and the Philadelphia physician Benjamin Rush.[74] That is, however, inaccurate; it was a constant undercurrent in earlier Christian history.

In medieval canon law, having had anything to do with shedding blood, even having served on a court to try a person for a capital offense could disqualify a man from the priesthood. Honored by Russians as their first Christan king, Prince Vladimir of Kiev eliminated the death penalty to mark his conversion in 988.

On January 5, 1527, when Felix Mantz of Zurich was condemned to drowning as the first radical Protestant to be executed by a Protestant government, part of the accusation was that he testified "that a Christian should not be a ruler, nor execute anyone with the sword, kill or punish." Menno Simons, Frisian leader of a movement like that of Mantz, wrote to the Calvinist Martin Micron in 1556 that civil killing ill becomes a Christian ruler.[75]

When in 1682 William Penn wrote his "Great Act," the Crown charter for his Quaker colony, the death penalty was eliminated for all crimes except premeditated murder, and even that was only included because it was demanded by the Crown. Thus, what Beccaria began to articulate in 1764 and Rush in 1787 was but a new phase, adjusted to the Age of Enlightenment, of a much older and more specifically Christian tradition of pro-life criticism. That tradition has worn thin recently, as many Christians have not seen past the prevalent linking

---

74. Benjamin Rush, "An Enquiry into the Effects of Public Punishments upon Criminals, and upon Society (1787)" and "Considerations on the Injustice and Impolicy of Punishing Murder by Death (1792), in *Reform of Criminal Law in Pennsylvania: Selected Inquiries, 1787-1819.*

75. Menno gives the following reasons: if the offender has repented of his sin you are killing your Christian brother; if he has not, you are consigning him prematurely to hell. Even the pagan Lacedaemonians did not kill offenders, but imprisoned them and put them to work.

of faith commitment with political conservatism. Some have oddly thought that concern for the dignity of the life of offenders was incompatible with concern for the wrongness of sin. What our study has shown is that if we take more seriously the original cultural rootedness of the death penalty in primitive rituals of retaliation, we must also acknowledge, in the light of the cross, our unworthiness to kill even the guilty.

CHAPTER 5

YOU HAVE IT COMING: GOOD PUNISHMENT

THE LEGITIMATE SOCIAL FUNCTION OF PUNITIVE BEHAVIOR

PREFACE: THE SHAPE OF THE FOLLOWING PIECES

What follows is a coherent package in subject matter, though quite mixed in terms of form.[1] Its several constituent pieces make the same point in parallel ways within several subcultures or subdisciplines. The way in which the several sections run parallel, without the material in one being derived from that in another, might prove something about there being a "deep structure" common in them all.

The package is not at present (summer 1995) to be thought of as "a book," since book marketing dictates choices among a limited number of possible literary models. The cross-disciplinary nature of this survey may well not meet those requirements. Nor is it a paper apt to fit any one journal. Putting it together in a "desktop" package is motivated by the thought that despite its heterogeneous and incomplete nature it might be worth circulating for critique.

---

1. [Editor's note: As indicated in the introduction, "Good Punishment" was never polished and formally published, but was made available online though Shalom Desktop Publications in 1995. http://theology.nd.edu/people/research/yoder-john/. Yoder began this work in 1992, released the first twelve parts in 1995, and then added an addendum in 1997. Yoder's own preface sufficiently establishes the unique nature of this material.]

In none of the subcultures or subdisciplines on which the following pages draw am I an expert, except in the indirect sense that my own field, that of Christian ethics, is itself a dialogical discipline that demands synthesis and critical listening to other disciplines.[2] In the reading to which the notes under the following texts testify, I have been struck by how narrow each of the subdisciplines and subcultures is, and how little the writers within each mini-world attend to being understandable outside the coterie of their own clients or to handling the questions an outsider normally would ask of them.

In some of the annotations to some of the mini-chapters, there are signs of my effort to cross-reference from one sub-disciplinary realm to another. Sometimes, but not usually, one chapter leads into the next. These connections and the occasional cross-references are vestiges of an earlier drafting phase when I thought I might be writing just one paper. More recent drafting, however, has led me to renounce that cross-referencing effort. Nor are all the footnotes complete.[3] There is no one logical sequence in which the chapters should come. They appear rather (roughly) in the order of my (chronologically) first getting to work on them.

Fellow Christian ethicists may note in the above title a reminder of the title *Good Anger* given a recent book by John Giles Milhaven.[4] In more than one careful reading of that book, I have not been able to find in it a precise thesis in moral theology put clearly enough that it could be either accepted or rejected; yet I share with Milhaven the intent counterculturally[5] to open up for another look

---

2. One exception to this disclaimer might be the fact that Sebastian Franck, with whom part 2 begins, represents the field of my dissertation research, namely the Radical Reformation of the sixteenth century. I first came upon the phrase about what "befits a king" when translating Franck into Spanish in 1971.

3. [Editor's note: Effort has been made to fill in as many of Yoder's footnotes as possible.]

4. John Giles Milhaven, *Good Anger*.

5. Or rather counter-sub-culturally. Our society at large is quite unabashed about punitive behavior. Especially in the United States, the public-politicized confidence in punishment as the cure for all kinds of offenses

the case that can be made for a category of human responses to conflict that we cannot handle as long as we deny their legitimacy.

"Legitimacy" may not be exactly the right word to identify the social and moral place of punishment. Taken straight, it means "according to the laws." But the laws vary widely. "Good" is certainly too strong, since we are talking about a response to evil and to intentionally causing pain, which may be held at best to be a lesser evil. Yet we do need to use a term from the moral realm. Perhaps "tolerability" or "sufferability" would be better.

Another title could have been "The Case for Punity." There is no such word as "punity" in the dictionary, and that very absence tells us something. The opposite term, "impunity," is most often used pejoratively; that there should be punishment is thus presupposed for its neglect to be wrong. Only because punishment is imperative is "impunity" seen to be wrong. It is that presupposition which I suggest needs further respectful study. The "imperative" may be thought of as grounded theologically, or psychologically, or sociologically; we need not choose among possible explanations. They may well all be valid.

Yet to recognize that is but the beginning of our task. There are quite varied forces that militate against punishment being inflicted. Some of these are spiritually profound, like forgiveness. Some are philosophically extreme, like anarchism. Some are politically defensive, like efforts by friends of the guilty to protect them. Thus, "impunity" becomes a term of reproach, used to condemn some or any or all of the reasons for the guilty party's not being punished. Since the reasons for the impunity may be good or bad or debatable, there can be no simple way through our problem.

Punishment is, to capsule the thesis of these pages, something that we do better to acquiesce in or to suffer than to ignore or to seek to wipe it out.[6]

---

and dangers is on the rise in the mid-'90s. It is the enlightened, Christian, academic, modern, and post-modern elites who are ashamed of it and whose embarrassment this study will critique.

6. Patience is the virtue that accepts suffering, or there is the old English term "longsuffering." "Sufferable" would seem to be in English the best word for "that with which one is patient."

As the reader will soon see, much of the learning process to which these pages testify was sparked by the work of René Girard. I am grateful for Girard's most creative contribution to the field of study and for his impetus to my own search, although I have had to conclude that the effort of some of his admirers to make of his analyses something like an Einsteinian "general field theory," capable of explaining everything, has done a disservice to Girard by overreaching.[7] I have therefore felt free to liberate some of the sections of what follows from needing always to dialogue with the Girardians, as some of the paragraphs drafted earlier did.

---

7. Girard himself denies that claim. He disavows the intention to provide "a reductive notion" or "a rigid mold into which to fit the diversity of forms." Cf. Robert G. Hamerton-Kelly, *Violent Origins: Walter Burkert, René Girard & Jonathan Z. Smith on Ritual Killing and Cultural Formation*, 106-11. Girard uses his own tools very freely and confidently over a wide variety of themes, but he disavows the claim, which some of his devotees seem to assume, that they explain everything.

PART 1: DÜRKHEIM: IN GOD'S NAME OR IN OURS

In 1893, Émile Dürkheim, one of the fathers of modern sociology, wrote his classic *The Division of Labor in Society*.[8] In a way that is only partly understandable to the lay reader, beginning under the odd heading "Mechanical Solidarity Through Likeness," Dürkheim focuses much of his study on the penal system. Without providing much documentation for his generalizations, yet on the grounds of his broad background in comparative cultural studies, Dürkheim describes punitive behavior as a key constituent of any society:

> [P]rimitive peoples punish for the sake of punishing, [they] make the culpable suffer particularly for the sake of making him suffer and without seeking any advantage for themselves for the suffering they impose. . . . they seek neither to strike back justly nor to strike back usefully, but merely to strike back. . . . That is because the passion which is the soul of punishment ceases only when exhausted.[9]

The escalation of the punitive response is thus part of the nature of things, of persons and societies; that is, the measure of the "passion" that enlivens the collective or common conscience.[10] "A simple restitution of the troubled order would not suffice for us; we must have a more violent satisfaction. The

---

8. Citations are from the English translation by George Simpson (New York, Macmillan, 1933), a version based on all five French editions.
9. Dürkheim, *Division of Labor in Society*, 85-86. Dürkheim argues that this is proven by the fact that animals, inanimate objects, or innocent persons may be the objects of punishment.
10. Translator Simpson notes (ix) that others would translate "collective or common consciousness" rather than "conscience." He is right in discerning that the two terms are not distinguished in French as they are in English. Yet it must mean more than "consciousness" in the sense of "awareness"; it has to include some kind of moral claim.

force against which the crime comes is too intense to react with very much moderation."[11]

The way most cultures explain to themselves the power of that "force," which makes penalty imperative, is their appeal to some transcendent authority.

> [A]t the bottom of the notion of expiation there is the idea of a satisfaction accorded to some power . . . which is superior to us. When we desire the repression of crime, it is not that we desire to avenge personally, but to avenge something sacred which we feel . . . above us. . . . Sometimes it is a simple idea, as morality, duty. . . ; most often we represent it in the form of one or several concrete beings: ancestors, divinity. That is why penal law is not alone essentially religious in origin, but indeed always retains a certain religious stamp. It is because the acts that it punishes appear to be attacks upon something transcendent.[12]

The editorial "we" here signals that Dürkheim is claiming to describe something common to all cultures, including both his own and earlier ones. This demand is perennial, even though the analysis that our modernity brings to bear will proceed immediately to challenge its basis.

> Assuredly, this representation is illusory.[13] It is ourselves that we . . . avenge, ourselves that we satisfy, since it is within us and in us alone that the offended sentiments are found. But this illusion is necessary. Since these sentiments have exceptional force because of their collective origin, their universality, their permanence, and their intrinsic intensity, they separate themselves radically from the rest of our conscience whose states are much more feeble. . . . they bind us to objects which are outside of our temporal life.[14]

---

11. Dürkheim, 99-100.
12. Ibid, 100.
13. I.e., from a modern perspective.
14. Dürkheim, 100. The value of Dürkheim's classic formulation does

There is much about Dürkheim's analysis that we need not pursue here. He is interested only in how society as a whole represses deviance. He does not seek to root the repressive process exhaustively in intra- or inter-personal drives or models or analogies (as will Girard). As our point of entry into the realm of "good punishment," it suffices to take note that Dürkheim, as one of the pillars of the discipline,[15] has described as not subject to any debate the pervasiveness of the punitive behavior of which he says five things that we can take with us into the encounter with other disciplines:

- The activity is vengeful. It is not at its base either caused or justified on grounds of the health of society or the rehabilitation of the offender.[16]
- The activity claims a transcendent validation, even in a society where the primitive and classical notions of divine will or an absolute moral order are no longer creditable.
- That there is such a process seems to be held by public opinion or "the common conscience" to be indispensable for the life of the society, even when the social scientist can make no moral case for it.[17]

---

not depend, for our purposes, on our being able to go into his use of the personality theory of his time ("alienation" and "mirage," 101), or his neurology ("nervous current," "cortical centers," "plexus," 97). His claim to show how a non-transcendent punitive drive claims a transcendent validation is independent of those causal explanations in terms of the "science" of his time.

15. David Garland, whose *Punishment and Modern Society: A Study in Social Theory* is the most respected recent broad survey (to which we shall return), begins his account with Dürkheim.

16. Garland points out as well that it is never claimed by its advocates or its agents that the punitive system is economically beneficial. It is in fact something that a society is willing to pay for, 106.

17. Not only does Dürkheim call the process an illusion, he goes to no trouble at all to apply to it the sociologist's explanatory concern (which is the topic of the rest of his book) for the complementary way in which labor is divided. He does not analyze separately the complementary roles within the punitive processes of legislator,

- This pattern obtains in all societies; it is a general human phenomenon, which some would call "natural," rather than a provincial or particular phenomenon.
- Any society seeks to reinterpret the drive, hiding its primitive simplicity by giving more respectable reasons for it.

Garland cites Nietzsche: "Pleasure in cruelty is not really extinct today; only, given our greater delicacy, that problem has had to undergo a certain sublimation . . . [punishment] has to be translated into imaginative and psychological terms in order to pass muster before the tenderest critical conscience."[18]

This is one way of affirming that we have to come to terms with the primal fact that punishment is constitutive of human existence. There is no point in arguing with its facticity. Our own moral sensitivity to the unworthiness of the punitive drive in our own hearts will not make it go away, even though that sensitivity has moved many to seek to ignore it or to hope that Enlightenment might make it fade away. Nor will our demonstrating the harm it does weaken it.

---

policeman, lawyer, judge, jailor, and offender. He does not (as does Foucault later) ask how the rulers benefit from the penal system.

18. Nietzsche, *Genealogy of Morals* (in *The Birth of Tragedy and the Genealogy of Morals*, 200; in Garland, 63).

PART 2: THE CULTURAL IMPERATIVE OF LÈSE-MAJESTÉ:

A LITERARY-HISTORICAL RECONNAISSANCE INTO THE HISTORY OF A DICTUM: CLASSICAL PREFACE TO A MULTIDISCIPLINARY ENQUIRY

It Befits Royalty to Be Defamed by Evil People

Sebastian Franck of Donauwörth (1499-1542), one of the so-called "Spiritualizers" of the Protestant Reformation, earned his living partly by making soap and partly by compiling and printing encyclopedic chronicles. One of his compilations was a collection of adages.[19] Another was a list of "roman heretics," i.e., persons condemned by the papacy as heretical. Of these persons Franck said that he had

> no doubt, that among them are many dear, blessed people, who have more Spirit in their little finger than [has] the Antichrist [i.e., the pope] in all his sects and bodies. These [the Antichrist's sects and bodies] merit well their place in the pope's calendar of saints—while those others [i.e., the "Roman heretics" Franck cares about] appear most honorably in his [the pope's] list of heretics,[20] since to be defamed by evil people is an honor (Luke 6:22), whereas it is a curse when one is blessed by them (Luke 6:22; Mal 2:2; cf. Ps 109:28; Matt 5:11). For to have all sorts of evil said of one-self by them is praise and blessedness. As that philosopher also said, "It befits a king, to be defamed, when

---

19. *Sprichwörter / schöne / weise / herrliche clügreden / vnnd hoffsprüch / darinnen der alten vnd nachkommenen / aller nationen vnnd sprachen gröste vernufft vnnd klügheyt* (Frankenfurt am Meyn: Fetruct bey Christian Engenolffen, 1541), cited here from the 5th ed., 1560, in the holdings of the Mennonite Historical Library at Goshen, Ind., courtesy of Nelson P. Springer and Joe Springer.

20. "Figure with honor" means in Franck's eyes, not the Pope's. It is an honor to these people that the Pope condemns them.

you speak and act rightly, especially [to be defamed]
by those, by whom to be praised would be a shame."
Christ testifies likewise (Matt 5:11; 10:17-25; John
15:18-25). Therefore they figure with great honor in
this [papal] register.[21]

Franck thereby took his place in the long line of those for
whom suffering, especially when unmerited, is a mark of truth.
Later historians of the same style, reading the story of salvation
from below, were Gottfried Arnold (1699)[22] and in our century
Walter Nigg and Leonhard Ragaz.

In a broad sense, this note of the reversal of all values is a
standard rhetorical move made by many thinkers in any time of
upheaval. That suffering is a mark of the true church is the broadest way to say it.[23] Yet something more precise than this general
vision of suffering as a mark of fidelity is also being expressed
by the dictum that Franck cites anonymously from "that philosopher." The particular form of suffering being described is
defamation, which relates to the fact that the person suffering is
a person of some status, and that the reason for it is the good he
has done.

---

21. Cited from the modern German edition of Franck's text in Heinold
    Fast, *Der linke Flügel der Reformation*, 234, drawn from 334
    and following in Franck's *Chronica, Zeytbuch vnd geschychtbibel*
    (Strasbourg, 1531).

22. Gottfried Arnold (1666-1714), *Unparteiische Kirchen- und Ketzer-
    historie*, 1688.

23. I reviewed the notion of "marks of the church" and the conviction
    that the cross is one of them in my 1967 paper "A People in the
    World" (reprinted 1994 in *The Royal Priesthood*, 86-101). How
    the Anabaptists of the sixteenth century inherited the same notion
    from Zwingli and probably from Erasmus is noted in my *Täufer-
    tum und Reformation in Gespräch* (Zürich: EVZ-Verlag, 1968),
    191-200. [Editor's note: This work is now available in English as
    *Anabaptism and Reformation in Switzerland: An Historical and
    Theological Analysis of the Dialogues between Anabaptists and
    Reformers*, trans. David Carl Stassen and C. Arnold Snyder (Kitch-
    ener, Ontario: Pandora Press, 2004).]

"That philosopher" to whom Franck alluded without naming him was probably Antisthenes (444-365),[24] a pupil of Socrates and the teacher of Diogenes. He is counted as founder of the "cynical" school. None of his writings have survived entirely, but several score of fragments are cited throughout the classical literature.[25] This particular apothegm is recounted in the most straightforward version of Diogenes Laertius: "Hearing then that Plato spoke ill of him; 'It is royal,' he [Antisthenes] said, 'when doing good to be spoken evil of.'"[26]

The phrase was cited as well by Epictetus,[27] by Marcus Aurelius,[28] and by Albertus Magnus.[29] Plutarch weaves the same thought, without crediting Antisthenes, into his life of Alexander the Great, who he says was patient with the way his courtiers spoke ill of him: "He was very mildly disposed at first toward this treatment of himself, and used to say that it was the lot of a king to bestow favors and be ill-spoken of therefore."[30]

The emperors Alexander and Marcus Aurelius may stand, for our purposes, for the notion that the authentic king will be ready to accept with a stoic serenity this component of the

---

24. It is not excluded that Franck might be referring to one of the later sources to whom we shall be coming, such as Epictetus or Marcus Aurelius, who, when they used the phrase, did not always credit Antisthenes. In the days before copyrights, to borrow a proverb from a predecessor was not a vice.

25. Fernanda Decleva Caizzi, ed., *Antisthenis Fragmenta*.

26. *basilikón, ephé, kalôs akoúein*; Caizzi Nr. 150; Diog L. VI/3.

27. Caizzi Nr. 20A, 30, from Arrian. VI/6/20; *prátein mèn 'eû, kakôs d' 'akoúein*.

28. *Meditations*, VII/36, Caizzi 20B, 30. The verb is the same as in Epictetus. One finds other parallel expressions in the *Meditations*. "Do everything as a disciple of [his own adoptive father T. Aurelius] Antoninus; Remember how he bore with those who blamed him unjustly without blaming them in return (VI/30)"; "When someone has done you wrong consider with what opinion . . . he has done wrong . . . you will pity him (VII/26)."

29. Cited in Sebastian Franck's own anthology of proverbs and adages, cited above, 43: *reguim est benefacere et malem audire*.

30. *Plutarch's Lives*, Loeb Classical Library (1971), 344-47.

cost of his role. Even one who is not a king (e.g., in the original usage of Antisthenes) is kinglike when he or she accepts that this is the nature of things.[31] The king does not *merit* that defamation, but he accepts it; it goes with the territory.

The value of this material, one lonely proverb making its way down through the classics with no clear connection to mythology or cult, or to civil punishment or prison, to which our other sources give more attention, is that it parallels from another angle the material we shall be observing in other disciplines. It affirms a kind of cosmic fittingness to the fact that the bearer of authority should be cut down. Such suffering *ex officio* is not in contradiction to but part of the dignity of the role.

---

31. I do not attempt to explain why Antisthenes, with no relation to government and when the person mistreating him was Plato, assumed that being like a king, having a royal attribute (*basilikón*), would be a good thing. This might well indicate that the dictum had a prehistory before Antisthenes.

PART 3: AFTER ANTISTHENES

The Cultural Reality Underlying the Classical Dictum: the Chieftain as Scapegoat

The notion that it befits royalty to be defamed is not a self-evident or necessary part of the general countercultural reflex of the cynic in ancient Greece (Antisthenes) or of the humanist in sixteenth-century Strasbourg (Franck), even though those are the people we saw repeating the proverb at each end of its trajectory, each in his own setting and for his own reasons. That it is fitting that powerbearers be defamed is a more narrow and precise kind of observation about the real world. The upsetting of standard values to which it testifies bespeaks a different cultural location from Franck's general vision of the place of suffering,[32] namely the special realm of liminal rituals whereby a society rehearses both the precariousness and the indispensability of social office.

The current term for this process is "scapegoating," yet the term demands great care in definition. The usage comes from Leviticus 16:9-22, where it may well represent a linguistic mistake. The Hebrew, which is usually translated "goat to be sent away," originally probably meant "goat for Azazel," Azazel being the proper name of some devil or spirit living out there in the desert, to whom the animal is sacrificed. There is nothing royal about the goat that is chased away. Nonetheless, the usage has become established in the language of anthropology or ethnology, which uses the term "scapegoat" to designate the entire field of ritual practices in many cultures that "send evil away."

---

32. Most interpreters of Franck's thought would derive his general thought about *Gelassenheit* (yieldedness or letting-go) and the place of suffering in the Christian life, following Christ, from the last pre-Reformation mystics. Yet it is also found in the thought of Renaissance figures like Erasmus and Zwingli. For cynics and stoics like Antisthenes and Marcus Aurelius, the basis for accepting suffering had to be different.

Frazer's *Golden Bough*,[33] the mother of all ritual encyclopedias, catalogs countless modes of "getting rid of evil" by killing a god or goddess, by placing the evil (or the devil) on a boat that one sends downriver, or on an animal, or on a person one chases away or kills. The variety of forms is so great that the reader despairs of finding a clear commonality in all of these practices. Readers seeking to "understand" such diverse cultures seem to be called to a leap of faith if they are to trust a particular anthropologist to make some sense of them all.

René Girard, literary critic turned culture historian and philosopher, has sought to bring greater coherence to the notion of the scapegoat by making distinctions among the many related but different practices on the basis of his understanding of how the event or practice that he calls *mimesis* describes the propagation of violence in simple cultures.[34] Girard's synthesis draws from three primary sources: ancient Greek myth, the practices of primitive peoples like those described by Frazer, and the medieval persecution of Jews and witches.[35]

---

33. James George Frazer, *The Golden Bough* (New York: Macmillan, 1922). In the perhaps more accessible 1940 abridgment, the killing of kings is chapter XXIV, 264-83, and other modes of expelling evil are chapters LV-LXIV, 538-658.

34. Girard first came to be widely read thanks to his *Violence and the Sacred*, trans. Patrick Gregory; and then in *The Scapegoat*, trans. Yvonne Freccero; cf. my review in *Religion and Literature* 19/3 (Autumn 1987), 89. For a good introduction to Girard's thought, see James G. Williams, *Religious Studies Review* 14/4 (October 1988), 320-26. For a more recent summary, see Hamerton-Kelly, ed., *Violent Origins*. Biblical analogs were first pursued by Raymund Schwager, *Brauchen wir einen Sündenbock?* 3d ed. A most recent update of Girard's version, going beyond the scapegoat themes, is his plenary lecture on "The Satan of the Gospels," presented at the American Academy of Religion in November 1992.

35. In each of these realms, the way Girard selects what data to use and how to read it goes beyond my capacity to evaluate. I here report on his synthesis without being clear about how one might expertly validate or invalidate it. That absence of a recognized disciplinary grid obligates the reader to enter in an amateur way the

Girard's overarchingly ambitious theory addresses in one sweep two fundamental issues:

- the origins of civil organization, which arose primevally as a way to keep the peace by breaking the viciously escalating circle of violence mimetically by punishing violence and directing the community's hostility unanimously against one victim;
- the origins of myth and ritual, which commemorate the death of the hero/victim by recounting and at the same time reinterpreting the foundational sacrificial event.

Once this vision has won some credibility, it may throw new light on other questions as well. Most original, and surprising to the French, post-modern, intellectual world he addressed, has been Girard's claim that the Hebraic worldview in general and the death of Jesus in particular represent a radical break in the otherwise universal fabric of scapegoat-based cultures. Thus, he constructs something like a historical demonstration of the uniqueness (and in some sense the truth) of Christianity based neither upon the authority of Scripture nor any traditional notion of revelation or magisterium, but on the historical facts as ethnography illuminates them.[36] His work has been so stimulating that there has already been formed an interdisciplinary circle of scholars who meet to read to one another's papers in a Girardian mode.[37] Most of the work of this circle of Girard's friends and admirers centers on a few topics: analyz-

---

conversation Girard has opened and thereby justifies my amateur access, despite the difficulties of such an enterprise, to which I shall refer more fully below.

36. In *Things Hidden Since the Foundation of the World* (trans. Stephen Bann and Michael Metteer, 158-63, 180-85, 205-15), Girard first made the strong case about the impact of Jesus.

37. The Colloquium on Violence and Religion has a membership list, a bulletin, a journal, its own international conferences, and its own sessions in the context of the American Academy of Religion.

ing the primitive origins of social structure, myth, and ritual; reinterpreting the biblical notions of atonement; and describing the uniqueness of the crucifixion of Jesus.

Girard has given less attention to a different set of questions that would seem to some to merit more, namely, the dimensions of mimesis and scapegoating that have survived beyond the primeval crises to reach into our ordinary contemporary experience whether or not some primeval purge can be claimed to have set them aside.[38] Might the mechanism of mimetic violence explain, as other psychological perspectives do not, why American society is so devoted to the death penalty? Might this perspective help to understand domestic abuse? Race riots? Renewed religiopolitical "Fundamentalism," whether in Iran, Egypt, Israel, or Texas?

A yet narrower question (which Girard does have in view, and which I should think his vision could helpfully interpret further, but which he does not seek to pursue) is the subset of scapegoats who would most properly fit the proverb from Antisthenes—namely, violence directed against the chieftain. Sometimes the scapegoat is not a leader but the outsider: Jew, witch, gypsy, or cripple. This best fits Girard's primeval and medieval examples.[39] Sometimes it is an anonymous innocent: a handsome

---

38. In "Generative Scapegoating" (in *Violent Origins*, ed. Robert G. Hammerton-Kelly, 73-105), Girard refers to some of this glancingly, as if these dimensions were hardly a problem. The maze of his bibliography obliges the part-time reader to continue the conversation without chasing down any other places where he might have said more. I did ask several others of his admirers for help in finding where he might have written on some of these issues. Girard is quoted as saying that social-science or social-service applications of these insights are not his field.

39. The starting point for the account of his book *The Scapegoat* is a cultural crisis in medieval Europe. The most obvious victim there was "the Jews." Similar evils befell the gypsy and the cripple, since their theologically qualified differentness was also already taken for granted.

young man or woman, or a person seized at random.[40] Yet at
another end of the scale, if it should be thought of at all as a
single scale, there is the other more focused set of scapegoating
rituals where the victim is the king.[41] A society finds ways, simul-
taneously or in sequence, to dishonor and to honor, to kill and to
resurrect its king. Sometimes the killing is literal and sometimes
it is ritual/symbolic.[42] Sometimes it is done to the real, legitimate
tribal chieftain himself, resulting in the transfer of power. Other
times the victim is a surrogate dressed like him, or a son. His
being defamed and rejected somehow purges the community's
hostility; his restoration (or the celebration of his memory) then
renews the unity of the people and (in primitive settings) hides

---

40. Even the goat in Leviticus 16 is chosen by lot. Cf. Shirley Jackson's
    short story "The Lottery," in *The Lottery: And Other Stories*. Thus,
    there can be no question of the victim's being "guilty" in any sense
    but that of some kind of ritual transfer.

41. Frazer, *Golden Bough*, 267-93. Frazer also describes other kinds of
    scapegoats (540-90). Girard gives the most attention to Oedipus and
    Dionysus, but there are also African and Polynesian models, includ-
    ing Captain Cook. More cases of anti-king violence are provided in
    Mark R. Anspach, "Violence Against Violence," in Mark Juergens-
    meyer, ed., *Violence and the Sacred in the Modern World*, 11-25.
        It is one of the shortcomings of Girard's account that he does
    not analyze seriously the structural or situational differences
    between the "royal" and the "anonymous" types. He says (in
    Hamerton-Kelly, *Violent Origins*) that the other categories (youth,
    Jews, cripples, foreigners) are outsiders *prima facie* [at first sight]
    whereas the king is the outsider *par le haut* [at the top]. That is
    hardly a sufficient description to override so profound a category
    difference. The types differ importantly at the point of blame. The
    anonymous scapegoat and the arbitrarily chosen outsider are per-
    sonally innocent; the chieftain, on the other hand, must somehow
    be declared guilty, or made guilty by some ritual act, so that his
    destruction is perceived as cosmically imperative.

42. Frazer describes cultures in which the regicide is imperative every
    eight or twelve years; others in which it occurs when the ruler's
    vitality begins to fail, and others in which it is annual. Greater
    frequency tends to reduce the number of candidacies for the office.
    Cf. Frazer, *Golden Bough*, 264-93.

from the celebrants in later generations the reality of the primeval murder.

In short, it does something for the community's cohesion to gang up on the power figure (thereby deflecting and cutting off the vicious spiral of successive retaliations dividing clans from each other at the same time that it purges the resentments against his rule) and to destroy him. Once they have sacrificed him, then they honor him for his gifts to them. Although Girard interprets at some depth a few classic cases of purgative regicide, he does not discuss the social utility of continuing to scapegoat leaders in modern societies.[43]

A Closer Look at the Two Kinds of Scapegoats

One way Girard tries to clarify categories is by distinguishing four different uses of "scapegoating."[44] He sets apart as not normative the Leviticus usage from which the term comes, which is quite correct (as already indicated above). Also convincing, though not argued adequately, is his setting aside the usages (which Frazer connects here) whereby "evil" is sent away as if it were a substance by ritually loading it on a boat or an animal.[45] But there are two other important differences, which, as already indicated, Girard does not really clarify, and which must also be important if the system is to cover its field.[46] To identify them will bring us closer to our present concern.

In his most brief and matter-of-fact formulation,[47] Girard refers to the ongoing presence in our ordinary societies of pro-

---

43. This may be because Girard wants to make more of the finality of Jesus. That is fine for a normative statement: after the cross of Jesus there should be no more scapegoating. Our concern, however, is descriptive: scapegoating does in fact continue and we want to know how and especially why it works.

44. "Generative Scapegoating," in *Violent Origins*, ed. Hamerton-Kelly, 73-105.

45. It is only in this connection that Frazer uses the word "scapegoat."

46. It remains possible that there are passages in the less accessible Girard literature that speak more to these questions.

47. "Generative Scapegoating," in *Violent Origins*, 73-105.

cesses of a scapegoating kind. Here the victim is anonymous and innocent, not a leader. Yet he seems to think that such processes can hardly ever really be carried out, since the people doing it would be ashamed of themselves.

> [T]he victim or victims of unjust discrimination are called scapegoats, especially when they are blamed or punished not only for the "sins" of others . . . but for tensions, conflicts, and difficulties of all kinds. . . . But scapegoating must not be regarded as a conscious activity. . . . Scapegoating is not effective unless an element of delusion enters into it.[48]

This is certainly too simple. The same ability a society has, which Girard so ingeniously documents, to fool itself about a lynching that occurred in the distant past can or could no less credibly reinterpret in a good light the way a recent leader has had to be cast down for the sake of the well-being of the people.[49] The acts of the community that charge him with some guilt, thereby justifying his defamation or expulsion, can be understood as proper social hygiene, as teaching society a lesson, or even as paying a debt to other victims. It is at this point that I propose to go beyond Girard in a Girardian mode by disentangling what he keeps together.[50]

---

48. "Generative Scapegoating," in *Violent Origins*, 74. This reverence to an "element of delusion" reminds us of Dürkheim's aforementioned statements from *The Division of Labor in Society*, that a deceptive attribution to God of what is really the community's self-defense is necessary to the credibility of the myth.

49. Obviously Jesus, like the servant of JHWH in Isaiah, would fit rather under the category of the prominent person declared guilty than under that of the anonymous innocent chosen by lot for a surrogate suffering role.

50. The mark of the "Girardian mode," within which I claim still to be working, is that one begins with the social science facticity of the punitive drive, honoring its reality rather than explaining it away.

I.   There is the difference between (a) "scapegoating" as a routine, ongoing social process, by means of which societies continue to handle internal tensions, and (b) the primeval paroxysm whereby Girard believes social organization began. The former is regular, repeatable, and observable, while the latter is hidden from consciousness and must be unearthed by Girard's shrewd sleuthing. On the latter subject, I do not propose to challenge or add to his account.

II.   There is the difference already noted, but inadequately exposited, between (a) killing the anonymous, arbitrarily chosen outsider (or a member of a special victim group, like the Jews in medieval France or the youths whom the Aztecs sacrificed), and (b) killing the chieftain. The former are in fact personally innocent; the chieftain must be made worthy of punishment by special means that define his guilt.

In the case of the randomly chosen innocents, our attention as observers is drawn to the arbitrariness of the choice and to the hiatus between the dramatic immolation and ordinary real life. That leaves us with a malaise, a feeling of injustice. The distance between the celebration and normal life is assured by that hiatus. When the victim is a power-bearer, on the other hand, the case for the sacrifice must be made differently.

The case with which we began in the Antisthenes citation is I/a and II/b among the variations noted above. Girard touches on all of the variations, but does not sort them out as much as he might or as much as we may need to if we wish to move with this wisdom into ethics or social action.

Girard's most recent reference to the scapegoating phenomenon is the one we already noted in the Hamerton-Kelly collection.[51] He continues to suggest, as earlier statements had, that the process of scapegoating, i.e., punishing individuals on other grounds than real personal guilt, is something of which our cul-

---

51. "Generative Scapegoating," in *Violent Origins*, 73-105.

tured contemporaries would be ashamed, so that the only way to unearth the truth is his kind of crosscultural sleuthing. This is the point I have already called into question, which will lead us on to the point of this treatise.

More Thoughts About Method

The challenge that René Girard represents to the ordinary cross-disciplinary reader is not subject to ordinary criteria of credibility. This calls for a parenthesis about intellectual etiquette. Girard's selection of which specimens to consider typical (whether drawn from classical literature or from anthropological field data) and notion of how to ascribe meaning to symbol or story does not convince me as the kind of "proof" I would ask for within a discipline I knew better. Rather than being more critically careful about tiny details, the way Girard demonstrates his expertise is by claiming the benefit of the doubt; the less ordinary hypothesis seems easier to entertain.

Girard's mode of presentation sometimes leapfrogs genially over parts of the argument where a skeptical reader would call for some kind of "proof." The wide background reading to which he appeals is seldom documented. This style is made still harder to follow by the format of *Des Choses Cachées depuis la Fondation du Monde*,[52] a seminar transcript marked by "in" language, and by his Gallic ways of arguing by indirection, allusion, hyperbole, and ricochet. I am half-French and I find the Gallic style fun to read. Nonetheless, it does make it harder for the neophyte, even the most benevolently disposed, to get on board. Thus, what a favorably pre-disposed critic in my shoes should not try to do is to test every point that could be doubted. I rather try to leap into Girard's frame of reference and to test the synthesis for its coherence.

I do not write this as grounds for rejecting Girard unheard, but by way of apologia to explain why it is not easy to give him a fair yet critical hearing and why I make no effort to touch every base in a point-by-point critique. Nonetheless, I take his

---

52. The French title of Girard's work, which was translated into English as *Things Hidden Since the Foundation of the World* (1987).

agenda and his mental mode seriously as provocation. There remains in his work a kind of heightened capacity to convince that makes its way not by slowly accumulating one brick at a time, but rather by a long leap to a gestalt that is impressive and illuminating as a whole, yet leaves the onlooker unclear about how to follow and the serious doubter out of the loop.

But that means also that in order to appropriate the promise of Girard's creative perspective, respecting the way he has changed the landscape, one need not review yet again all of the data he had reviewed. It must suffice that I seek to extrapolate an additional set of observations like his along the lines of his synthesis but beyond its limits.

Alternative Approaches to the Same Theme

Paul Ricoeur, another brilliant Frenchman with many admirers in America, has also given attention to the theme of punishment as a foundational cultural reflex. His "Interpretation of the Myth of Punishment" figures prominently in *Le Mythe de la Peine*, produced by a conference convened in Rome in 1967 by Enrico Castelli[53] as a part of a series of studies around the theme of myth. Concentrating on religion and penal justice, Ricoeur pursues many of the same themes as Girard, yet with little common vocabulary and no dialogue. Ricoeur's frame of reference is deconstruction and reinterpretation in Hegelian terms. He shares with Girard the starting point: an embarrassment with the phenomenon of punishment as something needing to be explained so that it can be left behind though not forgotten. He also shares a concern to respect Christian commitment although developing a philosophical system with its own rules.

---

53. Enrico Castelli, *Le mythe de la peine: Actes du colloque organisé par le Centre international d'Études humanistes et par l'Institut d'Études philosophiques de Rome: Rome, 7-12 janvier 1967.* The technical meaning of the term "myth" in this connection would seem to be not that the social phenomenon of punishing is at all unreal, but that the reasons a society gives itself for the practice are imaginative constructs, subject to being reinterpreted.

PART 4: THE POWER OF INNOCENT SUFFERING

Broadening the Base of Girard's Description

Before returning to carry further the conversation with Girard, it will be helpful to widen our picture by attending to another set of concerns that are directly germane to his theme although not discussed in his writings. The quotation above, "The Power of Innocent Suffering," is the way Martin Luther King Jr. frequently described the moral and social principle he had learned from Gandhi. That suffering has power can be affirmed in more than one way. Despite King's own avowal that he had derived the notion (i.e., his way of thinking about it) from Gandhi, the connection between the suffering and the power did not have the same shape for the two men.[54]

For King, the black Baptist with the Boston University doctorate, the explanation is a person-like providence behind the scenes; in the words of James Russell Lowell, which King often recited, God is standing in the shadow behind the cross.[55] I am less

---

54. By Christmas of 1955, King was referring to Gandhi as a source. Cf. David J. Garrow, *Bearing the Cross: Martin Luther King, Jr., and the Southern Christian Leadership Conference*, 32. Gandhi in turn said he got the idea from Tolstoy. Yet to that tradition Gandhi had added much: he rooted it in a religious cosmology, as Tolstoy did not, and he implemented it in tactically self-conscious ways, as Tolstoy did not.

55. "Though the cause of evil prosper / Yet the truth alone is strong. Though her portion be the scaffold / and upon the throne be wrong / Yet the scaffold sways the future / And behind the dim unknown / Standeth God within the shadow / Keeping watch above his own." James Russell Lowell, "Once to Every Man and Nation," in *Boston Courier* (Dec 11, 1945). Lowell is cited six times in James Melvin Washington's collection of King's best-known speeches: *A Testament of Hope: The Essential Writings and Speeches of Martin Luther King, Jr.* (San Francisco: HarperSanFrancisco, 1991). Garrow's *Bearing the Cross* is one of the leading King biographies, yet despite the use of that image in the title and on the frontispiece, Garrow does little to clarify its meaning. It is better interpreted in James H. Cone, *Martin & Malcolm & America: A Dream or a Nightmare*, 125-31.

clear about understanding Gandhi, but it would seem that there was in his Hindu mind some kind of cosmic web of energy transfer whereby the investment in prayer, fasting, brahmacharya,[56] and menial labor somehow pressures the oppressor to change sooner or later[57] in ways that reach deeper than the overt political dynamics of public opinion and judicial appeal.[58]

The other body of tradition with which it would be fruitful to interlock would be the theories referred to as "atonement"; i.e., the way Christian thinkers before Girard thought of the death of Christ as having been necessary and/or as bringing about its saving effect.[59] For some, sin is an offense against the order or balance through which the righteousness of a divine governor rules; the metaphor used is then that of an adult act of lawbreaking, and "satisfaction" is needed to restore the balance.[60]

---

56. Brahmacharya is sexual abstinence, seen neither as self-privation nor rejection of evil lust (as some Western asceticism might understand it), but as a channeling of moral energy.

57. Gandhi made the point that the eastern mind was more patient than the western and therefore more able to sustain a conflict for the long haul. Gandhi would not have titled a book *Why We Can't Wait* as King did. Cf. Romain Rolland, *Mahatma Gandhi*, 60-62. In *War Without Violence: The Study of Gandhi's Method and Its Accomplishments*, 167-72, Krishnalal Jethalal Shridharani built up from ancient Indian cultural roots a simple but impressive portrayal of how aptly that culture had laid the foundation, layer after layer, for Gandhi's vision.

58. James W. Douglass, in his *The Non-Violent Cross: A Theology of Revolution and Peace*, affirms this kind of hope. Water will find its way to the sea; truth is a force as sure to have its way ultimately as is the wind or the sun.

59. The word *atone* originally meant to bring severed bodies together, no different in substance from *reconcile*. Yet, somehow in theological English, it has come to designate the entire field of explanations of the cross of Christ, including punishment and expiation.

60. *Satisfy* is another term later theological usage has redefined. Literally and legally it meant "doing enough," meeting some quantitative requirement. In our ordinary usage it has come to mean making someone who had been offended feel all right or have some need met.

For another stream of thought, the metaphor for atonement is that of an adolescent's rebellion. What matters is not that a law was broken but that a bond of creaturely allegiance was violated. The remedy is the suffering of the Father (or of the Son whom the Father sends), which touches and turns the heart of the sinner. Theologians (classifying from the sinner's perspective) call this the "subjective" view.

The third classical stream sees the offenses as a diversion of the righteous flow of history; the "lost" human may be like a strayed child (or sheep) or a rebellious adult. What counts is that humans have become the captives of powers from which only the suffering of the righteous Servant can redeem them. Gustav Aulen and Anders Nygren called this the "classic" view.

What the three views of atonement and the two previously noted visions of the power of suffering have in common, which I propose to take account of as an initial enrichment of Girard's analysis, is that in ongoing social experience the phenomenon of blaming is functional.[61] Girard concentrates on ways in which that act has been hidden by later cultures. In that detective work, he is guided by his own refined liberal sensitivity, which assumes it is something of which to be ashamed. Ancient societies must have been somehow ashamed of it too,

---

61. Of course there are more types and subtypes, but most classifiers agree in the way they describe the main families. Here I follow the summaries of Robert S. Paul, *The Atonement and the Sacraments,* and J. W. McClendon Jr., *Systematic Theology,* vol. 2, ch. 5. The large body of discussion on the subject of just how Jesus' death "works" on our behalf testifies that the punitive agenda is perennial, that the sense of a need to explain it is pervasive, and that the ways to do so are unavoidably multiple, none of them simply satisfying. [Editor's note: Yoder's most extensive treatment of atonement, originally a collection of mimeographed course lectures available in Duke Divinity School's Cokesbury Bookstore as *Christology and Theological Method: Preface to Theology,* has subsequently been edited by Stanley Hauerwas and Alex Sider and published as *Preface to Theology: Christology and Theological Method,* 281-327.]

so they transformed it in their memories. We are ashamed of it, so it needs to be explained in ways that do not give it moral approval. These assumptions do fit our cultural heritage, but only for part of what Girard is interested in.

I here suggest that it would be no less worthwhile to recognize with a less judgmental empathy that there are also ways, in other aspects of our experience, in which blaming and punishing behavior still "works." It would be too much to describe this "working" as "redemptive," as might be said by Frantz Fanon,[62] and as is assumed by the advocates of capital punishment. The term "functional" does not mean simply "good"; yet conflict and the prison system, anger and ostracism do in fact continue to discharge a social function that cannot be wiped away by a declaration that it is morally unworthy. We understand a social process better if we do not try to lock or talk past the awkward realities.

---

62. What Frantz Fanon said in the setting of Algeria's war of independence about the rebel's need to destroy the symbol of his prior servitude is mirrored in the affirmative valuation of "rage" in some feminist therapeutic visions. A person educated always to be nice and to yield may experience standing up and striking back as a kind of salvation. [Editor's note: Yoder never cites his source, but two possibilities include *L'an v de la révolution algérienne* (Paris: F. Maspero, 1959) and *The Wretched of the Earth*, trans. Constance Farrington (New York: Grove Press, 1965; French 1961).]

PART 5: WITH AND BEYOND GIRARD:

Toward a Less Judgmental, More Descriptive Frame of Reference for Understanding and Accepting the Place of Punishment in Our "Fallen" World

Until better informed, then, I suggest that, despite the embarrassment this fact evokes among decent people, there are major sectors of our culture where it is not the case that scapegoating is *only and exclusively* something societies cannot bear to avow, so that it is buried by redefinition and then must be unearthed by Girard's kind of sleuthing.[63] In some settings, punishment for the sake of maintaining some kind of sacrally warranted social order still occurs, overtly and with a good conscience, in our own culture. This is where we began, with the patterns of punishment described by Dürkheim.

The most widely celebrated instance of this irreducible reality in the United States is the legislative return of capital punishment.[64] The value involved in our society's wanting to kill killers is not a conviction that *all* individuals guilty of killing should or do, for the sake of their own dignity, want to die.[65] Most public advocates of the death penalty adjust, in

---

63. The most special kind of sleuthing, in which Girard is uniquely creative and most difficult to critique fairly, operates in the cases where he argues that the absence of proof is itself the proof. He claims that the fact of a cover-up, such that in the surviving myth or legend we do not even see the foundational murder, is the way we know that that is what happened. Neil Elliot, in *Liberating Paul: The Justice of God and the Politics of the Apostle*, is one of those who have commented that such a scheme makes logical validation impossible. Elliot engages Girard on pp. 103-104, 130, 167-68, 198, 253-54, and 280.

64. This case differs somehow in the USA in ways we ought to seek to interpret creatively, not only to bemoan, from the rest of the developed world where capital punishment has largely been done away with. It is one theme on which Gingrich and Clinton agree to pander to popular anger; in March 1995, New York reinstated the death penalty.

65. That would be the necessary implication, if the deepest justification were a properly theological sense of the demands of a righteous

fact, with some equanimity to the facts that most killers are not killed, that the choice of who gets killed is enormously uneven (varying especially with geography, race, wealth, publicity, and intelligence), and (a different moral issue) that some innocent persons are executed. What they want is the continuing presence *in principle* of the supreme penalty *as an institution* within our society with only enough actual executions needing to be carried out for the *possibility* of legal death to be present as a spooky shadow on the edge of our culture. They are convinced (in a way that is impervious to information from other cultures or from statistics) that if the spooky shadow were taken away the world would go over the edge.

This psychic need for the celebratory possibility of execution, as symbolic backdrop to the civil order, is not a matter of social hygiene or cultural progress. It is what the ethnologist or the ethologist would call ritual or mythic. That is why the liberal activists in the Legal Defense Fund—who for generations, sacrificially, patiently, and with ultimate success used the courts and the Constitution of the USA to disqualify capital punishment on the grounds of unfairness—were winning the wrong battle.[66] It is why discussion of whether punishment rehabilitates or deters is ultimately a red herring.

Girard's rapid dismissal of possible good-conscious grounds for representative punitive ceremonies explains another relative

---

God. There are of course some killers who do believe that for themselves. There are also thinkers who believe that desire on the part of the killer is morally proper. Some of them read that view, I think abusively, into one rare argument of the Anglican apologist Clive Staples Lewis (cf. the numerous references to Lewis in H. Wayne House and John H. Yoder, *The Death Penalty Debate*).

66. Michael Meltsner, *Cruel and Unusual: The Supreme Court and Capital Punishment.* Through painstaking and creative advocacy work over decades, using moral leverage through the courts rather than convincing voters or legislatures, the death penalty was practically abolished in the USA in 1972. But then it was reinstated in most states by new legislation so formulated as to defend the practice against the old attack.

lacuna in his system, namely his not elucidating substantially *why* the punishers feel good about punishing.[67] His phrase "mimetic desire" is a label, not an explanation. The way he locates the most striking examples in the barely discernible past seems almost to reduce punishment to a barely controllable, unthinking (almost animal, primitive, or at least prehistoric) reflex,[68] which societies soon conceal behind a screen of legend because they are, after all, ashamed of it.[69] I suggest that we can only be fair to the facts and (it might follow) can only be able to change them if we can empathize less judgmentally with our neighbors' need to punish.

There must then be some kind of truth, however unworthy it feels to our civilized sensitivity, to the conviction that the divine order demands pain for pain. To locate the genesis of mimetic impulse to give what one got in early anthropoid culture (i.e., in phylogeny),[70] or in a young child's becoming a separate person (i.e., in ontogeny), does not mean that it is not also

---

67. "Generative Scapegoating," in *Violent Origins*, 73-105.
68. Girard regularly uses the term "mechanism," an oddly modern metaphor. It signals the absence of thought on the part of the actor, but also an abdication of explanation on the part of the interpreter.
69. While I call for a more adequate description of contemporary scapegoating, I must leave it to the anthropologists to test out the primitive parallels. The little I have read about Papuan intertribal vengeance indicates no embarrassment on the killer's part about whether the institution is humane. Retaliatory murder is in fact the basic source of the warrior's dignity. They do not try to hide it or transmute it in myth or memory. Nor is it unthinking; it is rationally planned and institutionally supported.
70. I apologize to the users of ordinary language for this very apt shorthand borrowed from the jargon of biology. Phylogeny speaks of how the species became what it is through change over time, with the root meaning located in Darwinian evolution. Ontogeny speaks of how the individual becomes the self he or she is, especially during the growth of the embryo. Here, of course, both terms are used metaphorically. All through this study we should ask regularly both how *persons* become who they are, and how *social patterns* come to be. Presumably the two etiologies will overlap, but they can and must nonetheless be conceptually distinguished, and different disciplines usually pursue the two kinds of questions.

a moral order. The fact that several classical Christian efforts to explain why Jesus had to die have constructed several different understandings of God's just demands, which we consider unworthy of our own advanced humane self-respect,[71] does not free us from the work of understanding the valid grounds that there might be for considering the cross necessary.[72] That is why I have argued that it makes more sense to agree with the letter to the Hebrews and with Karl Barth that the demand for death as penalty was somehow legitimate and that the cross of Jesus Christ has met that need,[73] rather than to reject with moral outrage,[74] as we are inclined to do, the entire notion of a vindictive demand.

What I have just argued with regard to the ancient institution of the death penalty would then, if we want to be consistent, be likely to find some analogy as well in other modes of vindictiveness as our society moves from one class of victim to another and from one kind of punishment to another. Any society under

---

71. Already above I alluded to the traditional Christian theme of explaining "atonement." I renounce any effort to make this correlation thorough as we go along, yet as this review proceeds, glancing references to the classical answers in that field may sometimes clarify. Modern Christian thought is largely embarrassed by the fact that Christians between the second century and the nineteenth, in order to explain the need for the death of Jesus, ascribed to God (the father, the judge) motives or demands that we today consider unworthy of a gentleman. I share the embarrassment, but I deny that that is a reason not to empathize with the culture we are studying. Cf. below the reference to C. S. Lewis, for whom there was no embarrassment in appropriating the primeval mythic mood.

72. I made this point also in "Against the Death Penalty" [ch. 4, part 9, in this volume], citing also Stephen Nathanson.

73. Yoder, "Against the Death Penalty" [ch. 4, part 6, in this volume]. Cf. Barth, *Church Dogmatics*, vol. III/4 (Edinburgh: T. & T. Clark, 1961), 437-46. This understanding would also be quite compatible with Girard's understandings concerning the impact of Jesus.

74. Or, one might add, with the smug moral superiority of the enlightened, as Dürkheim does.

stress needs to "take it out on" some kind of outsider. During WWII, it was ethnic Germans and (even more) Japanese who had to be rejected in the USA; before that, and again afterward (McCarthy), it was socialists. Despite progress on the legal level, neither Jews nor Blacks (nor Asians) in America are permanently safe from being the victims of our society's relapses.

More recently, men as a class have come to be vulnerable in a new way, as compensation for pain and suffering by women, when that pain can be blamed upon the prior patriarchal tilt of our society.[75] Here, too, to understand would be better than to bewail. We should expect the genesis (whether in phylogeny or in ontogeny) of women's need to punish to be different from what drove male avengers in primitive culture.[76] There is no *a priori* reason to assume that in every culture the same needs will surface. Then what it would take to satisfy those needs would also fittingly be different,[77] and the gospel cure for it might be different.

If there is as I have suggested a lacuna in Girard on the level of foundations or causal explanation, there may be another on that of ethical consequences. Girard is very clear, and right I believe, in arguing that Jesus did away with the "legitimacy" claimed by the social authorities of his time, including the Sad-

---

75. There should be room, logically, for the objection that beneficent patriarchal care, properly understood and benevolently exercised, would not be harmful; that what has hurt women has been the violation, not the implementation of proper fatherly caring. This excuse would, however, not change the retaliatory dynamics, since the root of the power of the punitive drive is located not merely in a mistake the stronger party made but in the weaker party's anger.

76. When Genesis 9:6 or the Mosaic Laws provided for punitive kill-ing, that was not done by a civil state but by the "avenger of the blood" who was often the next of kin. "Avenger" (*goel*) also meant "redeemer." Most ancient tribal cultures seem to have had such rules and roles.

77. The word "compensation" just used hides the variety of possible meanings of how the cure would need to fit the reason for the demand. I shall return below (part 8) to "victim compensation" as an especially complex form of punishment.

ducees and the Romans, for killing offenders. But what does that mean for us as we go on living in a world where that message has been rejected?

Some who have welcomed Girard's contribution connect it with the rejection of violence in social ethics.[78] Some have seen a connection to conflict resolution and corrections in domestic society.[79] Is bearing a cross constitutive of discipleship, as Luke 14:25-35 says it is? If so, would such a validation of human suffering as morally worthy apply legitimately only to persons prosecuted for doing the good of which an evil social order disapproves (1 Pet 2:20)? Might it also apply to other forms of innocent suffering (poverty, disease, catastrophe)? Or might it also fit those who are chosen for suffering by virtue of their visibility as office-bearers to be vicarious victims (as above, from Antisthenes to Frazer)?

One last question, a more formal, academic one perhaps, to which I proceed before returning to consider other kinds of punishment, is whether Girard's notion of *mimesis* is merely one more explanation of "atonement," an additional one to set beside all the others, or rather a mode of approach or appropriation, which can in some sense cover them all but without distinguishing among them. I suggest that the latter may well be the case. To say that punitive mimesis occurs is to label a set of phenomena formally, not to explain them genetically. When we go on to ask *why* it occurs, the answers may very well still be multiple, as we shall seek to itemize later, since the social settings are many. Punitive mimesis may be needed to teach a

---

78. John S. Dunne, *The Peace of the Present: An Unviolent Way of Life*, 21-25, 40.

79. Vern Redekop, *Scapegoats, the Bible, and Criminal Justice: Interacting with René Girard.* Redekop transposes the Girardian system very uncritically; in a projected doctoral project he will have occasion to be more thorough. As far as I have seen, I am alone in making the contemporary connection to the death penalty (cf. also "Against the Death Penalty" [ch.4, part 6]), but it would seem to be implied in Schwager, *Brauchen wir einen Sündenbock?*

lesson, to restore cosmic balance, to purge moral pollution or shame, to let off wrathful steam, or to restore maternal control (see part 6 below). All of these functions are compatible with Girard's vision of the primeval crisis, or of the cross of Jesus, or of blaming Jews for the Black Death (these are Girard's cases); but they are not identical in their logic, nor does "mimesis" characterize them all equally well. The roster of functions that punishment can have, to which I propose now to proceed, is not a pure typology in the sense that the diverse modes and roles would never overlap; yet disentangling them will help to surface important real differences.

Another point where the various metaphors might differ is that some might be more able than others to throw some light on America's special affection for the death penalty or on the possibility that certain forms of scapegoating, rather than having to be suppressed or repressed, might continue to be socially functional.

The point of the present text is, as said, to suggest that this just mentioned possibility is in fact the case. Within the turbulence of modern cultures, scapegoating mechanisms will continue to have a role. Like the culture's other powerful forces, that role is neither morally satisfying to us, nor "redemptive." The same is true for prisons, or for the just war tradition and the Pentagon, or for ethnocentrism, or for social-climbing ambition, or for greed, all of which we also consent to live with—but it cannot be done away with, and it is part of what makes the real world work. Revolting crimes, especially multiple murders, will continue to evoke demands for blood. Abuse of the defenseless underdog will continue to evoke demands for compensatory pain.

Christians correctly say that scapegoating is incompatible with Jesus. True. Psychologists say that avenging yourself really doesn't make you be a better person or feel better about yourself. True. Liberal defense lawyers correctly say that judicial punitiveness, especially the death penalty, is "cruel and unusual." Such critical claims are true, but as answers they are not in tune with the question. Politically such arguments win the wrong battle. The social function of punishing abides; it proclaims that some abuses are intolerable and it retrieves for victims their sense of their own dignity.

I reiterate here, without pursuing it further critically, that our society's very modern and very pragmatic concern to punish stands in some kind of strong analogy to very ancient notions of a divine order in which innocent sacrifice is a moral demand of the cosmos. Perhaps the most widely known metaphor for it is the "Deep Magic from the Dawn of Time," which C. S. Lewis describes in *The Lion, the Witch, and the Wardrobe* as giving the witch a claim against the very cosmos, a claim that the Christ-figure Aslan is willing to die for: "You know that every traitor belongs to me as my lawful prey and that for every treachery I have a right to a kill. . . . [U]nless I have the blood as the Law says all Narnia will be overturned and perish in fire and water."[80]

In an analogous way, classes of people shaking off the pain of their past involuntary subordination (whether that be the Algerian rebels for whom Frantz Fanon wrote, the masses of Eastern Europe after 1989, the families of the "disappeared" when Latin American countries return to legality, or women victims of male privilege) will demand that a symbolic patriarchal figure be toppled. To raise questions in that setting about being fair to the old man may be to ask the wrong question.[81] To this we shall need to return.

Christian interpreters of the figure of the "servant of JHWH" in Isaiah draw attention to the fact that although his suffering was not freely chosen, still the "servant" accepted it.[82] The same is true of the Gospels' interpretation of Jesus' fate.[83] Similarly, it does not occur to the chieftains in Frazer's accounts in *Golden Bough* to

---

80. C. S. Lewis, *The Lion, the Witch, and the Wardrobe*, 114. The still deeper "magic" of vicarious innocent sacrifice is described on 132-33.

81. [Editor's note: The designation "old man" refers to the patriarchal figure in the previous sentence. Yoder discusses this figure at length in part 7.]

82. Isaiah 42:1-9; 49:1-12; 50:4-11; and 52:13–53:12.

83. The Jesus of Luke 22:37 alludes to the Isaiah description in predicting his own passion.

raise doubts about whether it is just that the cosmic order calls them to be cut down when their time has come. Likewise, to redescribe the lay of the land as I here propose to do would indicate that it may be imperative to acquiesce in continuing socially authorized punishment as institutionally legitimate, where the offense is profound enough, *even though* the demand contradicts the most sensitive moral sensitivities, not only of Christians.

PART 6: MOTHER KNOWS BEST

Girard empathizes with the reflexes of embarrassment that
led societies, back in prehistory, to divert the "mimetic" punitive drive and to repress the memory of those primeval bloody
events.[84] His sensitivity to that embarrassment has led him to
his most fruitful revisions. Here, in contrast, I have begun to
propose that the punitive drive(s) and the events they produce
should continue to be considered socially functional and that
we should come to terms with the fact that they cannot be
banned completely.

Whether it would be ethically good or socially hygienic to
ban them completely is not something I care now to argue. In
any case, for the present we live in the world that they govern.
I do not see that this image of things and the agenda of Girard
are in any conflict; I propose to assume his schema and apply it
to a different set of data.

What distinguishes the scapegoating phenomenon from other
kinds of royal suffering (e.g., Phil 2; Isa 52–53) is that the need/
drive that demands or validates the punishment is located, without apology, in the punishers.[85] There is in these cases no appeal to
a divine command, as in the "satisfaction" theories of the atonement where it is God who wants the suffering. Nor is there a claim
that the offender will be morally restored, as in the "moral influence" theories of atonement or in the "rehabilitative" theories of
prison. Nor is there any intention to impact the cosmic/historical
order, as in the "dramatic" or "ransom" theories. The retaliatory
reflex or punitive drive (for Girard, "mimetic desire") is located,
for the case we are interested in now, within the persons who iden-

---

84. "We never catch ourselves in the act of scapegoating. . . . Scape-
     goating by others . . . appears to us an evil so stupid, so senseless
     . . . that it arouses our indignation," in Hamerton-Kelly, *Violent
     Origins*, 78.

85. Again we are at our starting point, with the problem stated the
     way we saw it described by Dürkheim. The claim is made that the
     need for retaliation is founded in the cosmic or the moral order,
     but it is operative through the avenger's own calling.

tify themselves (or their kind, or their protégées) as victims and who on that ground alone claim the authority to vindicate.

I therefore propose to describe, in an intentionally, utterly amateur and straightforward way,[86] some of the most obvious modes of such validation of punishment, which seem to me to command respect on the grounds that they are socially functional.[87] People do actually act like this in the confidence that for them to do so is good for the community or for the victims of past injustices or even (in the case with which we begin) for the one punished.

I shall not include the legal death penalty here, as I have already done elsewhere, since most of those who call for it claim a cosmic or transcendent mandate, as the other styles of punishing to which I shall now give more attention do not necessarily do.[88] Yet, as far as the method of argument is concerned, I stand by my earlier plea that the adversaries of the death penalty would do better to grant the deep cultural bona fides of their fellow citizens who feel that killing can somehow compensate cosmically for killing.

The first effective reason for punishing is the one I here propose to call "maternal," yet the adjective must be set apart in quotes because what it describes should not be taken as the fundamental or ideal definition of mothering.[89] We are asking

---

86. To be amateur in this setting calls for no apology since in a widely multidisciplinary conversation everyone is an amateur in most of the fields. The amateur's advantage is the ability to notice discrepancies and oddities, things taken for granted and gaps in the arguments to which the expert in each sub-discipline is accustomed.

87. The term *functional* has multiple shadings. It designates something that in fact is going on and producing an effect. Or it may bespeak the observer's evaluating the activity as useful and its results as not all bad, if not desirable, or as inevitable even if unpleasant.

88. In the conservative Protestant instances, the cosmic claim may be made for the "maternal" mode to which I now turn, but hardly for the "filial" to which I shall turn later.

89. I would be grateful if someone offered a better label. The only advantage of this one is that it renders the awareness that basic

about modes of and reasons for punishing with a good conscience. The prototypical child needing punishment "for his own good" is the infant. The punishing is done not by the victim of some offense, but by the mother (or someone else discharging the same role). Sin is understood at root as refusing the mother's benevolent care. The offenses and the punishment cannot be separated. The sanction to withhold the breast or the loving embrace from the rebel child, the restoration that the mother wills for the child's own good,[90] is the child's yielding to return to the same dependency on the mother's overwhelming benevolence. As the child ages, the mother may seek to prolong her control by other forms of the patient, benevolent denial of the embrace until the child has become so independent as no longer to yield to that sanction.

It is not sufficient to describe this pattern as the parent's desire to have the child do the right thing at one particular time. The objective is to force upon the child a posture of submissiveness, a recognition of parental authority in principle, which in the classical sources is spoken of as "breaking the will" of the child.[91]

---

behavior models are carried by elementary biological relationships and are learned when very young. In this respect it parallels Girard's interpretation, though of course it is in no way "mimetic," except in the special case where the mother does to the child what the child just did.

90. Some might argue that the mother also has needs and drives, other than the child's well-being, which punishing also may serve. Of course she does; some of them may be morally worthy and others less so. For present purposes I do not argue that; that is not the reason the mother gives (to the child, to herself, or to society) for the punishment.

91. As Philip J. Greven demonstrates in a chapter entitled "Broken Wills: Discipline and Parental Control," this act of submission by the child/victim is understood in direct analogy to the unconditional submission of the sinner to an angry though loving God. The child's yielding to the parent is patterned after the adult sinner's conversion, except that the child is given no choice. Cf. Greven, *The Protestant Temperament: Patterns of Child-Rearing, Religious Experience, and*

The fact that the mother's intention is purely benevolent—she has no other desire than to give to the child again what she is now withholding[92]—makes the punishing mother less likely than men might be to escalate the conflict ideologically into claims about the divine order they are enforcing, or into political explanations like proximate political goals to be forced onto the other by the punishment or the threat thereof, or into lethal levels of harm. All the mother wants is for the child to want to be babied again, to reaffirm the child's dependence and her authority.[93] But this fact that the mother's intention is pure benevolence[94] also makes it unlikely that there will be any strong internal self-criticism by the mother of the rightness of her reading of things.[95]

---

the Self in Early America, 32-43, cited from William G. McGloughlin, "Evangelical Child-Rearing in the Age of Jackson," 35-39.

92. This need to impose control is often justified in conservative Protestant circles by an appeal to the doctrine of original sin, such that the self-will of the child needs to be broken as an essential part of moral education. A classical statement of this is often cited from Susanna Wesley, mother of the founders of Methodism. The parent's will is assumed to be right: "In order to form the minds of children, the first thing to be done is to conquer their will and bring them to an obedient temper. . . . I insist on the conquering of the will of children betimes, because this is the only strong and rational foundation. As self-will is the root of all sin and misery, . . . so the parent who studies to subdue it in his child works together with God in . . . saving a soul." Susanna Wesley, "On the Education of Her Family" (1732) in Phillip J. Greven, ed., *Child-Rearing Concepts, 1638-1861: Historical Sources*, 47-48.

93. The contemporary feminist corrective strategies that punish older males for harming younger females may be understood as extrapolating the maternal motivation. The (older) mother may identify with the (younger) victim(s) and act on behalf of the class of such victims, yet the motivation can still be maternal—i.e., the intent is to bring the one punished into line—and is understood by both the controlling person and the environing observers as utterly benevolent.

94. Note above Susanna Wesley's characterization of breaking the will as "working together with God."

95. For obvious cultural reasons, the prototype of this kind of punishment is the biological mother (or the wet nurse or nanny). Yet a

Primeval Matriarchy

Medieval and scholastic exegesis interpreted JHWH's threat to the serpent—"I will put enmity between you and the woman; and between your offspring and hers; he will strike your head, and you will strike his heel" (Gen 3:15 NRSV)—as a pre-gospel, prefiguring the defeat of the serpent, Satan, by Christ. That is a meaning those words could not have had for the first Hebrew bards who recited them, nor for the scribes who wrote them. The meaning *then* had to be that the act of mothering, of giving birth and nurturing,[96] and raising offspring who will combat the serpent, would begin to restore for woman, through the offspring she raises, the morally effective governing role she had had over Adam in prefall Eden.[97] Every man-child's life is formed in a time of absolute dependence upon the benevolent and omnipotent mother. Thus, it was too simple, and premature, but it was not wrong, when Eve described Cain's birth (4:1) as JHWH's gift and, thus by implication, as the beginning of the fulfillment of the promise of 3:15.

The author of 1 Timothy has the Genesis account in mind when he writes, "the woman was deceived and became a trans-

---

father who is in a position to exercise absolute control of an infant can act in the very same way. Cf. the dramatic case of paternal absolutism, which Baptist minister and college president Francis Wayland boasted about, cited by Greven, *The Protestant Temperament*, 38-42. The combination of omnipotent control and utterly self-confident benevolence can also characterize the discipline exercised by a clan or an institution.

96. Sara Ruddick, *Maternal Thinking: Toward a Politics of Peace*, 18-22, breaks down the role of "mothering" into three components: preserving life, fostering growth, and training for social acceptability. All three, of course, are modes of control, and all three are unselfish. Ruddick does not study at any length how any of them might be overdone and become destructive.

97. I am by no means original in reading the Genesis account as describing the prelapsarian world as matriarchal. The serpent came to Eve not because she was morally weaker than Adam but because she had made the decisions in the family. The Adam of Milton had to wrestle with the decision to eat the fruit; the Adam of Genesis ate what was set before him.

gressor. Yet she will be saved through mothering" (1 Tim 2:15 NRSV, substituting "mothering" for "childbearing"). This cannot mean that women who bear children have a different access than do men (or childless women) to what modern piety calls "salvation," i.e., to forgiveness of sins and fellowship with God beyond death.[98] Nor can it possibly mean that the biological act of giving birth is "salvation" in some special sense.[99] It must mean (i.e., it must have meant for "Paul"—even more clearly than in the original Genesis text taken alone) the restoration (partial, gradual, under the conditions of history) of the same shalom that Eve had lost, namely matriarchy. That control is in fact restored (partially, gradually, under the conditions of history) not by the single event of giving birth, but through the universal phenomenon of costly mothering.[100] "Paul" in 1 Timothy says this not about one woman at a time but about women as a class (v. 15b, in fact, shifts to the plural). A childless woman is no less able than is a biological mother to govern an infant by the stick of withholding and the carrot of restoring a nurturing embrace.

The man-child will be weaned after a few years and taken off by the men of the tribe to be taught to be a hunter or a warrior. That will remodel his personality in the interaction with the adult male, but will not change the mother's. Her need to restore control and her way of doing it when she can will remain.[101] This

---

98. The majority of interpreters who are embarrassed about this text, or who simply reject it, assume that this is what the author meant. This is silly. Even if the "Paul" of the pastoral epistles was not the real Saul/Paul of history, and even if he was not very original or very bright and was patriarchal, he cannot have meant that.

99. A few original interpreters think it meant the mother's being saved from death during childbirth, which was, of course, much more life-threatening than now. I doubt that Paul thought that Christian women would be less physically vulnerable than others in labor.

100. Lady Nancy Astor (1879-1964) is said to have said, "Let's not blame the men: we created them."

101. It is no accident that even secular culture uses the phrase "Jewish mother" for a particular pattern of control seeking the son's well-being. The human prototype has a male offender and a governing

model differs from the others in that the battle for ultimate control can never be finally won; the older the son gets, the more the mother's recourse to external coercion is a sign of defeat. Control works best when it has been so internalized that no outward enforcement is needed.

In sum, it can hardly be argued that this "maternal punitive" pattern, including the most elemental punishment, does not have a natural (i.e., primitive biological) origin and an abiding social function.[102] In no serious way can the metaphor of "mimetic desire" describe it. We may ask for it to be limited or channeled, but hardly for it to be eliminated. Then when it leads to scapegoating we shall do better to define its place in the social process than to ban, ignore, or merely deplore it.

I already noted that it is peculiar to maternal punishment as a mode of retaining control (as contrasted with the other forms to which we shall soon turn) that it finally cannot win out. The son (or the daughter) will, ultimately, leave the nest. It

---

mother, but when we consider this metaphor in the realm of atonement, that may change. The dynamics between Hosea and his wife are analogous, but with the genders reversed.

102. Sara Ruddick's *Maternal Thinking* is a work of landmark importance, but it is striking that the author does not address this issue directly. The great value of her book is the connections Ruddick makes to the wider social realm. Her concern is not with the possibility that maternal power, like other power, could be abused. She does allude to, but only very thinly in passing, "dominating moments" (182) and to being "accused of control" (173). There are a few lines on spanking (167); she is critical of it but is more concerned to acknowledge that the mothers who do it mean well. There is no passage on breaking the child's will or on punishment. Maternal power, as Ruddick describes it, is all-wise and all-benevolent—to that extent she does approach the Wayland model (cf. Greven, *The Protestant Temperament*, 38-42). I much welcome her broadening impact on political philosophy; yet the outside possibility that maternal nurturing might also be oppressive would merit more attention than she gives it. It is fascinating that in the vast expansion of feminist consciousness there is so little critical attention to the power of mothering over the very young.

may, however, be possible to extend maternal control by means of coalitions, a recourse to which we shall return.[103]

I noted before that one of the intellectual challenges of cross-disciplinary study is the way one becomes more easily aware of odd gaps. In most feminist literature, the form of the offense of power abuse that matters is that committed by the father, and the most traumatic typical experiences see the girl as half-grown, as if life began with puberty. Yet developmentally we almost all begin life under matriarchy.

Taking Stock: The Difference Between Punishing and Taking Charge

Looking back over the concepts used in the several settings we have been reviewing, it has become visible that there is one major structural discrepancy in the descriptions of which none of the major disciplines seems to have taken account. The other types and disciplinary cross-references pay little attention to this dimension either, but our analysis will be served by bringing it to the surface now.

Whether the more familiar term be "punish" or "vindicate" or "avenge," the discussions and descriptions usually proceed as if the pain being inflicted, which we are seeking to explain, comes after the prior offense, which it mirrors or sets right. That was the case in Genesis 4:9 (Cain's murder of Abel) and is foreseen in the threat of Genesis 9:6 ("Whoever sheds the blood of a human, by a human shall that person's blood be shed," NRSV).

Yet once we get into the realm of the pain inflicted by the parent seeking control, that is no longer purely the case. A contest of wills is going on, and the pain being inflicted is part of the contest. This is dramatically the case for Francis Wayland with-

---

103. In the ideal case, punishment that confirms maternal governance meets needs on all sides. The subjugated child can lick its wounds, the mother can enjoy her being in charge, and the society can rejoice, since the event of punishment assures them of the wholeness of the system.

holding food from his child.[104] It is the case for exclusion and
ostracism when used by church communities to bring the devi-
ant into line.[105] It may even still be called "punishment" without
seeking to hide it under euphemisms. The person or institution
inflicting it clearly believes that the person being pressured has
earned the pain being inflicted and thus "has it coming," yet
the contest is still going on. The purpose of the pain is to incite
that person to yield, without which the moral equilibrium of the
system cannot be restored. The phrase "teach him a lesson" may
seem appropriate, but the lesson to be taught is not so much
"you should not have done that bad deed [in the past]" as it is
"you have to recognize [from now on] who is boss."[106]

This conception of the positive function of punishment as
struggle for control might be called *agonic*.[107] That is, it is part
of a contest in which the forces for good must first gain control
before anything else can be set right. It has very clear pathological forms, like the parent beating an infant to make it stop
screaming, but there are also very rational ways of putting it,
like General Sherman marching through Georgia destroying

---

104. Cited by Greven in *The Protestant Temperament*, 38-42.

105. Some of the most striking recent examples are provided by the
writings of former members of the communal Society of Brothers:
notably *Torches Extinguished*, by Elizabeth Bohlken-Zumpe (San
Francisco: Carrier Pigeon Press, 1992), and *The Community That
Failed,* by Roger Alain (San Francisco: Carrier Pigeon Press, 1993).
These witnesses are biased, yet the church authorities who threw
them out do not deny exercising discipline in this way because they
are convinced of its benevolent intent.

106. Accepting who is boss is not merely a power question. It includes
a set of ideas. The one who yields must accept, on other grounds
than truth/proof/argument, the system of ideas and descriptions
of reality that the punishers are enforcing. The concern of Job's
counselors was that he should affirm that his suffering was something he "had coming." Bringing someone to change consciousness
on grounds not of conviction but of control has recently come to
be called "brainwashing," but most pre-liberal societies and some
post-modern ones do not consider it a bad thing to do.

107. *Agon* means wrestling.

everything in his path in order to get the people of the South to see they should surrender.[108] The mother who withholds the breast represents the most benevolent and the most irresistible form of this constraint.

This agonic dimension makes clearer the argument against due process or "fairness" to which we shall later need to return. When the issue is taking control, procedural concerns that call for a level playing field can get in the way of making things right.

Another Classical Side Glance

Girard's single-key approach finds the same kind of original explanation behind most of the classical literature. Sensitized by Girard's example, a more flexible or less self-confident reader may well find differentiated modes of punishment in others of the old lays. Some of the examples are maternal.

In Aeschylus' *Eumenides*, the second play in his reworking of the legend of Agamemnon, the title personalities (Eumenides), who speak collectively as the chorus,[109] begin as primeval, sub-terranean, numinous powers or "furies" that are responsible for retribution in general but especially for punishing matricide.[110] The special theme of this version of the story is the blood-guilt claim laid by the furies against Orestes, who had killed his mother, Clytemnestra, because she had treacherously killed his father, Agamemnon, when he came home from the wars to find her unfaithful. Even though the execution of Clytemnestra

---

108. It is part of the insanity of war, and of William Tecumseh Sherman, that the victims of his destruction had no say in how long the Confederate armies would continue the struggle. That is also why Sherman counts as one of the founders of the notion of "total war."

109. Cited here from Richard Lattimore's translation in *Complete Greek Tragedies*, vol. 1 (Chicago: University of Chicago, 1953). Usually they are three; they have snakelike hair and can inflict either death or madness.

110. Their precise name was "Erinyes," from the verb *to strive* or *to wrangle*. The euphemism "Eumenides" (from "to speak well of") is a specimen of primitive religion; it is bad luck to speak the actual name of a malevolent deity.

was merited and had in fact been commanded by Apollo under the authority of Zeus, the Eumenides are unrelenting in their demand for vengeance since matricide is worse than other kinds of killing.[111]

The stage is set for a compromise by the split vote of the jury of men of Attica. Orestes cannot be found guilty, but neither can the claims of the furies be overruled. Athena, to whom the case goes on appeal, decrees that, instead of being sent back to the underworld unsatisfied,[112] the furies can be promoted to a role of benevolent peacekeepers.[113] So the retributive, chthonic, maternal energy is not overruled or wiped away, but domesticated,[114] transformed into a force for stability. "Let them render grace for grace. Let love be their common will."[115] This picture is compatible with the Girardian vision of mimesis in that a chain of killing-for-killing can only be interrupted by a divine peacemaking intervention. It is like Girard's account in that a euphemism (Eumenides means the gracious ones, those well-spoken of) replaces the real name(s) of the furies. It differs from Girard in that the special claim, which must be redirected, is that of goddesses defending by punishment the special status of the mother.

In Euripedes' *Bacchae*, Pentheus is a royal scapegoat. He is personally innocent of evil-doing, except by virtue of his princely

---

111. Line 210. Killing one's husband as Clytemnestra had done is less evil because he is not kin (line 212, 605). If matricide were not sanctioned, all society would fall apart (495-496).

112. *Eumenides*, 870. Apollo calls them "foul animals" (644). Athena says they are older than she; i.e., their numinous authority is more primitive than hers (848).

113. "[Y]ou shall sit on shining chairs beside the hearth to accept devotions offered by your citizens" (*Eumenides*, 806-7).

114. This is something like the way in which, according to Hendrik Berkhof, the "principalities and powers" in the thought of Paul can be brought into a subordinate place within the divine purposes (*Christ and the Powers*). This is a theme Walter Wink underplays in his ongoing work on the powers, most notably *Naming the Powers: The Language of Power in the New Testament*; *Unmasking the Powers*; and *Engaging the Powers*.

115. *Eumenides*, 984.

status. Dionysus, who leads him to destruction, is neither good nor bad; he stands for raw power, life force. In terms of cultural history,[116] he represents the invasion of Greece by Asiatic models of religious enthusiasm. The offense of Pentheus is his not being shrewd enough to cope with the invasion by the cunning and brutality of the dionysiac mode of enthusiasm. He rejects the vital force but cannot control it. When he becomes curious and goes up to the mountain pastures alone to see the crazed women, young and old, "wild with divinity," they tear him apart, thinking he is a lion, and his mother Agave returns to the city with his head on a stick, a gruesome parody of empowerment through possession.[117] There is nothing mimetic in the frenzy.

There is also no happy ending; everyone loses. Dionysus as victorious divine judge condemns the women for killing Pentheus, although they did it under his impulsion. He condemns as well Cadmus who had been the voice of sobriety. Nothing of Thebes survives. The victory of vitality is utter destruction; the implement of the destruction is the crazily "liberated" women, especially the king's own mother.

If Euripedes had written a half-century before Aeschylus, we could be tempted to project a line of cultural evolution, beginning with maternal power being raw destructive passion, then moving to its being justified vengeance, and then onward and upward to its being tamed into peacekeeping. Unfortunately for such a project, Aeschylus wrote a half-century before Euripedes. Abandoning such an evolutionary vision is good; ancient drama is not to that degree univocal or transparent or on a natural uphill slope, nor is ancient moral culture. Each of the themes stands alone; each is perennial. Mothering can correlate with crazy passion or with punitive repression in the defense of matriarchy or with peacekeeping. Any one pattern can progress or degenerate into any other.

---

116. Most accessibly described in the introduction by William Arrow-smith, *Complete Greek Tragedies*, vol. IV, 530-542.

117. "All your daughters are brave, but I above the rest. I have left my shuttle at the loom; I raised my sight to higher things—to hunting animals with my bare hands" (Euripedes, 1235-36).

The Moral Claims of the Defense of Order

In the setting where the abuse of power is prevalent, it is not easy to be fair to the points at which the proper use of power can be held to be a duty, even an unwelcome and onerous one. The son who takes over from the old man may be proud and power hungry, but he may not.[118] He may also be doing, with regret, something that for the sake of the community needs to be done and which costs him some pain. The old man may be tired and ready to go, or he may want the son to take over. The Oedipus of the ancient myth did not know he was killing his father, but in our society the younger supplanter knows very well what he is doing and regrets it.[119] "This hurts me more than it does you" is not a farcical claim. More than that, the son/supplanter may be burdened for the long future not only by feelings of guilt but also by external job descriptions taken on when the old man was cut down, which were not what the supplanter would have most wanted to do.[120] The reason the "son" takes over cannot be reduced to hunger for power; the intention is to shore up the system.

---

118. Here we reach into the theme of part 8.
119. I use the masculine here only because the prototype does; the supplanters may be female.
120. I can think of men whose entire later life work was skewed by the sense of duty to take over from someone senior and then be governed by that person's calling instead of his own. But then there are others for whom cutting down the old man became an occasion for gratification and professional promotion.

PART 7: THE OLD MAN MUST GO

A second model of positive punitive function may be described somewhat more briefly here because its place may be easier to see since it is more familiar in our pop psychology. In any rapidly developing culture, there needs to be a way for the coming generation of power-wielders to move their predecessors out of the way. Compulsory retirement or limited terms in office may do this in some sectors of culture and society; in others it is less smooth. In the broadest sense, well established in our culture, some might call this power more oedipal.[121]

In many ways and for many reasons, which in a more traditional society could be identified with the cosmic order, the older man governs as long as he can. New reasons, having to do with cultural change, numbers, and self-esteem, lead men of the next generation to want the older man to move aside before he is ready.[122] That is a socially functional reason for scapegoating. Despite the exceptions like a J. Paul Getty, an Armand Hammer, or a George Burns, it is generally better for a changing society (and not only for the young man's mental health or self-esteem) that the old man be replaced.[123] What Freud called a "complex,"

---

121. Just as the current use of "scapegoat" has moved away from the origins of the term in Leviticus, so too this common usage is far removed from both Freud and the Greek drama. As noted above, the ancient Oedipus did not know the man he killed was his father, and he did not kill *in order to* take either his father's throne or his wife. Likewise, the prototypical patient for whom Freud created the category was not trying to move an older man out of office. Letting the metaphors shift in this way would be wrong only if it were not conscious.

122. Obviously when we move from the traditional to the metaphorical usage, some of the "younger men" may be women. The "old man" needing to be forced out may also be a woman (e.g., Golda Meir, Indira Gandhi, or Margaret Thatcher).

123. As noted above that the "maternal" mode is not gender-bound so that one of its dramatic instances is the account of a Baptist minister father, so in our time the "filial" mode of displacement may be exercised by younger women as well as men.

leading us to think of it as pathological, may in fact be whole-some. This type of punishment may be closer to "mimesis" than is the "maternal" form and closer to the regicides in Frazer.[124]

There is another distinguishable frame of reference for demanding punishment. This one might be considered an organic outgrowth of the "maternal," or the "filial," or an overlapping of the two.[125] It will, however, be clearer for our purposes that we name it separately, while being aware of the logical and perhaps developmental connectedness. Let us call it the "governmental." Not only parents punish in order to show who is boss; others do it in the name of public order. The next generation does it in the interest of its claim that the old man was tyrannical.

I do not allude here primarily to punishment by the state, although the state does it too. To "teach him a lesson" means primordially that the individual being punished must learn who is boss. Only derivatively does it also mean that the group wants

---

124. In the intention, in the imagery, and in the modern counterparts, the next generation does in fact effectively take over the rule. To see or to say this too simply would, however, be to miss other important dimensions:

a) One fact that is quite obvious in the ancient myth, namely that after taking down the old man Oedipus does not rule happily ever after. The destructive mechanism which he bought into, unwittingly and perhaps unwillingly, when he brought down the old man, will bring him down in its turn. Serious moral testing of "theologies of revolution" in our generation does not fail to note that the tactics used to seize the throne may also make it vulnerable.

b) Although often the younger person does replace the "old man" in an institutional role (e.g., church, state, school, and business), there are other punitive modes that inflict pain without taking any-thing over (e.g., journalism and public mockery or defamation).

125. I noted in part 6 above that the maternal, punitive drive may pro-long its concern for control when the son outgrows the original con-straints by means of coalitions. That may occur either with the "fil-ial" form now being discussed (i.e., the classical oedipal triangle) or with the "victim" style yet to be studied. Or the mother may enlist her daughter-in-law to function more like another mother than like a spouse, as they conspire to control the man they share.

to teach its rules as to acceptable behavior and force people to obey them. The person punishing does it not on impulse or out of anger, but for the sake of the guilty one: "this is for your own good. It hurts me more than it does you." This rationale differs from the maternal in that the order being enforced is understood as not merely personal but social and just, functional.[126] It differs from the merely "filial" in the claim that what the younger man seeks is not mere selfish desire for power for himself. He rather believes himself called to wield said power in the defense of righteous order.[127]

Good Measure Versus Due Process

We are now in a position to observe an important trait common to the three forms just observed: maternal control, filial takeover, and reinforcing governmental legitimacy. This common characterization will apply as well to the "victim empowerment" category yet to come.

It is characteristic of all these types that in addition to the amount of penalty needed to attain or maintain control, or to restore the balance, a further amount of punishment is called for "for good measure." More is needed not only in order (pragmatically) to be successful in seizing power, but in order to celebrate the legitimacy of that control and to "rub it in" in the awareness both of the offender and of the watching world who must be *shown* who is now boss.

It is thus precisely inappropriate, in this setting, to ask ordinary "liberal" or "due process" questions about whether the punishment "fits" the crime. The whole point is that more than equal measure is needed to make the point. "Making the point" is more than "restoring balance." The point is not that "every offense demands equal compensation," but that "you are no

---

126. Of course, in conservative Christian circles it is understood as also being divinely warranted.
127. Cf. above (part 6) the recognition of the "agonic" type of conflict, which is not strictly "punishment" since what it does is to set things right—the infliction of pain being only a means to that end.

longer in control." Again this is a point where the need to punish leaves mimesis behind.

A parenthesis on the theme of "due process" is called for here.[128] The label "due process" is purely formal; it has numerous applications.

One set of meanings for due process is derived from the civil justice system, but we usually expect them to be understood and respected also with respect to other forms of conflict:

- The accused should be able to confront the accuser.
- It should be assumed that there is not only one account of the facts of the case, so that the truth of the matter needs to be established by open debate and the use of witnesses, documents, challenging the accuser, etc.
- The one accused is not bound to provide evidence against his/herself on his/her own.
- The one accused is presumed innocent until proven guilty.
- Each party should have an advocate.
- The judge should be impartial.
- Records should be kept, with documents available to the accused.
- On actions taken there should be a minute record.

Another set of "due process" notions are derived from the New Testament tradition, which some churches take more seriously than others:

- Matthew 18:15 instructs the accuser to speak first privately to "the brother."[129]
- Matthew 18 assumes a forgiving intention and expects a reconciling outcome.

---

128. I shall return to this theme in part 9.
129. This provision is also in the Notre Dame Honor Code guidelines, and in most such codes.

Yet other procedural understandings are tacitly assumed, but are also often articulated as prerequisites for valid socially shared work on complex issues of fact:

- Newspapers should not publish libel.
- Promises of confidentiality should be made and when made should be kept.
- Professionals are bound to specific codes.
- Some professionals, such as priests and journalists, have an obligation to protect their sources.
- Conflict of interest should be avoided by not letting one person have several roles or loyalties (or concealed interests) in the process.

Yet other sets of guidelines are developed by particular entities or movements or communities:

- The rule of St. Benedict makes procedural requirements much like those of Matthew 18.
- The Society of Brothers founded in the 1920s in Germany by Eberhard Arnold codified, under the label "the first rule of Sannerz," the prohibition of gossip and the obligation to take one's accusations directly to the accused.
- Any modern organization may make its own rules for decision process and membership status; e.g., a university or a government agency may prescribe in detail how to process matters of status and tenure, or sexual harassment.
- Other cultures will have still other rules: some centering on the "wisdom" of the elders, some with conceptions of the power of "shame" or "impurity."

Whatever be the *content* of the "due process" notion, what matters *formally*, within all the diversity of the many phenomena here listed, is that it is thought to be indispensable to the viability and dignity of a society that conflicts should be resolved and decisions made in ways that are commonly understood and accepted by all parties to the conflict as procedurally valid. If not, the alternative is (or looks like) naked "might makes right," whereby not only the victims but also many third party observers consider the outcomes invalid and the community weakened.

In most societies, until very recently, the acceptance of these due process standards in vigor was largely taken for granted or common sensical; i.e., it did not need to be formally defined or studied or negotiated. When cultures are in flux, on the other hand, and when there needs to be renegotiation or redefinition, those procedures for changing the rules usually do not try to begin from scratch, but seek to "mend" or "restore" what it is assumed was already in effect.

It is important to have taken note of this, as we come back to our topic from this detour. As we seek to understand the vindictive power of the scapegoating process, we learn that the refusal of due process criteria may often be part of the point at stake. The protestors who want the "patriarchal" system destroyed include in their accusation the due process system itself. They do not want justice in the terms that the system offers. They want to redefine the system.

- The "innocent until proven guilty" principle favors the accused.
- "Confronting the accusers" is tilted against the victim, as long as the accused is seen by the victim in the light of his powerful past.
- Prosecuting the abuse of police power tends to be done in such ways as to favor the police.
- The rules of evidence and the Anglo-Saxon habits of argument, in for example the prosecution of rape accusations, tend to favor the accused.
- The breach of confidentiality, especially if joined to the defamatory power of gossip and the press, is one way to bring down the powerful.
- A mother or a professional counselor does not need to keep a promise made to a child, since she knows better

and her intentions are irreproachably benevolent. The same may be true for a therapist, an educator, or a court.
- The intention to forgive may cheapen the needful recognition by the perpetrator of damage and guilt.

The moral authority for thus setting aside such standard rules of due process is the maternal or the oedipal or the "governmental" claim, which we were just describing, that there must be a change of regime. The "maternal" form assumes that the offender is the child whose rebellious will must be broken, and due process considerations must not stand in the way of imposing that surrender. The infant's challenge to parental authority is wrong in principle, regardless of what particular act of obedience the mother is enforcing at the time. The "oedipal" form, on the other hand, assumes that the offender is the old man whose authority is oppressive, independent of any evaluation of the rightness of his particular governing acts.

Although the familial metaphors of "mother" and "oedipus" are sociologically opposites, they have in common the kind of self-evident and unqualified moral claim that they make against the one previously in charge. In the new phase, which this conflict has taken in the American 1990s, the two streams may also coalesce concretely when the person claiming unrestrained authority is at the same time both a junior person talking of taking power over those who had it before and a woman talking in coercive terms of the "healing" that will ensue when the accused yields to her control.

For many purposes, due process remains indispensable. It is needed to establish formal guilt in a court of law. It is needed in procedures of mediation. In a therapeutic setting, it is needed if the healing or the re-education of the accused is desired. It is needed for a journalist or historian to come as close as possible to establishing "facts." It is needed if there is to be ethical evaluation of right and wrong actions. These considerations make it all the more important that we take account of the "oedipal" and/or "maternal" considerations, which count against due process in some cases.

This intentional disregard for due process is present as well in the older cultural history of scapegoating.[130] What dictates that the leader must be cut down is not some particular evil he has done, not a specific culpable act of tyranny or bad management, although there may be a formally or ritually inculpating procedure to justify the punishment. It would, however, be wrong to ask fairness questions, either procedural or quantitative, since fairness defends the prior structure.

Or to say it another way: concepts of fairness have developed over the centuries in light of the notion that the various parties to conflictual relations are somehow peers or are committed to equal regard for one another. The purpose of "due process" at the heart of the law is to keep the playing field level. Roman citizenship law, Christianity, open conversation in the Holy Spirit,[131] Anglo-Saxon common law, Enlightenment, and other liberation visions have each developed their own ways, significantly different ways yet congruent, of defining why we should treat each other as peers and why that calls for leveling the field. Yet they call for leveling. That makes it important that the maternal and oedipal imperatives of punishment or control should escape *by definition*, not merely by inadvertence or error, from the scope of the imperative of maximizing parity. They want precisely to tilt the field in order to correct for what they denounce as the previous tilt in the wrong direction.

I have attended thus far to three models of estrangement and punishment (and thereby potentially of atonement) at greater length than to the ones more traditionally dealt with in theology.[132] I have attended to them first because traditional

---

130. This fits most closely the scapegoat who is the chieftain, the Antisthenes figure against whom "mother" and "son" join. The other kind of scapegoat, the innocent outsider, fits less with this rationale. This latter kind of scapegoat is seen as collectively guilty by virtue of who they are, so that due process questions do not arise.

131. 1 Corinthians 14 (esp. vv. 26-31).

132. Such would be those located in the order of things, or in the demands of God's anger or honor, which were referred to above

theologies have noticed them less, but also because they are "closer to the ground" anthropologically and because the argument that they have a legitimate place in functioning cultures is serious.

Thus, there are more ways than one in which it can be argued that social patterns that punish or remove a leader may be socially functional.[133] For none of them does the metaphor of "mimesis" standing alone illuminate much. Our analysis may then, I claim, be aided more by further describing their naturalness, as I have begun to do, than by letting our embarrassment repress them.

(part 4), and which are regularly found in the traditional atonement theories. A full analysis might need to correlate those reasons to these.

133. As said above (part 4), the term "functional" chosen here is intentionally less positive than "good," yet more affirmative than "legitimate." Even many pacifists recognize that in the world as it is, in peacetime, police have a function. The penal system has a function. The market economy has a function. This is affirmed even though each of these systems falls short of gospel love and each of them hurts many people.

PART 8: EMPOWERMENT

After having made the case, with the two or three anthropologically most elemental illustrations, for recognizing that retribution may be socially in order, I need to move on to add two additional reasons to the basic list. The best label for the next form is probably "victim vindication."[134] The reason for the punitive response in this case is the inner psychic need of the victim of abuse to return pain for pain. The victim may affirm that this demand of pain for pain is identical with that of the divine order, but, of course, in the conflict situation not everyone sees the demands of that order the same.[135] The victim's perspective is the best way to see the point.[136] This need may underlie the primitive "mimetic desire" in Girard, but in Girard's case it is not usually the victim who strikes back, but the system, the order of things.[137] Further, in many settings the "striking back" is often not symmetrical, so that even here the mimesis metaphor may not be the most appropriate, although it is less out of place than in the other cases.

Before reaching back to the resources of the dictionary, I can best begin with the simplest of metaphors. I have often heard it recounted as true, and as often as poetically apt, that a child who resents being overpowered by the authority of an older sibling will state the complaint in the form "Just wait until I am big and you are little!"

---

134. This would be the fourth form, following the maternal, the filial, and the governmental.

135. The previous sentence is an understatement. What is precisely wrong is that someone who has held and used power has held its use to be validated by some divine order.

136. Liberation theologies speak of "the epistemological privilege of the oppressed." Seeing the skewed world from below is the way to see it most accurately. The point is not that the underdogs are morally better people, but that they are better placed to see things as they are.

137. Nor in the case of Frazer (*The Golden Bough*) or Anspach ("Violence Against Violence").

This would appear to be one of the most elementary forms of moral discourse. A state of affairs or a deed is evaluated as bad by the person whom it hurts, and its having happened is attributed to a power imbalance. This is a moral appeal. The complaint is clothed in the hypothetical scenario of a future turning of the tables, which somehow, sometime, the universe is obligated to provide. This complaint can of course be addressed as well to a parent or other power-bearer. The child does not say "that hurts!" but "that was wrong!" and the way to clarify that wrongness is "what you did to me should be done to you." Symmetry, tit for tat, is an image for justice. The mimetic dimension is strong here, but at the time the injustice is felt, the punishment is not meted out, since the demand or the hope is articulated by the child in the face of her frustration at not being able (now) to satisfy it. This is not a mere testimony to anger but a moral appeal. It demands that the cosmos should in the future intervene to restore the balance.

The inherited meaning of the word "victim" demands further elucidation, since in modern applications the term can be used much more widely. Despite the formal similarity, the term "victim" does not come from the same root as "victor."[138] It does not mean simply, as the verbal similarity may make one think, the party who lost out in a conflict. "Victim" comes from the same root as "witch," and it refers to a sacrifice that is understood by those who impose it to be effective within and by virtue of a superstitious or numinous worldview.[139] The claim is made, by those who cause the victim to suffer, that such suffering is good for the system or within the order of things. It is this posi-

---

138. This similarity of the English words has been used to good effect in theological discussion of atonement. Cf. John Seldon Whale's classical book on christology, with those two words in the title: *Victor and Victim.*

139. Other English words beginning with "vic-" come from still other old indogermanic roots; the four occurrences of this three-letter root within the words *vicious, vice president, victor,* and *victim* all have different original indogermanic derivations.

tive value claim, made on behalf of the oppressive order by those whom it serves, which becomes so offensive when the victims become aware of its injustice and retrieve their self-esteem. Not the pain itself but the "order of things" claim, which was supposed to justify the pain already suffered, is the evil demanding vindication. To be "victimized" is thus worse than merely to suffer pain. What offends the victim most is the fact that the pain is justified; it is inflicted in the name of the way things are and should be by power-bearing persons and/or structures that claim some cosmic mandate. That validation claim, more than the pain itself, is what constitutes the scandal and demands that the corrective be more than a mere reprimand.

Frantz Fanon, whose *Wretched of the Earth* came out of the Algerian uprising against France (1955-62), wound together in one cord several forms of victimization:

- classical political colonialism and the response of national liberation;
- racism: Fanon was black, from Martinique, although living and working in Algeria; and
- neocolonial economic and cultural domination of the "third world" by the "first."

Although all of these offenses are institutional and his study included dimensions of economic and political science, Fanon the therapist responded in terms also drawn from individual psychotherapy.[140] His vision of the "healing" or, better, of the celebratory "empowerment," which the underdog has the right to claim by acting violently in the ordinary case, can be formulated by means of the oedipal image of the son whose dignity is linked to his supplanting his father.[141]

---

140. This part of Fanon's argument got the most attention because it was accentuated by Jean-Paul Sartre, who wrote the preface.

141. In "Modes of Human Violence," *Irish Theological Quarterly* 41 (July 1974): 185-204, Edna McDonagh reviewed sensitively the deeper roots of Fanon's kind of argument (199-203). He perceived

It is this component that I propose we need to recognize as real and extend to understanding other modes of victimization rather than the three listed above, especially those with a sexual or physical dimension. The victims' demand that the perpetrator of a prior abuse be punished is part of the victims' retrieval of their dignity.[142] Social hygiene, protecting others against the same depredations, may be part of the concern but is not its root. The root is the dignity that was wounded when the victims' suffering was wrongfully interpreted as being properly part of the nature of things. The punishment not only expresses their resentment; it sets right the skewed cosmos.[143] It does not mirror the wrong deed so much as reverse it. Again, "mimesis" is not the best label for this.

There is also a macro social counterpart to victim vindication, which we can perhaps define best by some recent negative examples. When Gerald Ford, as one of his first actions once in office as president of the USA, pardoned his predecessor, Richard Nixon, church spokespersons joined politicians and journalists in deploring that Ford had thereby short-circuited the national experience of truth and healing that a judicial process might have provided.[144] When, after a generation of fascist

---

them in the revolutionary thought of Georges Sorel (1908), the playwright Aimé Césaire, and parallels among Irish and Palestinian rebels, all of whom link violence with salvation. One could add the romantic irredentists of nineteenth-century Italy or Poland, for whom the imperative of heroic violence was not restrained by any "just-war" considerations of probable success.

142. One friendly critic has pointed out to me that the language reference made above might be misunderstood. The linguistic link between "victim" and "witch" does not mean that the victims demanding compensation are in the role of witch. It is rather that the system oppressing them, against which they rebel, claims numinous or spooky validation, so that their rising up to resist it is comparable to disenchantment or exorcism.

143. That the need is located within the victims, even though they project it into the cosmic order, fits with Dürkheim's thesis with which we began (part 1).

144. Cf. William Hamilton and Charles P. Henderson, "Theology and

military dictatorship, civilian government returned to Argentina, there were strong voices among the conservative Catholic bishops, the civilian politicians and bureaucrats, and among the higher military themselves calling for "reconciliation." By this they meant that the thousands of murders and "disappearances" that could be documented should go unpunished.[145]

Over against this call for cheap reconciliation, those who cared for an authentic return to social peace insisted that it could not come without stating the truth.[146] The killers might not need to be killed (again not literal mimesis), but they needed to be named and, properly, they should not be in line for continuing privileges of office. The same issue arose again early in 1993 when the report of the UN truth-finding operation in El Salvador was shunted aside by the Cristiani government's hasty declaration of "amnesty."[147]

---

the Pardon," *The Christian Century* 91, vol. 33 (October 1974): 900-902.

145. Cf. Lawrence Weschler, *A Miracle, A Universe: Settling Accounts with Torturers*, who compares "transitional justice" problems in Argentina, Brazil, Chile, and Uruguay.

146. As Hannah Arendt indicates in her *Origins of Totalitarianism*, the first step into tyranny is the destruction of "the juridical person" in the citizen. Then "the first essential step toward liberty is the revival of the legal impulse in man." As Arendt indicates elsewhere, this need for rehabilitation is not in conflict with the role of forgiveness to which she gives foundational importance (*The Human Condition*).

147. Any country moving from blatant tyranny to law and order must face this problem somehow: Chile, Eastern Europe, South Africa. A "Rule of Law" study project under the auspices of the United States Institute of Peace has documented in great detail the importance of some kind of "justice" in the transition from tyranny to decency (Neil J. Kritz, ed., *Readings on Transitional Justice: How Emerging Democracies Reckon with Former Regimes*). Currently the most helpful overviews of this theme are José Zalaquett, "Confronting Human Rights Violations Committed by Former Governments: Principles Applicable and Political Constraints," in *State Crimes: Punishment or Pardon*, 23-69; Lawrence Weschler in *State Crimes*; and Aryeh Heier, "What Should Be Done About the Guilty," in *New York Review of Books* (Feb 1, 1990).

There are thus strong justice claims that ought to count against the cheapening of grace by calling for reconciliation without restitution, forgiveness without pain. The nature and extent of the punishment are not what matters for this type, but that the offense be named and known is a condition of life's beginning again. This explanation might be thought of as a modern equivalent of the scholastic atonement theory, which used to be called "rectoral." That was, in turn, a subset of the "satisfaction" family of theories, according to which the reason God as ruler needs to insist on punishment is not that God is angry or that there is a cosmic scale of recompenses to be balanced (e.g., pain for pain), but that the illegitimacy of those behaviors needs to be acted out publicly and dramatically as a part of the definition of the society's moral identity. This then approaches the "governmental" notion listed above. Yet it says more than the offenders *themselves* must be taught a lesson. The "lesson" must be acted out celebratively for the whole society to see or for the sake of "history."

René Girard sees the meaning of all of world history, growing in momentum and breadth since the cross of Christ, as consisting in the progressive unveiling of the injustice of all scapegoating and victimization. As he notes, there is a particularly painful paradox just at this point to which our culture has come, since the newly developing reason for punishing a new victim is the punitive demand of the former victims.[148] The cause of victim vindication turns in on itself.[149] Can it avoid being a vicious circle? Does the victims' revindication not tend to validate, by replacing it, the very offense it seeks to rectify? Both the fact that the victims affirm victim status as a self-definition and that in return they mimetically victimize others reinforce the very structure they denounce.[150]

---

148. Cf. Girard's plenary lecture on "The Satan of the Gospels," presented at the American Academy of Religion in November 1992.

149. This is particularly the case in the special mode I shall later be calling "tectonic."

150. The popular psychodynamic view of personality is torn between "hydraulic" metaphors, according to which pain or evil is "pent up"

PART NINE: ENTERING A NEW AGE

In times of tectonic cultural shifting, in settings where whole blocs of cultural meanings are being moved, a particular dramatic punitive event may mark a major transition thanks to more violence than usual or thanks to violence erupting into a setting where it had been absent. The execution of Charles I of England and of Louis XVI of France were such tectonic pivots. One does not ask whether either of those men merited the death penalty. Likewise, the deaths of Gandhi and Martin Luther King or those of John F. and Robert Kennedy or Steve Biko or those of Oscar Romero and Ignacio Ellacuria came to mean more as historic hinges than as acts of political criminality. In this sense (as already noted), a special corrective wave of feminist initiative may be found by many to be indispensable in America in the mid-1990s in order to make sure that the legacy of patriarchy has been banished.

By the nature of the case, the justification for this kind of punishment will not be *merely* that it dramatizes a change of regime. It will be natural that at the same time it should make "maternal" or "filial" or "governmental" or "victim empowerment" claims for its rightness. We noted above that while "mother" if standing alone will lose out in the end, the maternal drive can enter coalitions with other patterns. The mother can ally herself with her daughter-in-law, who thereby becomes more like a mother than like a spouse and partner to the man they both want to control. Or the "mother" can ally herself with the "son" when the time has come for the chieftain (her spouse, his father) to be brought down. Already, under the heading of

---

and can be "vented" to keep it from "exploding," and "behaviorist" explanations, according to which if you are rewarded for acting in a particular way once, you are more likely to do it again. The notion of victim vindication by "getting it out," described above, buys into the "hydraulic" or "venting" metaphor and is challenged by those who find the "behavioral" image more realistic. Thus, the "vindication" demand buys into one school of psychology at the expense of another.

the "governmental" mode of "showing him who is boss," we noted the possibility that the different kinds of punishers could make common cause. In the case of the tectonic shift, to which we now turn, the sense of mission with which punishment is demanded will be strengthened not by coalition alone but by exceptional timing and a sense of historical mission.

Not only does the process have to be painful to the former patriarch to be satisfying to the victims, there are also patterns ordinarily associated with due process that may need to be over-ridden. This can be the case, as we saw in part 7, for ordinary "maternal" or "filial" righteousness; even more will this obtain for the "tectonic" case. "Innocent until proven guilty" is a pillar of the rule of law, as are the laws of evidence. Yet in skewed situations these safeguards may protect the rapist, the abusive policeman, or the oppressive old boy. Likewise, judgments of proportion are subject to abuse. Both the "maternal" (including the "governmental") and the "filial" reasons to punish demand as we have seen not "that the punishment fit the crime,"[151] but rather that the party newly in charge must not only possess but celebrate—brandish total control of the offender—whether that be the "mother's" control of the infant or the "son's" overwhelming the old man.[152] Therefore, concern for matters of proximate fairness, proportion, and proper procedure may appear as seeking to frustrate the necessary outcome.[153] For the one being pun-

---

151. This is another way in which we see that "mimesis" is an insufficient designation and explanation.

152. This is especially overt in the "break the evil will" theme in the discipline of Susanna Wesley or Francis Wayland (part 6).

153. Anita Hill, a public embodiment of the tectonic drama, is supposed to have said, "the woman should be supported whether there is proof or not." Her admirers welcomed that idea, as an expression of the view just being described. Her detractors pounced on it as a sign of unconcern, odd for a lawyer, for justice. Actually Hill did not use those words in the context of finding someone guilty judicially without proof and therefore punishing him. She was saying that a single mother should have financial support for her child regardless of whether she can prove the father's identity, which is

ished, to ask for fair play can be condemned as just one more mode of patriarchal control.

It should thus by the nature of the case be expected that when such a pivotal execution happens it is immaterial whether there was one specific crime committed to merit it. As René Girard learned from the anthropologists, sometimes the chieftain is declared ritually guilty of some impurity in order for his execution to be mandatory, but often the offense and the "trial" are rigged.[154]

On the other hand, when the "scapegoat" is not a chieftain but an anonymous innocent or outsider, there is no pretense at all of finding that person morally or juridically guilty. When the scapegoat is "the Jews" or the gypsies, their guilt is stipulated for the entire class independent of any personal accountability. In general, whether for the chieftain or for the anonymous scapegoat, the punishment is not linked and should not be linked to juridically proven guilt on the scapegoat's part for it to be morally valid or for it to be legally imperative or for its saving effect on the cosmos to "work."[155]

Again, with this case of the tectonic shift as with the earlier cases ("maternal," "filial," "victim vindication") of which it is so

---

certainly morally right for the child's sake. But the fact that the wider anti-due-process reading was picked up and welcomed by many reinforces the present point. It is natural in this special setting that women should want more harm to be done to the patriarch than he can be proven guilty of having caused.

154. Cf. Mark Anspach, "Violence Against Violence," 17, and James Frazer, *The Golden Bough*. We already noted that the juxtaposition of the "chieftain" and "innocent outsider" models of scapegoat is the weakest part of Girard's explanation.

155. The point should be made yet more strongly. It is constitutive of the drive for punishment, especially in the "maternal" and "filial" modes, that no questions of due process should even be raised. Notions of "due process" and fairness assume a vision of parity among the parties, whether the origins of that call for parity are to be found in Greek or Roman civic culture, in Anglo-Saxon fairness, or in Christian or enlightenment egalitarianism. But neither the "mother" nor the "son" wants to be treated as a peer (cf. part 7). The power of the "mother" or "son" to get away with being unfair is part of the point needing to be acted out dramatically.

to speak a cumulation, it would be wrong to seek a simple moral judgment on the phenomenon. Events are socially functional, and they contribute to the maintenance or movement of a society without being easily qualified as right or wrong morally. The impact of the 1992 Los Angeles disorders or that of the Clarence Thomas hearings has to be assessed as a global cultural-historical phenomenon (both as cause and effect), without our needing to reduce that assessment to a simple moral evaluation of whether any one actor or any "constituency" or "the way things went" was morally right or properly found guilty.[156]

It has been illuminating for our purposes to disentangle and to name severally the diverse types of reason to punish. They can occur alone, and each can make sense to the respective actors. Each has its place in anthropology (whether in the person or in the society). Each should be discerned, labeled, and evaluated in its own right. None can be simply reduced to a subform of the others. "Mimesis" does not explain most of them. Of most of them, however, it should also not be surprising that in special settings there can/could be some special power constellations and cultural turning points where more than one of these dimensions would coincide. We need not affirm "all of the above" as equally valid morally or heuristically, nor need we distinguish carefully among them as if only one at a time could apply in real cases. It suffices to see that each type exists, that these types are different, sometimes deeply, from one another, and that in a specific conflictual nexus they may coalesce.

---

156. If I were the therapist or a moral advisor of a person bent on vengeance, I would want them to see that the punitive drive is counterproductive, not something they will remember with pride. If I were their pastor I would want them to see that the punitive drive is not Christian. If I were a social theorist or legislator, I would work against building that vindictive drive into the laws. But for now, whether what I am doing in this essay be called social psychology or ethics, the prior need is to face the fact that this phenomenon of punishing with a good conscience is part of the order of things. Should I be called to be the scapegoat, my making the point that it is unfair to treat me that way would be out of order.

PART 10: WHAT THEN SHOULD THE OLD MAN DO?[157]

When Socrates was accused by the authorities of an offense that in the worst construction would be worthy of death, he had more than two options. He seems steadily to have chosen the worst.

1. He could have left Athens before the trial. No one would have stopped him. He did not even consider this. Why not? Perhaps because the people in power would have been glad to see him go, would not have minded not having to kill him, and would have been glad to be able to interpret his escape as a victory. Their control of the system would have been confirmed at less cost and trouble than if there had been a trial; and his leaving could have been interpreted as a tacit confession of his guilt and an acknowledgment of their rightness. Instead, Socrates stayed in the city and thereby forced the authorities to follow through with the process.

2. In the trial process, he could have been less stubborn. He could have pleaded that those who denounced him were exaggerating, that he was misquoted, and that his words were taken in the wrong light. He could have brought his children into the courtroom to make an emotional plea. All of those arguments in defense would have been true.[158] Instead, he made no conces-

---

157. [Editor's note: Part 10 was originally the last chapter of the original online version of this work (before Yoder added an additional chapter in 1997). We moved it, despite the fact that it does not fit perfectly in this new position, because it extends Girard's framework rather than bring the various sections of this essay to a close as the following chapters do. It is as if Yoder had previously wrapped up his piece with the chapters to follow and then, having later identified an important extension of Girard's work, simply appended it to the end rather than organically weave it back into the collection in a more appropriate place. This is consistent with Yoder's confession in the preface to this present chapter (154) that the chapters of the original work appear when he wrote them and not necessarily in a strictly logical sequence.]

158. To bring in his children to inspire pity might have been considered as corrupting the judges (*Apology*, Loeb Classical Library [1943],

sion and affirmed his integrity in a way that they could take as proving his guilt.

3. Once found guilty, the court offered him the possibility to propose his own sentence. If he had proposed something sufficiently onerous, they might have been able to interpret that as an acceptable compromise and an avowal of guilt and to back away from the death sentence. Instead he proposed that, since what he had done was not wrong, the punishment should not be a punishment. He should be positively rewarded, like the winners in chariot races, with maintenance in the Prytanaeum.[159] This made it impossible for them to back away without total loss of face.

4. Once condemned to death, he could have escaped. His friends were preparing to help him take that way out.[160] As with option 1 above, he could have looked forward to a hero's welcome in some other city and a new start for his teaching career. He refused. Why?

Why was it right, in Socrates' mind, to accept the punishment rather than to avoid it in any of these four available ways? He was not yielding to the cosmic imperative of regicide, like the chieftains going uncomplainingly to their ritual death in Frazer or Anspach. Yet his acceptance of death as the price of his integrity, as a fate not to be cheated, was in some sense like those elite victims of Girardian sacrifice. Socrates saw his submitting to the sentence in the light of the imperative of the shape of things as they are and must be, *even when* the system is in the wrong hands.[161]

It is not that Socrates "believed in the system," trusting that the institutions that claim to grind out justice will do so, ulti-

---

123-25). He could properly argue that in other cities a capital case cannot be decided in one sitting; with more time he could have convinced them (*Apology*, 131-33).

159. *Apology*, 129-31.
160. *Crito*, Loeb Classical Library (1943), 153-63.
161. "Better die innocent and be justified before the princes of the world below" (*Crito*, 189). The account in *Phaedo* (Loeb Classical Library [1943], 200-205, 218-21, 289-91, 301-307) adds a different and extraneous argument, namely welcoming death because the soul is imprisoned in the body.

mately, most of the time, so that it is better to support the system, even at the cost of a few misfires, rather than to challenge its control. There are people who believe that. That is the humanistic or "liberal" reason for accepting punishment. Such believers submit conscientiously to civil courts or to church courts in that mentality without insisting on due process for themselves, thinking that even with a few injustices mixed in, which happen to fall on them, it is better that the system be working than not. Or they may think "I promised to work by these rules" and decide that sticking by the promise is itself so important that the promise must be kept even when the rules don't work fairly.

Neither for Socrates nor for Jesus, whose decision was formally similar and has been alluded to earlier in this study,[162] was such a "belief in the system" an adequate explanation. The reason for accepting the suffering was deeper, or even opposite. Because one does *not* trust the system, one challenges it by suffering. An analog, more enlightening, would be the way Gandhi obliged judges, who would rather have let him out by a loophole, to imprison him.

For Socrates, any avoidance of the price of truth-telling would have been a denial of the told truth. Any of the "ways out" would have meant disavowing who he had been and what he had been saying. Had he been a judge, he would have been a just judge and would have found himself innocent (as he showed when they asked him to suggest a penalty). But once the unjust verdict had fallen, it was not his role to prevent its being executed.[163]

Nor can we ease the explanation by ascribing to Socrates a partial avowal, like what is sometimes done in our courts with

---

162. Nor for Gandhi or King, whose stances were analogous and in a way derived from the above.

163. My attempting to understand Socrates in his own terms would not include approving of his administering the poison himself. He would better have obliged them to send an executioner. Jesus did not crucify himself. Gandhi did punish himself by fasting, but that was a different dynamic.

a "no contest" plea, saying in effect "I am not worthy of death but I probably am guilty of something, and I am sorry, and the difference is not worth the cost of a lengthy, noisy, costly truth-finding process." It was constitutive of Socrates' posture that he was not at all guilty of the crime of treason and that those who pronounced and followed through on the condemnation very well knew that to be the case. The injustice of the condemnation was part of what made it imperative that he bear the penalty. It was imperative for them because their claim to legitimate power would collapse if they granted that his condemnation was unjust. It was therefore imperative for him to refuse to meet them on their terms.

Socrates' death is another part of the classical tradition that does not fit closely to the Girardian categories as to why he needed to die. Yet, once it is clear that he must die, his reasons for accepting that fate are quite parallel to the kings in Frazer and Anspach.

PART 11: FURTHER AGENDA IN THE GIRARDIAN SYSTEM:

TOWARD A "THICKER" FRAME OF REFERENCE FOR POST-GIRARDIAN ANALYSIS OF THE ROOTS OF PUNISHMENT

The theoretical system that René Girard has developed around his special understandings of scapegoating and sacrifice has now grown beyond the dimensions of a "school" to those of a discipline (perhaps more precisely an interdisciplinary subdiscipline), with its own international conferences, its membership lists and fees, and its sections at the annual meetings of the American Academy of Religion. That attests to the strength of the victim, but it also has the shortcoming that mere mortals like myself, without the time or the mobility to give full time to the subdiscipline, tend to be left behind.

After reviewing the multiple ways that punishment functions, I now return to the conversation with the system created by Girard. I have had to conclude that there is a gap in the Girardian system. The gap is worth working on, since other parts of the system are convincing. Three parts that I find convincing and do not challenge here are as follows:

- the notion of a primeval constitutive social event, the *lynchage fondateur* [founding murder], the original or primeval crisis at the origins of all societies, which purchased social peace at the cost of sacrifice. Its components are the punitive drive or "mimetic desire," the event of sacrifice, and the need for a victim not part of the spiral. These elements are conceptually separate, but they interlock in Girard's theory. The primeval event can be traced, though only indirectly, through the depth level interpretation of primitive cult and ancient myth and legend. It needs thus to be dug up because its being hidden is part of the way the society defends itself.
- a new way to identify and interpret the uniqueness and cultural effect of the cross of Christ, both as historical

event and as gospel.[164] This implies a historical reading of why in fact the power-bearers of his time killed
Jesus, namely because he unveiled the falsity of their
claim to be just punishers, and a vision of the meaning
of history since Easter as the widening ripples from the
breakthrough of that cosmic debunking.

- the intellectual charm of a general theory about the entire
  human drama, which others whom Girard inspires can
  unfold through the standard agenda of other disciplines
  (Schwager in Old Testament, Williams in New Testament, and others in sociology or psychology).

I have had to observe, however, through ordinary lay real-
world analysis, that there are many forms of punitive behavior
that cannot be explained as mimetic and have not been concealed in the primeval forms of myth and ritual. They can also
be considered as constitutive of society as a whole, but they are
also part of the person. One can discern their constitutive quality by attending to the ontogeny of the person in such elemental
ways as the biologically nuclear relation of mother and son,
son and father.

The gaps in the Girardian scheme may be summarized as
follows:

1. There seems to be a gap in the interpretation of *why* people want to hurt people. The term "mimesis" has the advantage
of being purely formal; it says that one does as one was done to.
The same is true of the term "re*tal*iate." That is what the root *tal*
means. But *why* this is done and why it is done with a good conscience is not self-evident. There is a difference between anger-
provoked vengeance, maternal or paternal notions of how and
why to make a child submit,[165] and forensic notions of enforc-

---

164. I agree with Mark I. Wallace [Yoder's source uncertain] that Girard
     makes the claim to have proven "uniqueness" a little too easily
     and too often here, but that is not my present concern.

165. I noted above (in the Wayland case, part 6) that a father may very
     well punish for the same kind of benevolent reason that I here typi-

ing a judicial order. All of these may lead to inflicting pain for pain, but their implications will differ, as do the cosmologies they presuppose. Classical doctrines of atonement, as I have noted, disentangle several theories of why "being done to as one did" should be proper, even imperative. What counts as an answer to the "why" question (including why the Girardian primeval crisis or the cross of Jesus should "work" as an answer) will be different from one setting to another, depending on which answer to the "why" question is most adequate.

Some of the simplest ways to answer the "why" question are less complicated than Girard's story. People who draw on parallels from zoology or from early childhood development may believe that simply imitating blow for blow needs no further explanation. I have shown why I think that it does need explanation, that the question should be asked and can be answered, and that there may in fact be more than one right answer.

2. As was noted above, there is an overlap between two different kinds of cases in Girard's passages about scapegoating. One set of scapegoats are simply innocent and are "chosen" unfairly for punishment, like the Jews in medieval France and other kinds of outsiders, such as gypsies, cripples, and Aztec youths. The other kind are prominent people: tribal chieftain in Frazer, Oedipus or Dionysus in classic Greek drama, the king in Antisthenes, and Marcus Aurelius, Gandhi, King, and Romero. The chieftain may be substituted for by individuals chosen from the former category, but that calls for rituals to justify the substitution. The "chieftain" may be designated for punishment by virtue of his office, or he may be forced to perform some ritually offensive act that brings down the doom upon him. So one kind of scapegoat is anonymous and the other is *ex officio*; one kind is innocent and the other becomes guilty ritually.

Both of these forms ring true to *some* of the data of ethnography or of mythology and to real patterns of scapegoating in

---

fied as "maternal"; yet there may very well be other specifically patriarchal reasons for punishing that are not included in my survey.

our societies; nonetheless, they are structurally quite different. There is no reason to reduce one to a form of the other. If we ask *why* the evil must be done to the scapegoat (my first question above), these two types do not fit the same explanations. Nor do the same explanations work in the same way to connect with Jesus or to the primeval crisis or to the killings of Gandhi and King or to those of the Kennedy brothers.

3. A third kind of question, for which the Girardian system is promising, but to which René Girard himself does not choose to speak, is how we might understand the ongoing processes of scapegoating as they continue to take place in many societies or in our own. All the attention I have seen Girard giving to this matter is glancing. To say that either a primeval social contract or the cross of Jesus settles the question contributes nothing on this level. Some of us think that to understand scapegoating as a natural process might contribute to fruitful social action (e.g., to the choice of the most helpful modes of conflict resolution) illuminated by a vision of why the punitive reaction is in some sense natural.[166]

4. The first time I began appealing to the Girardian perspective was when I was assigned to seek to interpret why mainstream American society is so solidly devoted to the death penalty. The "liberal" angles on punishment, which did so much at such great cost to set the death penalty aside in the USA by the use of the courts (until 1972), have turned out in the longer run to be ineffective to overcome the deep cultural demand for retaliation, which has now reinstated the death penalty in many states. The liberal lawyers and sociologists have been arguing (quite correctly, in terms of Christian ethics, but ineffectively) that killing criminals is inhumane or ineffective. My reading of Girard would suggest that, beyond this moral condemna-

---

166. Mennonite interest in Girard has arisen largely in professional circles interested in the two related fields of corrections and conflict resolution. Girard himself does not disavow that kind of concrete application, but neither does he support it strongly. He would hardly see such applicability as needed for validation.

tion of institutionally killing killers, it would be more helpful to interpret how vengeance is anthropologically normal so that the need is not for enlightenment but for reconciliation.

The first two concerns just noted (1 and 2 above) might be called weaknesses in Girard's system; the latter (3 and 4) are rather themes to which his system might very well be able to be extended in such a way as to speak helpfully. As far as I can see, nothing of the original validity of the Girardian synthesis for the concerns that it illuminates so creatively would be weakened by recognizing that there is more than one strand in the causation underlying vindictive social processes or by acquiescing in the recognition that, although painful and costly and not particularly virtuous on the part of those who execute it, punishment does have a social role.

The point of the core argument of the present outline, when first drafted in 1992, was to test this compatibility claim with persons who know enough about the Girardian scheme to critique or correct me competently, without trying to barge into the inner circle of the most informed disciples. I did not propose initially to bother Professor Girard himself with these questions, since it is bad etiquette to ask a major personage for help with one's homework about him, and since this kind of "yes, but" question, which I am pursuing, is probably better answered anyway by a sympathetic secondhand interpreter or by other members of the disciple community.

Now, however, that (beginning fall 1993) my own ruminations have gone off farther in other directions, while none of Girard's interpreters have responded substantially to my queries, I see less need to connect all that I say closely to all of his system. My conviction that the Girardian perspective has been asked to carry too much freight has grown, so that to mesh with it at every point is less imperative than I once assumed.

If it should be the case that the position sketched in the above pages, although provoked and illuminated by reading Girard, is incompatible with his system, that might not prove that it is wrong,[167] but only that it is in another sub-discipline,[168] working with data that are not central for Girard's agenda. In that case the best way for me to pursue the theme further may well be to connect my exposition still more loosely to the interface with Girard that initially provoked it.

---

167. The papers in Hamerton-Kelly's *Violent Origins* make clear that in this kind of interdisciplinary search it is very hard to know what would constitute falsification. The papers by Walter Burkert ("The Problem of Ritual Killing," 149-76), René Girard ("Generative Scapegoating," 73-105), and Jonathan Z. Smith ("The Domestication of Sacrifice," 191-205) in that book talk past each other on such a high level of methodological abstraction and with such nonchalant insouciance as to validation that the reader is given no notion of what might count as a trans-systemic common court of appeal. Internal consistency, the ability to run whatever comes up through one's own grid, seems to be for each author the only validation needed.

168. The one place in the literature where I have seen a similar thesis is Lucien Scuble in "Girard's anthropology is valid but incomplete and *généralisable*." The latter adjective does not mean what "generalizable" would mean in English, but rather "subject to being taken up into a larger synthesis." [Editor's note: There is no essay or mention of Scuble in Hamerton-Kelly's *Violent Origins*, but Scuble (also Scubla) does affirm and critique Girard's anthropology in "The Christianity of René Girard and the Nature of Religion," in *Violence and Truth: On the Work of René Girard*, ed. Paul Dumouchel, 160-78 (Stanford, Calif.: Stanford University Press, 1988), esp. 170-78.]

PART 12: BACK TO THE REST OF SOCIOLOGY

By beginning with Girard and the modernity he presupposes, I may seem to have leapfrogged over the long, older debate about why it is socially desirable to punish. In law and in the philosophy and sociology of law, there is a routine, old debate about the reasons for punishing. My interlocutor, H. Wayne House, and I reviewed them in *The Death Penalty Debate*.[169] Usually there are four. Some philosophers reduce the categories to two: retribution and consequentialism.[170]

What is noteworthy for present purposes, a consideration that may justify the "leapfrogging" in the present survey, is that those standard lists do not include precisely *either* of the considerations that Girard takes most seriously:

- "mimetic desire" as a primitive reflex, which is not really the same as either personal vengeance or divine retribution; and
- social hygiene, the concern to protest the social peace from the chaotic impact of too much ad hoc retribution, which is the reason given in Girard's reconstruction for the primeval crisis that replaces, controls, and then hides the record of the *mimesis*.[171]

---

169. House and Yoder. House listed four types: "retribution, deterrence, protection of society, and rehabilitation" (16). I reviewed other similar four-point lists (155; cf. the beginning of chapter 4, part 6 of this volume). Our original accounts were intentionally standard and largely parallel. As I pointed out, House then went on to redefine some of the terms in an idiosyncratic and self-refuting way (198-99 [this part of the *Death Penalty Debate* is not reproduced in this volume]).

170. E.g., Edmund L. Pincoffs, *The Rationale of Legal Punishment.* Gertrude Ezorsky lists "teleology," "retribution," and the combination of the two in her introduction to the collection of classical texts she edited, *Philosophical Perspectives on Punishment.*

171. Whereas the effect and intent of the *lynchage fondateur* [founding murder] in order to teach a lesson was to diminish the total amount of violence in the social system, the effect of modern punitive escalation is the opposite.

Girard is certainly right in claiming that those dimensions belong in the picture, and the modern consensus ignores them to its discredit.

Nor do the standard sources on the reason for penalties discuss the other alternative, socially functional reasons to which my study then turned. Again, it is striking how cross-disciplinary reading makes us aware not only of the gaps *between* the cultivated fields but also of the explanations that are missing when one identifies questions within a discipline other than one's own.

An excellent survey of the theme of punishment in sociology from Dürkheim to the present is offered by David Garland.[172] His work further confirms my conviction that there is a lacuna in our critical, cultural self-understanding at the point of *why* people really punish. Garland and all the people he cites (as different as Dürkheim[173] and Foucault) assume that the entity that punishes is the state, acting on behalf of society as a whole.[174] The prototypical punishments are prison and the death penalty.[175] The prototypical offenders are adults, without asking how they got that way.[176] The prototypical punishers

---

172. David Garland, *Punishment and Modern Society: A Study in Social Theory*, brought to my attention by R. Bordt.

173. Émile Dürkheim, one of the fathers of the discipline, analyzed punishment in *The Division of Labor in Society*. He is supportive of Girard's project in the broadest sense, in that he attempts to describe the vindictive drive as somehow primitive and as somehow natural.

174. Foucault names villains within society (the bourgeois, the elites) who bear the most responsibility, but still, also for Foucault, the punitive institutions are society-wide and state-authorized (Garland, chapter 6). Cf. Foucault's *Discipline and Punish: The Birth of Prison*.

175. There used to be flogging and torture. They too were society-wide. Garland notices the illogic of our culture's being closed to the possibility of reinstating physical punishment, which would be cleaner, cheaper, and perhaps just as good a deterrent as prison. This note was drafted before the experience of April 1994 in which many Americans praised the use of flogging in Singapore.

176. Modern societies do make exceptions for the insane and others with diminished capacity for accountability. That only proves that

(i.e., the public standing behind the judge and the executioner) are assumed to be adults in positions of social authority, without asking how they came to hold that power or to believe that punishing is good.

This brief side glance at the traditional debate has been helpful as a reminder of how different are the several arenas of discourse on apparently overlapping subject matters. The older criminological debate, as expertly reviewed by Garland, is most concerned with understanding how the penal system administered and rationalized by the state works, especially prisons and the death penalty, and asks about general philosophical justifications "from the top down" in terms of total social well-being and theories of authority.

So when I propose in this connection to ask through what small-scale experiences humans in all cultures *come to be* believers in the punitive imperative, and when I answer the question by naming the prototypical roles of the mother and of the son, it should probably be no surprise that the literature on large-scale punitive institutions has little to say. There is nothing in these texts for me to argue with.

Another striking lacuna is that even René Girard has little to suggest (though in his 1992 AAR speech he came closer to saying something than in his books) about how to move society from here to there. It might seem at first that all scapegoating stands condemned, as both morally unworthy in the light of modernity and theologically overcome in Jesus Christ. Yet it won't go away. Would it then not perhaps be more promising to recognize that the scapegoating phenomenon is alive and well?[177]

---

the prototype is the adult offender. Yet all of us first have been infantile offenders.

177. I was redrafting this paragraph in December 1993. The Korean government had just agreed, in the framework of the General Agreement on Tariffs and Trade, to open four percent of Korea's domestic market to importing rice. Ministers' heads in the Korean cabinet had to roll because Korean rice farmers were offended. The trade agreement will not be revoked. Nobody claims that those

In every culture and in every age, the rulers will keep killing their Socrates. What matters in understanding the process is to gauge the point at which, with regard to a specific issue in a particular subculture, one particular bloody sacrifice may trigger or mark the awareness that the bloodletting should end.[178] Then in that particular subculture, with regard to that particular atrocity, the awareness that "this is too much" can take hold. So the shape of the primeval event repeats itself in one sector or another of the culture. Yet in other worlds and other cultures, this transforming crisis has not yet come. What we would challenge in Girard is his locating the phenomenon only in the primeval past instead of seeing it as a paradigm.[179]

After the bloodletting of the Civil War, chattel slavery in the USA is unacceptable, even though racism is not gone. After Auschwitz, no one can justify genocide in the name of progressive human values, even though we are still seeing retrograde and small-scale genocides and some even deny the world-changing fact of the Holocaust. The way the impact of the death of Jesus can enter the social process is not that it does away with punishment, but that it offers a paradigm whereby, in one place at a time, the awareness that "this is too much" can break through. None of these changes opens the new age, yet each of them partakes in a fragmentary way of the victory of resurrection and Pentecost, thus offering to others elsewhere, noncoercively, the power to replicate reconciliation.

---

imports will destroy the market for domestic rice. The political action of joining GATT was morally and economically right. Yet there needed to be a ceremonial acting-out of the country's objection to being forced to do the right thing.

178. Although Israelis had been killing Palestinians for a quarter-century, one particular mass murder in a Mosque in February 1994 sealed the Israeli readiness to conclude the peace negotiations. Although Bosnians had been killing each other for two years, one particular mortar blast in Sarajevo triggered the realignment of forces, which enabled the longest-yet truce around the city.

179. Chapter 7 of my *Politics of Jesus*, 2d ed., documents how widespread in the New Testament is the thought that the cross is a paradigm to be reflected in the lives of Jesus' followers down through history.

ADDENDUM: JESUS IN RELATION TO THE "SOCRATES" SECTION[180]

I have kept the above material [i.e., the twelve parts of "You Have It Coming"] on the general cultural level of the social science disciplines, whose self-understanding is "objective" or "scientific," because those terms were set by the interlocutors: Socrates, Antisthenes, Marcus Aurelius, Dürkheim, and Girard. There has been frequent cross-referencing to Christian values and vocabulary because of the (post-) established status of Christianity in the West, but there has been no reference to whether specifically Christian (i.e., christological) norms would illuminate independently the questions of whether and how to accept the punitive character of our world's structures.

It therefore should add something that my survey loops back to Christian origins to observe that there are christological norms that would speak to the same questions, whether saying something more or saying some of the same things differently. This is facilitated by my having had the privilege of skimming the dissertation *Christianisme et Société dans la Première Lettre de Pierre* by Larry Miller.[181]

It is helpful to take as the base for this New Testament reference the single specimen of 1 Peter. It cuts the problem down to a manageable size. This permits us to avoid the much more complex challenges of interpreting Jesus and the Zealots, Jesus and the Romans, Jesus and the Sanhedrin, Paul and the synagogue, Paul and municipal authorities, Paul and Rome. We have here just one writer addressing one circle of churches in

---

180. This chapter was not part of the original Shalom Desktop packet. It was added in 1997. [Editor's note: this footnote was in the original manuscript.]

181. *Thèse présentée en Vue de l'Obtention du Doctorat, Université des Sciences Humaines de Strasbourg, Faculté de Théologie Protestante* (1995). Miller's massive investment of erudition in the dialogue with past and contemporary scholarship in several disciplines need not be reviewed here.

a single brief document.[182] This provides a much simpler basis for analysis than if we were to take on a larger corpus from the canon. It bypasses perennially debated questions of Christian origins by locating the agenda of faithfulness in communities that already existed outside Palestine having been created by missionary preaching in a pagan world.[183]

The worldview of the author of the epistle, as it meshes with the setting of the Christians in Roman Anatolia, is characterized by the juxtaposition of two cosmic systems. One of them is based on reciprocity or retribution: "to punish wrongdoers and to praise those who do right" (1 Pet 2:14 RSV). It is represented not only by "the emperor" or the "governors" he delegates, but also by the other structures of authority represented by the slave-owner or the family patriarch.[184] This system will not go away and, although in a broad sense the Christians are "radical" or "utopian," they do not expect it to go away, nor do they attack it. It is right that Christians should submit to this system, not only when the sanc-

---

182. For his purposes, it is unimportant to Miller to investigate the author's personality. First Peter 1:1 names five provinces in what later geography calls "Anatolia." There is no basis for positing any significant diversity among the addressee communities with regard to either their social situations or their value commitments. But neither do we know much about whether or why Anatolia was different from the rest of the Mediterranean world or why it was to them that "Peter" wrote. The brevity and homogeneity of the text save the scholars the trouble of discussing the unity of authorship.

183. A major gap within the story, derived from Miller's choice of interlocutor disciplines, is that it is told without much reference to Judaism. "Pagan" is the polar opposite to "faith," rather than translating "Gentile" in contrast to the bearers of the Mosaic, Davidic, and Jeremianic heritages. This may overvalue the element of the addressees' respective conversions in the background to the letter's appeals.

184. It also relates in 1 Peter 3:22 to the "principalities and powers," which are prominent in the Pauline writings (to which Walter Wink has given much attention recently), but Miller's self-discipline left that not specifically Petrine theme out of his synthesis.

tions it imposes are fair,[185] but also (especially) when it unjustly punishes the believer for doing right (1 Pet 2:18-20). The reason for this submissiveness is not cowardice or fear, nor spiritual subservience to its values, but the believers' loyalty to the stronger claims of the other cosmic system.[186]

This alternative system is based on "gift" or grace.[187] The Christians return good for evil because they ascribe higher authority to the other cosmic system, implemented by a higher court,[188] where good (especially the "good" of accepting innocent suffering, not returning evil for evil) will be ratified and in whose ultimate judgment the vicious cycle of evil-for-evil that governs the world-as-it-is will be overruled.[189]

---

185. One signal of the acceptance of this jurisdiction is the concern to be ready to "make a defense to anyone who calls you to account." Miller reports that the question of who those people are is open, but his argument is stronger if this refers not merely to neighbors who wonder what Christians believe but to some kind of court which can blame and punish.

186. The alternative to the submission would, of course, be some kind of rebellion. Bo Reicke thought a specifically "zealot" temptation was present in the addressee churches. [Editor's Note: Yoder does not indicate his source, but he was likely referring to Reicke's *The Epistles of James, Peter and Jude: Introduction, Translation, and Notes.*] Miller posits a less clearly conscious alternative in order to make his point. Miller even retrieves the word "non-resistance," which has contested connotations in recent western ethical thought.

187. Miller's exposition of this "systemic" vision of the function of the epistle is aided by his borrowings from recent scholarly developments in semiotics and sociological exegesis.

188. Jesus "trusted him who judges justly" (1 Pet 2:23 RSV). Miller makes much of the image of each system having its ultimate judgment.

189. We need not be told how it will be overruled in order to understand the clash between the two systems and the claims of the "gift" system on the believers. Is the higher courtroom where that vindication of the good occurs to be understood as "heaven" or "history" or the believers' hearts? Miller is often ready to say simply that the sources do not answer some question that our culture thinks would need to be answered before we could understand or before we could believe.

Scholars have noted that the author is not very concrete about what the "good work" is that the addressees are invited to stand by. It seems to be neither a broad-ranging set of lifestyle prescriptions, nor a narrow range of liturgical actions. Those may be assumed or implied, but in any case they are not itemized or argued. The acceptance of unjust suffering is the center of what the Anatolian Christians are called to, even though the most pointed statement of this call is the one addressed only to slaves. The attitude taken toward the authorities in place is called "submission" (*hypotassesthai*) or "honor" (*timân*). It is not called "obedience" (*hypakouein*). That concept is reserved for the (countercultural) will of God.

This readiness to suffer is based not on some stoic or proto-Kantian moralism, but on the Jesus story. The prototype for accepting unjust suffering as the penalty for doing good is not a principle but a person, a narrative (1 Pet 2:21-24). Nor is there in this appeal any exegetical reference to moral instruction like that of the Sermon on the Mount, to virtue language like the hymn to *agape* in 1 Corinthians 13,[190] or to the lists of virtues and vices in Galatians 5:19-23.

Although it can be described with a view to the approval of the heavenly court of appeal,[191] the historical import of this stance is that it publicly proclaims the gospel in an incomparable and irreplaceable way: these set-apart people[192] "declare

---

190. Marie-Louise Lamau has found in 1 Peter a "hymn to the suffering Christ" analogous to the hymn in Philippians 2 (numerous citations in the Miller text). Even when rhythmic literary forms may be discerned, which might be older than the extant text, those texts too are narratives about Jesus' innocent, willing, and submissive suffering. [Editor's note: Yoder does not identify his source, but he may be referring to *Des Chrétiens dans le monde: communautés pétriniennes au ler siècle* (Paris: Cerf, 1988).]

191. Cf. 1 Peter 1:17 RSV, "who judges each one impartially according to his deeds"; 2:23, "who judges justly"; and 5:5, "opposes the proud and gives grace to the humble."

192. The four adjectives of 1 Peter 2:9 all accentuate differentness. Most of the other ways of describing them elsewhere in the letter also

the wonderful deeds of him who called you" (1 Pet 2:9 RSV). This posture does not merely "silence the ignorance of fools" (2:15) and "put to shame those who revile you" (3:16); like the "greater righteousness" of Matthew 5:13-20, this behavior communicates to outsiders something of the gospel that could not be communicated by any other means than the willing acceptance of unjust suffering.[193]

The earlier chapters of the above study laid out the claim that punishing is present in all society and is socially functional, so that it is better to come to terms with its place in the texture of things than to bemoan it or declare it immoral. Now the New Testament perspective just reviewed widens the case by saying that the punitive quality of power operations fits, by virtue of the willing submission of Jesus and his followers, within a longer historical process of redemption. As Joseph had said it, "you meant evil against me; but God meant it for good" (Gen 50:20 RSV). This may apply not only to Joseph's role in feeding Egypt and then (derivatively) also his brothers according to *Prima Petri*.[194] The same truth is at work in the ongoing proclamation that the economy of grace will have the last word—proclamation that can best (only?) be performed by willingly yielding the first word to the economy of penalty.

---

focus on difference. If Miller had attended more to the jewishness of their identity, it would only have added depth to this dimension.

193. Cf. "The Pacifism of Proclamation" in my *Nevertheless: Varieties of Religious Pacifism*, rev. and expanded ed.

194. I wrote at the beginning that the selection of a single small text made Miller's task more manageable. That does not mean, however, that any other major strands of the New Testament literature would contradict his results.

APPENDIX

THE WRATH OF GOD AND
THE LOVE OF GOD

The following lines are intended as a contribution to discussion, and not as a monograph.[1] The questions with which we have to deal are not easy questions. They are not new, but we must admit that neither within nor without pacifist circles have we come to a clear understanding that fits into the rest of our Christian life and work of what the wrath of God means to us. To save time and avoid misunderstandings, permit me first to note what I do *not* intend to say.

    1. It is not my intention to attack in detail the view, which is present among certain pacifist circles, that wrath is somehow a sentiment or character unworthy of God. I shall simply begin with the uncontestable observation that in the Bible's thinking about God there is such a thing as divine wrath. Nor, on the other hand, is it my intention to attack those who accuse pacifists of ignoring the wrath of God, which the state and the Christian in the state are called to serve. These two views, on the one hand the conviction that God is too loving for wrath to have any place in his being and on the other the belief that God is so wrathful that pacifism misunderstands him, are mirror images of

---

1. [Editor's note: This essay was originally prepared for the Historical Peace Churches and International Fellowship of Reconciliation Conference, Beatrice Webb House, England, Sept. 11-14 (Basel: Mennonite Central Committee, 1956). It was not published prior to this volume.]

one another. Both of them make the basic theological and logical mistake of thinking too soon that they know whereof they speak. Both views, that which seems congenial to some pacifists and that which hastily rejects a similar kind of pacifism, assume ahead of time that they know what "wrath" is and that they know what "God" is and what he wants. They come to the problem, therefore, with their decisions already made, having full information derived from their own philosophical and psychological background. The decision they finally make about whether or not to agree that God can be wrathful is simply an exposition of their prejudices and their postulates. We shall do well to avoid both views by refusing to come to our problem with too clear an idea of what "wrath," in human experience, in ordinary usage, or in orthodox doctrine, must mean.

2. Next on the list of things we do not intend to do is the exegetical analysis of those biblical texts in both Old and New Testaments that deal with the wrath of God. We avoid this task not because it is unimportant but because it is too important to deal with in a paper of this length. It has been largely done in the standard theological concordances and dictionaries. Our question is rather from what point of view we are to ask the Bible questions and what we shall do with the answers the Bible gives us.

3. We do not here intend to use the modern "shortcut" method, which is quite in vogue in certain Barthian circles (although it is not necessarily something that the Barthians have learned from Barth)—a shortcut that consists in simply saying that God's wrath and his justice, his love and his mercy are all the same thing; and that since we say so by definition, all kinds of verbal acrobatics and dialectical juggling with terms are permitted to the Christian theologian. That is a shortcut.

4. And lastly, what we attempt to say here is not the Mennonite position. It would be hard to affirm that there *is* such a thing as a Mennonite position; and if there were one, it would be hard to know on what grounds one could say that it was right. I do dare express the conviction that the thinking repre-

sented by these lines has been carried on in an effort to follow the same channels and to build on some of the same presuppositions as the sixteenth-century Anabaptists and the early Mennonites. But when I say that, I am saying at the same time that the thinking I do here is to the best of my knowledge consistent with the presuppositions and the starting points of an Alexander Mack or of a George Fox.

～・

If we are interested in understanding the wrath of God and in seeing in the clearest possible light the questions it raises for us, we shall not go far astray to begin with the most extreme form that that wrath can take and to begin the series of questions we must ask by trying to understand the Christian doctrine of hell. This is not an original idea. Some of you may be acquainted with the booklet written by Dr. Rachel King, *God's Boycott of Sin*, which is an attempt to demonstrate that there is some connection between the place of hell in God's working with man and Christian pacifism. What, in the last analysis, does hell mean? I think that Christian thought, when it has not sought to avoid the problem entirely, is generally agreed that hell means simply that you *can* be let alone if you want to be. God will not impose himself on humans. And that means that, if humans decide permanently, irrevocably, and sincerely (if that word can be used here), God will respect those humans' decisions, even if they decide to turn their backs to God. Humans who have chosen to reject God and who then discover that God will accept their decision against their own interest have found out what hell is.

The wrath of God could be described in similar terms. God's wrath is a description of the fact that humans can disobey God if they want to. Their disobedience will put them out of plumb, will put the world out of plumb, and nothing will run straight from then on. But God will let them do that if they will. It is the mystery of what we usually call "the freedom of the will," with which we here must grapple. It is *not* what the Bible talks about when it speaks of freedom. Strangely enough, when the Bible talks about human freedom, it means being *made* free to become a slave of God. The only "freedom of the will" of which the Bible speaks is freedom to choose the good. But those who do not choose the good are not spoken of by the Bible as being "free" to choose evil. They are spoken of as being slaves—slaves to their passions, to mammon, or to some other demons or idols to whom they have sold themselves. The Bible recognizes full well the phenomenon that we speak of as "freedom of the will," the fact that humans can choose the wrong. But the Bible does not call that freedom. The Bible calls that the "wrath of God" because, if we choose the wrong, God will let us choose it. God will let us get ourselves and the world about us off the track. And God respects our "freedom" to bring about chaos where he has willed order. God lets us choose "unfreedom," and if we have made the choice, he respects the choice we have made for ourselves. That is God's wrath.

The question arises, as it has arisen in the minds of philosophers all through the Christian ages and even before: Did not God make a mistake? Would it not have been wiser on God's part *not* to make humans free, or at least not to make humans *ultimately* free? Would it not have been better simply to let them be a little bit freer than a beast, be just slightly capable of influencing their own destiny, so that if they made too terrible a mess of things God could always cross it off the record and start over? This is the kind of question that every parent asks, for the temptation of every parent to force goodness upon the child, upon the adolescent, and upon the young adult is a temptation to save that child, that adolescent, and that young adult from the price of freedom. It is a question that every educator asks, for the attempt of schoolmasters to make the decisions and do the thinking for their charges because they can do it better is a temptation to consider freedom as a mistake. It is a problem faced by every administrator, for capable administrators know that they will do their job better if they do it themselves and if they use their subordinates not as human beings but as tools.

And yet we somehow know—not as Christian pacifists alone but also as Christian parents, or as Christian educators, or as Christian administrators—that we cannot say that freedom is a mistake. We know that parents have never done their job until they have learned to let their child be free completely, even to make mistakes, even to make *bad* mistakes. We know that teachers have never truly educated their charges until they have left them to struggle with error and even to fall into error. And yet a tremendous amount of thinking and acting in our western civilization has been carried out under the assumption that really, when God made humans free, he *did* make a mistake.

In order to demonstrate what I mean, it might be wise to list a number of examples in very disparate fields. In the field that is "purely religious," the doctrine known as universalism affirms that either because humans are ultimately too good to be lost or because God is too good to lose humanity there is no such thing as hell in any sense of the word; everyone will, in the end, wind up in the right place. It sounds very loving of God to save everybody. But saying this really means he made a mistake. It really means that history is a farce, because nothing is really decisive. It means that when humans stand before a choice (or think they do) and when they think, or when God tells them, or when their minister tells them that this choice is a choice between right and wrong, that again is a farce. It means that human freedom is a farce because, however clearly and intentionally and evenly humans turn away from God, they are sure in the end to find out that they cannot do so. In other words, this view denies really that God ever wanted to make humans free; or that if humans are free, they are so only in an unreal sense.

A second type of denial of this ultimate respect that God has [for] humanity's capacity to choose unfreedom is the orthodox Calvinistic doctrine of predestination. The Calvinistic conception of the holy sovereignty of God, which was drawn in some respects more from Roman and Greek philosophical sources than from Scripture (or at least from the New Testament), felt that it would be an insult to God if humans could lose themselves, could separate themselves from God. Calvinism felt that God would be insulting himself if he made humans who could talk back to him. And therefore the only answer for this extreme form of Calvinism, when it faced the problem of sin, was to say that God wanted it that way. God wanted humans to sin so that God could demonstrate his holy justice by condemning those who sinned. God wanted humans to sin so that he could demonstrate his holy mercy by saving some. The difference between those whom God would save and those whom God would judge was entirely God's decision. We should not criticize this orthodox Calvinistic view, as many moderns are tempted to criticize it, because it insists upon the inscrutability of God's designs, nor because it admits that somehow God saw this all coming; we must refuse it insofar as it affirms that God did not create humans with the capability of talking back to him. If there is anything clear about the scriptural view of humans it is that they *can* (and do) talk back to God.

Another general area in which we see this denial of human freedom—and now we turn to the sociological realm—is that form of Christianized society, which we have come to speak of as "Constantinian," that society in which every child is baptized at birth and [every adult is considered] a member of the Christian church. We all know many of the things we have to say against this kind of church strategy, but for the moment I am interested only in calling our attention to the fact that once again the assumption here is that it would be against God's will for humans to be free not to be Christians, and therefore the church does God a great service by putting his label on everyone without asking whether that label corresponds to anything in the will or the being of those whom we brand with it. Clearly enough, the working of this principle has, in European history, been just the opposite of its intention. It has been to create unbelief within Christian society. The way in which mass Catholicism has created, all through modern European history beginning with the Renaissance, forms of Christianized unbelief is one of the most significant facts of modern times. It is within Catholicism that atheism came to be. If the purpose is to "Christianize" society in the sense that that society is brought under Christian ethical norms, then it is one of the most indisputable facts of the sociology of religion that it is the free churches and the Protestant revival movements, refusing precisely to begin with the assumption that everyone is a Christian, that have Christianized society. One needs only to compare the morale of the public servant, of the professional, or of the common worker in a country whose thinking has been formed by a series of revivals and by the work and witness of Protestant free churches, such as is the case in much of the Anglo-Saxon world with similar attitudes in a Latin country, to see that the most effective way of bringing morale to society is in any case *not* that of Constantine, *not* the assumption that we must treat everyone as if they had no choice but to be Christian.

Coming back to the subject that interests us more nearly, we must admit that there is a certain kind of pacifism that also tends to say that God must have made a mistake. There is a kind of pacifism that we can find in our history books and in the history of our movements—I doubt if it is alive today, but it is alive in the minds of our opponents at least—that thinks (or thought) that Christian pacifism is for the whole world. Christian pacifism has been thought of by such people as a strategy for society, which is available and practicable also for non-Christians, not only for the church, but also for the world. No specifically Christian or even specifically religious starting point is necessary in order for a nation to disarm, to organize justice in a nonviolent way, and to bring peace to the world. No repentance, other than a kind of repentance of which all people are capable; no forgiveness, apart from a kind of diplomatic forgiveness of which all people are capable; no new birth, apart from the kind of fresh start of which all people are capable is necessary to live in the path of peace. The error of this kind of "pacifism" is again the failure to accept God's decision to let humankind be disobedient. The kind of "pacifism" that we see in a George Fox, that we see in the Anabaptists or in the Brethren, at least in their early periods, was a kind of pacifism which, clearly enough, knew that all the world was called to this way; but it was not the kind of pacifism that expected that all the world without repentance, without forgiveness, and without a new birth could follow the way.

Finally, there is a very deep though indirect way in which the concern for human justice somehow attempts to undo God's creation of humankind in freedom. We may very well (with the New Testament) agree that government, based upon the eventual possibility of recourse to force, is with us in this world as long as "this world" stands. We may well agree (with the New Testament) that this function of government somehow stands in God's hands; and yet at the same time, once we have understood something about the wrath of God and once we have seen that its nature is precisely that which permits humans to create chaos and to destroy themselves and the world around them, we see that there is a sense in which human justice, by preventing that chaos from going its normal course and preventing the worst kinds of sins and the worst kinds of crimes from being carried out unhindered, interferes with the freedom that God has given humankind.

Having seen, although briefly and inadequately, in a number of different ways what it amounts to to think that God must have made a mistake in creating humans capable of talking back, we may be ready for the other answer. And it is my conviction, although I have not yet been able to work out and to express all that it will mean, that if we think radically enough at this point we shall find the answer to the problem of wrath, insofar as there can be an answer, and find it in God's love. If we agree that God was *right* in making humans as he did, and we know that God is the definition of love, then, when we want to know exactly what God's love means, we shall come to the conclusion—difficult to understand but radically revolutionary if once we can seize it—that love means respecting the freedom of the beloved to reject love. Love, and we shall do well to use the term *agape*, since there is something peculiar about this love of God, does not impose itself.

The depth of God's love is measured when we see that he is willing to love even those who refuse his love. Human love seeks a response. We need not enumerate the differences between human love and divine love as Nygren has attempted to describe them, nor need we ask whether Nygren's analysis is adequate; but I think we may say at this point that the deepest difference between human love and God's love probably lies here. God's love respects the beloved so far that if those who are the object of God's love wish to destroy themselves, they can. If individuals think (erroneously we know) that their joy will lie in separating themselves from God, God will let them do so. And it is God's love that does that, because God's love respects the freedom of his creature to talk back and the freedom of his creature to respond to his self-giving love spitefully.

If this is the case and I think, without going too deeply into the specifically theological problems, that we would have grounds biblically to claim that this is what God's love really means, then we come to the startling conclusion that God's love and his wrath are the same thing. This is not the cheap shortcut of the theologians who take what they mean by love and what they mean by wrath and say that those two things are somehow both reconcilable in God. Nor is it the still cheaper shortcut of those who take what they mean by love and what they mean by wrath and let the two stand side by side as a paradox that must be accepted on faith. On the contrary, it is an identification of God's love with his wrath that comes from looking at the structure of his dealings with humanity, from asking what God means by creating humans, and from seeing the depths of God's respect for his creature in the fact that if that creature wishes to rebel, he or she may do so.

The reason God created humans in this way, we know clearly enough, was not in order to exercise his wrath. The reason he did it was that it is the only way to win his creature. The only way for human fellowship with God to have meaning is for that fellowship to be free and unforced, just as the only way for the fellowship between a parent and a child to be free and unforced and genuine is for the child to have been free to rebel, or the only way for the fellowship in learning between educator and pupil to be anything but a mechanical discipline is for the pupil to have come freely to ask for help. It is just so with the salvation of humankind. Salvation is true salvation only if it saves from destruction. Only if there is such a thing as a lost condition of humanity can we say that salvation is worth the trouble. God's reason for making humans free was not that humans could then lose themselves, but that humanity's true freedom would be in choosing to commune with God, to love him and to serve him, and to glory in his presence. But our interest, with reference to the present problem, is not to deal with this fact that God's love was the only way in which he could meaningfully and usefully create humans for his fellowship. What interests us especially, if we are to discuss the wrath of God, is the much more surprising fact that this love remains true to itself even when it is rejected. Even when individuals have refused (or we may also say as long as individuals refuse) to accept God's love, it is that love that lets them go on, that does not deprive them of his existence with a stroke of thunder, and does not bowl them over with some kind of miraculous conversion, but lets them be free to lose themselves. That love of God is the wrath of God.

Thus far we have attempted to describe God's love and his wrath in a way that looks philosophical. We have begun by discussing the way God created humankind. This is bad theology. We have done it only because it sometimes seems when a discussion has been wrongly carried on for centuries that, before being able to begin afresh, one must first convince oneself of the possibility of another beginning. But the final test of what we have been saying about God's love and its willingness to let humans go will come when we turn again to the Bible and ask whether the biblical writers thought that way. People have been reading the Bible, reading about God's love and God's wrath for so long with ideas of love and wrath that they had acquired somewhere else that it was necessary first of all to show that it is conceivable that we could describe God's wrath in another way. But now we must ask whether or not it is really the case that God's love, in the Bible and in the work of Christ, lets humanity be free in this way; whether or not it is the case that before human rebellion God would rather suffer himself and let humans refuse his love than to impose it on them. And there we must come back to the center of all Christian thinking, the ministry of Jesus Christ and his death.

Recent studies of the ministry of Christ and of the world in which that ministry was carried on have made it quite apparent, after theologians and historians had been confusing the question for a number of centuries, that Jesus had a very clear and definite attitude toward the problem of the state and of human justice. It now seems clearly demonstrated that Jesus was, as a human being, entirely apart from any deeper and more religious ways of stating the question, faced with the problem of whether he, seeking the good of humanity, should set up a just state. Judaism in its most faithful forms was awaiting a Messiah who would do just that. God had promised to the Jewish people that he would set up a just order among his children. The Pharisees and the Zealots knew very well what that meant. That meant a just state, organized by God's people, which would carry on a just war in the defense of its own freedom and divinely ordained social order and show to all of the world the glory of God through the community that would in that way be established. The Zealots understood Jesus, (when he preached about the kingdom of God), to be talking about that kind of a just state. The other Jews, whether they understood him correctly or not, told Pilate that Jesus had such intentions. Jesus was crucified as a Zealot. The writ of accusation explaining to passers-by the reason for this man's execution said, "Jesus of Nazareth, King of the Jews" (John 19:19). Nothing is clearer than that the ministry of Jesus must be seen within the framework of zealotism and the problem of the holy purpose of God to set up a state governed by his chosen people.

And yet that was a misunderstanding. When the Zealots thought Jesus was talking about the kind of a kingdom they wanted, they had misunderstood. When the Jews told Pilate that Jesus was seditious, they were either consciously lying or passing on a misconception. And when Pilate condemned the man, it was in the knowledge of his innocence.

The study of the life of Jesus brings us even closer to the recognition of the importance of the problem of the state in Jesus' work when we realize that the peak of the temptation experience was this political problem (Matt 4:1-11; Luke 4:1-13). Jesus was offered the possibility of taking over the Jewish people and, through the Jewish people, all of the world. He could do it by making an institution out of his powers to create bread. He could do it by the kind of gratuitous miracle in which, falling as if from heaven into the court of the temple, he would seem to be the Messiah coming from the skies. He could do it by accepting some sort of cultic confusion related to the pagan universalism of the Roman religion of his time. We may not, as moderns, be able always to understand exactly what is meant and how we should conceive of what the Bible speaks about when it says "Jesus was forty days in the wilderness and was tempted by the Devil." We don't know how that looked or how it felt, but one thing is clear: in the minds of the writers of the New Testament story, Jesus was faced with the temptation, which in his mind was a real human historical possibility, of taking over the world and running a just state. And he said "No."

The second crisis in the ministry of Jesus, which the work of Maurice Goguel has made especially understandable, occurred just after the episode we know as the feeding of the five thousand when, as we are told in the sixth chapter of John's Gospel, that people wanted to make a king of him.[2] He had done just about what the Devil had asked him to do. He had made bread. And the thousands of people who had eaten that bread thought

---

2. [Editor's note: Yoder does not indicate, but he is probably referring to Maurice Goguel's *Life of Jesus*, 359-99.]

that this was what they were looking for. They were ready to follow this man and make him king. Jesus said "No," and we are told that many of his disciples left him that day. It was from there that he went to Caesarea, that he asked his disciples if they knew who he was, and that he told them for the first time that the Son of Man would have to suffer. Once again we may find it hard as moderns to understand how people could think as that crowd did, or as Jesus did. We don't believe in miracles anyway. We may find it hard as moderns to make for ourselves a picture of how such a rebellion could have happened, and how people could have considered things so preposterous to be in the realm of the possible. Yet once again, nothing is more clear than that the writers of the New Testament accounts understood that Jesus had before him the possibility of miraculously taking the lead in setting up a just state, in fact a welfare state.

Once more, in the garden of Gethsemane (Matt 26:36-56), Jesus told Peter that if he were to defend himself, if that were his intention, he had enough angels at his disposal so that he would not need Peter's sword. Once again, we moderns do not know what it would have looked like for twelve legions of angels to come down into that garden. We do not know what they would have done to the troops of the high priests. But we do know one thing: Jesus, as far as he was understood by the writer of the Gospel, thought it was a real possibility that he could, even at this late date when everything in his ministry seemed to be lost, undertake a campaign of angelic violence and establish that just political order, which the Zealots were seeking and, up until then, Judas had been expecting.

It is interesting that, in all the pious things that have been written about Jesus' prayer in Gethsemane when he told his Father that he would prefer that it be otherwise, that "this cup should pass from him," no one has ever asked, very seriously at least, how that could have happened. How could his cup have "passed from him"? What would that have meant concretely? Once we ask the question, there seems to be only one possible answer. It would have meant a holy war. It would have meant that the Jews who were seeking for his life and the Romans who were willing to be made the tools of the Jews would be prevented from carrying out their evil designs. It would have had to mean, once again, some kind of divine and just political and military action. Thus, we see that, speaking humanly and historically, the reason for the cross of Christ was his constant refusal to accept as his final aim or as the guide for his life the establishment of that kind of human justice, which, we have already seen, is a way to limit human freedom and to prevent man from doing everything to which his freedom could lead him. And so the most innocent man who ever lived was condemned to death. And there again we see just this same kind of *agape* in action. His cause was perfectly just; he was God himself. Letting the perfectly just cause be utterly refused by man is the ultimate in *agape*, the ultimate in the respect for humanity's capacity to refuse God. In a sense, if we are to take at face value the epistle of John (3:12), killing is the worst kind of sin. Killing is typical of all sin, it is sin *par excellence*, because it is the most direct opposite to *agape*; it takes away most completely the freedom of its object. The extreme form of *agape* is thus to let oneself be killed, respecting most ultimately the freedom of the beloved to respond hatefully and spitefully to one's love.

One of the most common terms used in the New Testament to speak of the work of Christ is "obedience." We find it in one of the earliest descriptions of his work, Philippians 2, and we find it in one of the most theologically developed, the epistle to the Hebrews (5:8). Now when it is said that the ministry of Christ was his obedience, that means simply that it was his conformity to the nature of God. The reason Jesus had to die to save man is that God *is* that way. God is loving in such a way that he will let man's sin go so far as to kill God. God's respect for the freedom that he gave his creature is so great that he will permit that creature to go all the way to hell, to kill God himself.

Of course, God did not stay dead. That is the gospel. But God first of all had to let human sin do its worst, go all the way to the end of its capabilities. That is ultimately what it means, quite literally, when we read in Scripture of Jesus having "borne our sins." Not simply that he somehow covered up the deficit in our moral checking account but that our sinfulness, our human tendency willfully to turn away from God, was what killed him. And it is because he bore to the absolute end, to death itself, the tendency that we have to turn away from him willfully and spitefully, that he could meet us at the end of our willful, spiteful rebellion and, through the power of the resurrection, when we had reached the end of our capacity to rebel, resurrect us.

Before concluding we must ask two more questions. First of all, what does the Bible mean when it speaks of the "world" and uses the words "powers," "principalities," "thrones," "archangels," and all those other "mythological" terms, which are at first sight so embarrassing to the modern man? First of all, we might be helped to be somewhat less embarrassed if we noticed that moderns speak in a way that is just as mythological. Moderns speak of "fatality," of "probability," and "causality" in a way that is no more rational. Moderns speak of the "demonic," of "values" which in becoming autonomous become evils. That is what the Bible means to say when it talks about "principalities and powers." What the Bible describes when it speaks of the "world" is the order of creation under the sign of its disobedience. Yet the world is not chaos because God respects its rebellion. God lets rebellion stand before him, lets it exist independently, in a way, of his own will. He never willed rebellion, and yet he permits it. And the word "world" we can use philosophically to refer simply to God's respect for disobedience. Within this world what interests us most is the fact that violence is also somehow respected and channeled. In the Old Testament, the wrath of God used the powers, especially the foreign powers in this case. Assyria is the classic example. The wrath of God, even in the Old Testament, was not considered one of his personal characteristics. It was not connected with his holiness and with his justice in the way Protestant orthodoxy has often connected it. Even in the Old Testament, wrath is not a characteristic of the person of the revealed God; it is rather the fact that God used the powers, enemy nations, the storm, and the grasshopper, somehow channeling those disorders into something that would keep the world from falling apart, keep pride and sin from going too far.

In the New Testament this same channeling of violence takes the form of what we call the state. Again, the state, "the powers that be," the "principalities," and the "thrones" are considered in the New Testament as agents of the wrath of God—this is said in so many words in Romans 13:4—but somehow this wrath is not the same thing as God himself. Only seldom does the New Testament use the term "wrath of God." It prefers to say simply "the wrath." This is a reminder that it is not God's real intention to be this way. It is man who turns God's love into wrath. And because the powers of the world are the agents of the wrath of God, it can be very clear in the New Testament that the Christian is not an agent of the wrath of God. A Christian is rather a bearer of *agape*. A Christian, like Christ, would rather accept disorder than obtain order at the price of destroying his beloved. The Christian, like Christ, would rather accept mistreatment and disorder, injustice, than to take away from others, even a sinful and evil-intentioned other, the possibility of refusing God.

We are asking that same question once more in other terms when we ask what it means to be a Christian disciple. No one will argue with us if we say in general that the Christian should follow Christ. But everyone, including most pacifists, will disagree with us in practice if we say that this means that the Christian, like Christ, and like the Christians of the first centuries will be somehow inherently incapable of taking care of the needs of human justice and, at the same time, will refuse to say that the state has no right to exist. The Christians of the first centuries—and I think we can say that they were at this point faithful to the New Testament writers and to Christ himself— said that somehow if you are a Christian you will be led by love in such a way that you cannot be responsible for human justice.

But if you are not a Christian, if you are Caesar, for instance, then you shall and should have other, lower norms.[3]

This is shocking. It is scandalous. It was scandalous to Celsus in the second century; it was scandalous in the sixteenth century when the Anabaptists said it, and it was scandalous later when Fox and when Robert Barcley said it. But why is it scandalous? When we look at the root of the irritation that arises in the minds of people when we admit that government must somehow continue to exist as long as sin exists, and yet that we cannot consider ourselves, as Christians, called to carry out under all conditions certain of the functions of government, we find that the heart of the scandal lies first of all in legalism. Legalism would speak of morality and of moral principles without asking who is to act. Legalism would lay upon all people the same ethical requirements whether those people know about God's love or not. Whether people have been forgiven or not, it would require

---

3.   [Editor's note: Here Yoder contrasts the lesser norms practiced by the state in its rebellion with the norms of the church in its submission to Christ's lordship. The capital punishment writings in this collection make explicit, however, that Yoder believed that Christ is the actual single norm for both the church and the state. This is something Yoder believed before he wrote "The Wrath of God and the Love of God," as evident in his unpublished essay "The Theological Basis of the Christian Witness to the State" (not to be confused with an essay by the same title that was published in *On Earth Peace*, ed. Donald F. Durnbaugh, 136-43), which he wrote in 1955 and which he unpacked nearly a decade later in *The Christian Witness to the State*. The reason why the state "shall and should" have lower norms in practice is because in rejecting Christ's lordship, which the state will do until Christ returns, the state will lack the faith resources required for those who would live according to the norm of Christ (including repentance, forgiveness, and new birth). Yet, since believers possess those resources, they should never lower their standards, in Kantian fashion, to what everyone could and should be able to do in a given situation. That Yoder held fast to this conviction is evident in his 1997 addendum to "You Have It Coming," p. 233, where he restates it in a new context.]

them to forgive; whether they have repented or not, it would require them to change their lives; and whether they have been born again or not, it would require them to have a new kind of existence. That is legalism because it does not take into account the nature and the being of the ethical agent.

But more deeply, this New Testament "dualism," which makes a difference between Christians and other people, seems scandalous because we are used to making no difference between Christians and the world. We are not used to attributing to the world the dignity that God gives it in its rebellion. God gives the world the freedom to stand up and to say "No," to talk back to his love and still exist without being struck down by thunder, and to go on in its self-sufficient life. We are doing the same thing if as scandalous "sectarian" Christians we tell those who would be responsible for human government that we will respect their right and, in fact, proclaim it their duty to seek human justice and say at the same time that that is a part of the world. The ethics, then, of just statesmanship, just policemanship, and just hangmanship have a certain worth because God respects the world, but they are not specifically Christian ethics. For those of us who belong to Christ, they cannot be finally valid.

This kind of a recognition, that there exists a world, is what medieval Christendom and Constantinian state-church Christendom through the centuries have been unable to conceive. That is why it is no accident that the churches now known as the historic peace churches really should be called simply the "Historic Free Churches," because they are the groups that recognize the most clearly and the most consistently that there is such a thing as the world. The Anabaptists in the sixteenth century and George Fox in the seventeenth (Mack will not have been very different) had to go around all over Switzerland and all over England evangelizing—evangelizing *Christian* Europe—because there is such a thing as a world in a lost state. That is the starting point for the recognition that we as Christians of the free-church tradition can, without being inconsistent, without being self-righteous, and without being irresponsible, still admit that there can exist in the hands of God a state apparatus for which we as Christians are not ultimately responsible, but which nonetheless is in the hands of God.

Thus, the wrath of God and the love of God have an incidence upon sociology and ethics, even though this is not to be understood in the way the two mutually exclusive views we noticed at the outset would like. Love and wrath have a relationship to pacifism and to militarism, but if we understand that relationship clearly, it will be precisely in that we will have the nerve to be scandalous as the early Christians were and to accept as final for us the way of Christ even where that seems to some to be irresponsible. For it requires no Christians, it requires no church, and it requires no Christ for humans to be under the wrath of God. That takes care of itself. If there was a point in Christ's coming, if there is a point in the Christian church, and if there is a point to our being Christians, it is because we are called to express *agape* in the pure form, in the form that counts, and [to express] the reality of repentance, and forgiveness, and the new birth in a way in which the world cannot.

~·

It seems to me that the deepening of our understanding of our specific witness as historic peace churches, within the ecumenical context as well as within our own churches, will come by our forgetting our peace witness occasionally and reminding ourselves that behind that peace witness there is a doctrine of the church, a doctrine of the world, an understanding of the meaning of human history, a doctrine of the last things, a doctrine of the Christian life, and a doctrine of the atonement that are peculiar to those fellowships whose calling it has been to reject the Constantinian compromise of the church with the world. Precisely by this dissociation from the world, it has been our calling to give to the world a specific dignity and a place in God's plan as the bearer of his wrath, a relationship that the rest of Protestantism and the rest of Christianity as a whole have not been capable of understanding.

It is my contention, historically speaking, that although none of the founding fathers of any of our several communions ever theologized about this question, these understandings of the church and the world, of history and the Christian life are common to our three groups. And it might well be that the point at which we could be most helpful to one another would be that point at which we would seek—not for what we can say about pacifism either to one another or to the churches or to the world, but to seek—for that common, valid element in the church and its ministry that was held by the early Anabaptists, the early Friends, and the early Brethren. In spite of our weakness and tepidity, it has broken out ever again and keeps breaking out, thanks to the grace of God, in the other churches of the world.

BIBLIOGRAPHY

Aeschylus, *Eumenides*. Translated by Richard Lattimore. In *Complete Greek Tragedies*. Vol. 1. Chicago: University of Chicago Press, 1953.

Alain, Roger. *The Community That Failed*. San Francisco: Carrier Pigeon Press, 1993.

Anspach, Mark R. "Violence against Violence." In *Violence and the Sacred in the Modern World*, edited by Mark Juergensmeyer, 11-25. London: Frank Cass, 1992.

Arendt, Hannah. *The Human Condition*. Chicago: University of Chicago Press, 1958.

———. *Origins of Totalitarianism*. New York: Harcourt Brace, 1951.

Arnold, Gottfried. *Unparteiische Kirchen- und Ketzerhistorie vom Anfang des Neuen Testaments bis auf das Jahr Christi 1688*. Hildesheim: G. Olms, 1967.

Bailey, Lloyd R. *Capital Punishment: What the Bible Says*. Nashville: Abingdon Press, 1987.

Barth, Karl. *Church Dogmatics* III/4. Edited and translated by G. W. Bromiley and T. F. Torrance. Edinburgh: T. and T. Clark, 1961.

Bass, Clarence B. *Backgrounds to Dispensationalism: Its Historical Genesis and Ecclesiastical Implications*. Grand Rapids, Mich.: Eerdmans, 2005.

Beccaria, Cesare. *On Crimes and Punishments*. Translated by Edward D. Ingraham. Indianapolis, Ind.: Bobbs-Merrill, 1963; 1764.

Bedau, Hugo Adam. *Death is Different: Studies in the Morality, Law, and Politics of Capital Punishment*. Boston: Northeastern University Press, 1987.

Bedau, Hugo Adam, ed. "The Case Against the Death Penalty." American Civil Liberties Union, 1992. Available online at http://users.rcn.com/mwood/deathpen.html [accessed Jan 1, 2011].

———. *The Death Penalty in America.* 3d ed. New York: Oxford University Press, 1982.

———. *The Death Penalty in America: Current Controversies.* New York: Oxford University Press, 1997.

Bedau, Hugo Adam and Chester M. Pierce, eds. *Capital Punishment in the United States.* New York: AMS Press, 1975.

Bedau, Hugo Adam and Michael L. Radelet. "Miscarriages of Justice in Potentially Capital Cases." *Stanford Law Review* 40.1 (Nov 1987): 21-180.

Belousek, Darrin W. Snyder. "Capital Punishment, Covenant Justice and the Cross of Christ: The Death Penalty in the Life and Death of Jesus." *Mennonite Quarterly Review* 83, no. 3 (2009): 375-402.

Berger, Raoul. *Death Penalties: The Supreme Court's Obstacle Course.* Cambridge, Mass.: Harvard University Press, 1982.

Berkhof, Hendrik. *Christ and the Powers.* Translated by John H. Yoder. Scottdale, Pa.: Herald Press, 1962.

Berns, Walter. *For Capital Punishment.* New York: Basic Books, 1979.

Black, Charles. *Capital Punishment: The Inevitability of Caprice and Mistake.* New York: W. W. Norton, 1974.

Block, Eugene B. *And May God Have Mercy: The Case Against Capital Punishment.* San Francisco: Fearon, 1962.

Borchard, Edwin M. *Convicting the Innocent: Errors in Criminal Justice.* New Haven, Conn.: Yale University Press, 1932.

Bowers, William J. "The Effect of Executions Is Brutalization, Not Deterrence." In *Challenging Capital Punishment: Legal and Social Science Approaches.* Sage Criminal Justice System Annuals, edited by Kenneth C. Haas and James A. Inciardi, no. 24. Beverly Hills, Calif.: Sage Publications, 1988.

Boyd, George N. "Capital Punishment: Deserved and Wrong." *Christian Century* (Feb 17, 1988): 162-65.

Caizzi, Fernanda Decleva, ed. *Antisthenis Fragmenta*. Varese and Milano: Istituto Editoriale Cisalpino, 1966.

Capital Punishment, a scientific study contained in a special issue of Philadelphia's *Prison Journal* (Oct 1958).

Castelli, Enrico. *Le mythe de la peine: Actes du colloque organisé par le Centre international d'Études humanistes et par l'Institut d'Études philosophiques de Rome: Rome, 7-12 janvier 1967*. Paris: Aubier-Montaigne, 1967.

Clark, Gordon H. "Capital Punishment and the Bible." *Christianity Today* 4 (Feb 1960): 8-10.

Cone, James H. *Martin & Malcolm & America: A Dream or a Nightmare*. Maryknoll, N.Y.: Orbis Books, 1991.

Douglass, James W. *The Non-Violent Cross: A Theology of Revolution and Peace*. New York: Macmillan, 1968.

Dunne, John S. *The Peace of the Present: An Unviolent Way of Life*. Notre Dame, Ind.: Notre Dame University Press, 1991.

Dürkheim, Émile. *The Division of Labor in Society*. Translated by George Simpson. New York: Macmillan, 1933.

Durnbaugh, Donald F., ed. *On Earth Peace*. Elgin, Ill.: Brethren Press, 1978.

Ehrlich, Isaac. "The Deterrent Effect of Capital Punishment: A Question of Life and Death." *American Economic Review* 65 (1975): 397-417.

Elliot, Neil. *Liberating Paul: The Justice of God and the Politics of the Apostle*. Maryknoll, N.Y.: Orbis Books, 1994.

Eshelman, Byron E. *Death Row Chaplain*. Englewood Cliffs, N.J.: Prentice-Hall, 1962.

Euripedes. *Bacchae*. In *Complete Greek Tragedies*. Vol. IV. Chicago: University of Chicago Press, 1959.

Ezorsky, Gertrude, ed. *Philosophical Perspectives on Punishment*. Albany, N.Y.: State University of New York Press, 1972.

Fanon, Frantz. *L'an v de la révolution algérienne*. Paris: F. Maspero, 1959.

———. *The Wretched of the Earth*. Translated by Constance Farrington. New York: Grove Press, 1965; French 1961.

Fast, Heinold. *Der linke Flügel der Reformation*. Bremen: Schünemann, 1962.

Foucault, Michel. *Discipline and Punish: The Birth of Prison*. London: Allen Lane, 1977.

Franck, Sebastian. *Chronica, Zeytbuch vnd geschychtbibel*. Strasbourg, 1531.

_____. *Sprichwörter / schöne / weise / herrliche clügreden / vnnd hoffsprüch / darinnen der alten vnd nachkommenen / aller nationen vnnd sprachen gröste vernufft vnnd klügheyt*. Frankenfurt am Meyn: Fetruct bey Christian Engenolffen, 1541.

Frank, Jerome and Barbara. *Not Guilty*. Garden City, N.Y.: Doubleday, 1957.

Frazer, James George. *The Golden Bough*. New York: Macmillan, 1922.

Garland, David. *Punishment and Modern Society: A Study in Social Theory*. Chicago: University of Chicago Press, 1990.

Garrow, David J. *Bearing the Cross: Martin Luther King, Jr., and the Southern Christian Leadership Conference*. New York: Morrow, 1986.

Gerber, Rudolf J. and Patrick D. McAnany, eds. *Contemporary Punishment: Views, Explanations, and Justifications*. Notre Dame, Ind.: University of Notre Dame Press, 1972.

Girard, René. "Generative Scapegoating." In *Violent Origins: Walter Burkert, René Girard & Jonathan Z. Smith on Ritual Killing and Cultural Formation*. Edited by Robert G. Hamerton-Kelly. Stanford, Calif.: Stanford University Press, 1987.

————. *The Scapegoat*. Translated by Yvonne Freccero. Baltimore, Md.: Johns Hopkins University Press, 1986; French 1982.

————. *Things Hidden Since the Foundation of the World*. Translated by Stephen Bann and Michael Metteer. Stanford, Calif.: Stanford University Press, 1987.

————. *Violence and the Sacred*. Translated by Patrick Gregory. Baltimore, Md.: Johns Hopkins University Press, 1977; French 1972.

Gleason, Ron. *The Death Penalty on Trial: Taking a Life for a Life Taken*. Ventura, Calif.: Nordskok Publishing, 2008.

Goguel, Maurice. *Life of Jesus*. Translated by Olive Wyon. New York: MacMillan, 1933.

Gray, Ian and Moira Stanley. *A Punishment in Search of a Crime*. New York: Avon, 1989.

Greven, Phillip J. *The Protestant Temperament: Patterns of Child-Rearing, Religious Experience, and the Self in Early America*. Chicago: University of Chicago Press, 1977.

Greven, Phillip J., ed. *Child-Rearing Concepts, 1638-1861: Historical Sources*. Itasca, Ill.: Peacock Publishers, 1973.

Hamerton-Kelly, Robert G. ed. *Violent Origins: Walter Burkert, René Girard & Jonathan Z. Smith on Ritual Killing and Cultural Formation*. Stanford, Calif.: Stanford University Press, 1987.

Hamilton, William and Charles P. Henderson. "Theology and the Pardon." *The Christian Century* 91, vol. 33 (Oct 1974): 900-902.

Hauerwas, Stanley. "Punishing Christians: A Pacifist Approach to the Issue of Capital Punishment." In *Religion and the Death Penalty: A Call for Reckoning*, edited by Erik C. Owen, John D. Carlson, and Eric P. Elshtain, 57-72. Grand Rapids, Mich.: Eerdmans, 2004.

Heier, Aryeh. "What Should Be Done About the Guilty." *New York Review of Books* (Feb 1, 1990): 32-34.

Hoekema, David. "Capital Punishment: The Question of Justification." *Christianity Century* 96 (Mar 29, 1979): 338-42.

House, Wayne H. and John Howard Yoder. *The Death Penalty Debate: Two Opposing Views of Capital Punishment*. Dallas, Tex.: Word Publishing, 1991.

Jackson, Shirley. *The Lottery: And Other Stories*. New York: Farrar, Straus, Giroux, 1949.

King, Rachel. *God's Boycott of Sin: A Consideration of Hell and Pacifism*. New York: Fellowship Publications, 1946.

Klassen, William. *The Forgiving Community*. Philadelphia: Westminster Press, 1966.

———. *Love of Enemy: The Way to Peace*. Philadelphia: Fortress Press, 1984.

Koestler, Arthur. *Reflections on Hanging*. New York: Macmillan, 1957.

Kritz, Neil J., ed. *Readings on Transitional Justice: How Emerging Democracies Reckon with Former Regimes*. Washington D.C.: United States Institute of Peace, 1995.

Lamau, Marie-Louise. *Des Chrétiens dans le monde: communautés pétriniennes au Ier siècle*. Paris: Cerf, 1988.

Lasserre, Jean. "The 'Good' in Romans 13." In *On Earth Peace*, edited by Donald F. Durnbaugh, 130-35. Elgin, Ill.: Brethren Press, 1978.

Lawes, Lewis E. *Man's Judgment of Death: An Analysis of the Operation and Effect of Capital Punishment Based on Facts, Not on Sentiment*. New York: Knickerbocker Press, 1924.

Levy, Sandra M. "Primitive Symbolic Consciousness and the Death Penalty in American Culture." *Anglican Theological Review* 83, no. 4 (Fall 2001): 717-34.

Lewis, C. S. *God in the Dock: Essays on Theology and Ethics*, edited by Walter Hooper. Grand Rapids, Mich.: Eerdmans, 1970.

———. *The Lion, the Witch, and the Wardrobe*. New York: Macmillan, 1950.

Lind, Millard. *The Sword of Sheer Silence and the Killing State: The Death Penalty and the Bible*. Telford, Pa.: Cascadia, 2004.

Lowell, James Russell. "Once to Every Man and Nation." In *Boston Courier* (Dec 11, 1945).

Lucas, Charles. *Recueil des Débats des Assemblées Législatives de la France sur la Question de la Peine de Mort* (Paris: 1831).

McBride, James. "Capital Punishment as the Unconstitutional Establishment of Religion: A Girardian Reading of the Death Penalty." *Journal of Church and State* 37, no. 2 (Spring 1995): 263-87.

McCafferty, James M. ed. *Capital Punishment*. New York: Aldine, 1972; Lieber-Atherton, 1973.

McClendon, James W. *Systematic Theology*. Vol. 2. Nashville: Abingdon, 1994.

McDonagh, Edna. "Modes of Human Violence." *Irish Theological Quarterly* 41 (July 1974): 185-204.

McGloughlin, William G. "Evangelical Child-Rearing in the Age of Jackson." *Journal of Social History* 9 (1975).

Meltsner, Michael. *Cruel and Unusual: The Supreme Court and Capital Punishment*. New York: Random House, 1973.

Milhaven, John Giles. *Good Anger*. Kansas City, Mo.: Sheed and Ward, 1989.

Miller, Larry. *Christianisme et Société dans la Première Lettre de Pierre*. Thèse présentée en Vue de l'Obtention du Doctorat, Université des Sciences Humaines de Strasbourg, Faculté de Théologie Protestante, 1995.

Mouw, Richard J. and John Howard Yoder. "Evangelical Ethics and the Anabaptist-Reformed Dialogue." *Journal of Religious Ethics* 17, no. 2 (Fall 1989): 132-33.

Murder and the Penalty of Death, a scientific study in Philadelphia's *Annals of the American Academy of Political and Social Science* (Nov 1952).

Nathanson, Stephen. *An Eye for an Eye? The Morality of Punishing by Death*. Totowa, N.J.: Rowman and Littlefield, 1987.

Nietzsche, Friedrich. *Genealogy of Morals*. In *The Birth of Tragedy and the Genealogy of Morals*. Garden City, N.Y.: Doubleday, 1956; orig. German ed., 1887.

Nugent, John C. *The Politics of Yahweh*. Theopolitical Visions Series. Eugene, Ore.: Cascade Books, 2011.

———. "The Politics of YHWH: John Howard Yoder's Old Testament Narration and Its Implications for Social Ethics." *Journal of Religious Ethics* 39, no. 1 (Mar 2011): 71-99.

O'Donovan, Oliver. *The Ways of Judgment*. Grand Rapids, Mich.: Eerdmans, 2005.

Paul, Robert S. *The Atonement and the Sacraments*. New York: Abingdon, 1960.

Pincoffs, Edmund L. *The Rationale of Legal Punishment*. New York: Humanities Press, 1966.

Plato. *Apology*. Loeb Classical Library, 1943.

———. *Crito*. Loeb Classical Library, 1943.

————. *Phaedo*. Loeb Classical Library, 1943.

Playfair, Giles and Derrick Sington. *The Offenders: The Case Against Legal Vengeance*. New York: Simon and Schuster, 1957.

Plutarch. *Plutarch's Lives*. Loeb Classical Library, 1971.

Redekop, Vern. *Scapegoats, the Bible, and Criminal Justice: Interacting with René Girard*. Akron, Pa.: Mennonite Central Committee Office of Criminal Justice, 1993.

Reicke, Bo. *The Epistles of James, Peter and Jude: Introduction, Translation, and Notes*. Anchor Bible 37. Garden City, N.Y.: Doubleday, 1964.

Rolland, Romain. *Mahatma Gandhi*. New York: Century, 1924.

Ruddick, Sara. *Maternal Thinking: Toward a Politics of Peace*. Boston, Mass.: Beacon Press, 1989.

Rush, Benjamin. "An Enquiry into the Effects of Public Punishments upon Criminals, and upon Society (1787)" and "Considerations on the Injustice and Impolicy of Punishing Murder by Death (1972)." In *Reform of Criminal Law in Pennsylvania: Selected Inquiries, 1787-1819*. New York: Arno Press, 1972.

Ryrie, Charles C. *Dispensationalism*. Revised ed. Chicago, Ill.: Moody Press, 2007.

The San Francisco Friends Committee on Legislation's popular level piece, *This Life We Take*, 1965.

Schwager, Raymund. *Brauchen wir einen Sündenbock?* 3d ed. Thaur: Kulturverlag, 1994.

————. *Must There Be Scapegoats?* San Francisco: Harper and Row, 1986.

Scuble, Lucien. "The Christianity of René Girard and the Nature of Religion." In *Violence and Truth: On the Work of René Girard*, edited by Paul Dumouchel, 160-78. Stanford, Calif.: Stanford University Press, 1988.

Shridharani, Krishnalal Jethalal. *War without Violence: The Study of Gandhi's Method and Its Accomplishments*. New York: Harcourt Brace, 1939.

Smith, Brian K. "Capital Punishment and Human Sacrifice."

Journal of the American Academy of Religion 68 (2000): 3-25.

Stassen, Glen H. "Biblical Teaching on Capital Punishment." *Review and Expositor* 93 (1996): 485-96.

Stassen, Glen H., ed. *Capital Punishment: A Reader*. Cleveland, Oh.: Pilgrim Press, 1998.

Van den Haag, Ernest and John P. Conrad. *The Death Penalty: A Debate*. New York: Plenum, 1983.

Vellenga, Jacob J. "Is Capital Punishment Wrong?" *Christianity Today* (Oct. 12, 1959).

Washington, James Melvin, ed. *A Testament of Hope: The Essential Writings and Speeches of Martin Luther King, Jr.* San Francisco: HarperSanFrancisco, 1991.

Wenger, J. C., ed. *The Complete Writings of Menno Simons: Circa 1496-1561*. Translated by Leonard Verduin. Scottdale, Pa.: Herald Press, 1956, 1984.

Weschler, Lawrence. *A Miracle, a Universe: Settling Accounts with Torturers*. New York: Pantheon Books, 1990.

———. State Crimes: Punishment or Pardon. Papers and Report of the Conference, November 4-6. Wye Center, Maryland, 1988.

Westmoreland-White, Michael L. and Glen H. Stassen. "Biblical Perspectives on the Death Penalty." In *Religion and the Death Penalty: A Call for Reckoning*, edited by Erik C. Owen, John D. Carlson, and Eric P. Elshtain, 123-38. Grand Rapids, Mich.: Eerdmans, 2004.

Whale, John Seldon. *Victor and Victim*. Cambridge: Cambridge University Press, 1960.

Williams, James G. *Religious Studies Review* 14, no. 4 (Oct 1988): 320-26.

Wink, Walter. *Engaging the Powers: Discernment and Resistance in a World of Domination*. Minneapolis: Fortress Press, 1992.

———. *Naming the Powers: The Language of Power in the New Testament*. Philadelphia: Fortress Press, 1984.

———. *Unmasking the Powers: The Invisible Forces That Determine Human Existence*. Philadelphia: Fortress Press, 1986.

Wright, J. H. Christopher. *An Eye for an Eye: The Place of Old Testament Ethics Today*. Downers Grove, Ill.: InterVarsity Press, 1983.

Yoder, John Howard. *Anabaptism and Reformation in Switzerland: An Historical and Theological Analysis of the Dialogues Between Anabaptists and Reformers*. Kitchener, Ontario: Pandora Press, 2004.

————. "Capital Punishment and Our Witness to Government." *The Mennonite* 78, no. 24 (June 1963): 390-94.

————. "Capital Punishment and the Bible." *Christianity Today* 4 (Feb 1960): 3-6.

————. *Christian Attitudes to War, Peace, and Revolution*, edited by Theodore J. Koontz and Andy Alexis-Baker. Grand Rapids, Mich.: Brazos Press, 2009.

————. *The Christian Witness to the State*. Newton, Kan.: Faith and Life Press, 1964.

————. *The Christian and Capital Punishment*. Institute of Mennonite Studies Series, no. 1. Newton, Kan.: Faith and Life Press, 1961.

————. "The Death Penalty." *The Mennonite* (Nov 1959): 724-25.

————. "The Death Penalty: A Christian Perspective." In *Capital Punishment Study Guide*. Winnipeg: Conference of Mennonites in Canada, 1980, 44-49.

————. "The Death Penalty: A Christian Perspective." *The Interpreter* (Jan 1979), 5-6.

————. "Exodus and Exile: The Two Faces of Liberation." *Cross Currents* (Fall 1973): 297-309.

————. "Exodus 20:13—'Thou Shalt Not Kill,'" *Interpretation* 34, no. 4 (Oct 1982): 394-99.

————. *The Fullness of Christ: Paul's Vision of Universal Ministry*. Elgin, Ill.: Brethren Press, 1987.

————. *The Jewish-Christian Schism Revisited*, edited by Michael G. Cartwright and Peter Ochs. Grand Rapids, Mich.: Eerdmans, 2003.

————. *Nevertheless: Varieties of Religious Pacifism*. Revised and expanded ed. Scottdale, Pa.: Herald Press, 1992.

———. "Noah's Covenant and the Purpose of Punishment." In *Readings in Christian Ethics*. Vol. 2. *Issues and Application*, edited by David K. Clark and Robert V. Rakestraw, 471-81. Grand Rapids, Mich.: Baker, 1996.

———. *The Original Revolution: Essays on Christian Pacifism*. Scottdale, Pa.: Herald Press, 1971.

———. *The Politics of Jesus: Vicit Agnus Noster*. Grand Rapids, Mich.: Eerdmans, 1972; 2d ed., 1994.

———. *Preface to Theology: Christology and Theological Method*, edited by Stanley Hauerwas and Alex Sider. Grand Rapids, Mich.: Brazos, 2002.

———. *The Priestly Kingdom: Social Ethics as Gospel*. Notre Dame, Ind.: University of Notre Dame Press, 1984.

———. *The Royal Priesthood: Essays Ecclesiological and Ecumenical*, edited by Michael G. Cartwright. Scottdale, Pa.: Herald Press, 1998.

——— (translator). *The Schleitheim Confession*. Scottdale, Pa.: Herald Press, 1977.

———. *Täufertum und Reformation in Gespräch*. Zürich: EVZ-Verlag, 1968.

———. "The Theological Basis of the Christian Witness to the State." In *On Earth Peace*, edited by Donald F. Durnbaugh. Elgin, Ill.: Brethren Press, 1978.

———. *To Hear the Word*. 2d ed. Eugene, Ore: Cascade Books, 2010.

———. "You Have It Coming: Good Punishment: The Legitimate Social Function of Punitive Behavior." (Shalom Desktop Publications, 1995) http://theology.nd.edu/people/research/yoder-john/ [accessed Jan 1, 2011].

———. Review of *The Scapegoat* by Réne Girard, Translated by Yvonne Freccerò, *Journal of Religion and Literature* 19, no. 3 (Autumn 1987): 89-92.

Zalaquett, José. "Confronting Human Rights Violations Committed by Former Governments: Principles Applicable and Political Constraints." In *State Crimes: Punishment or Pardon*. Conference Report of the Aspen Institute, 1989, 23-69.

Zumpe, Elizabeth Bohlken. *Torches Extinguished: Memories of a Communal Bruderhof Childhood in Paraguay, Europe, and the U.S.A.* San Francisco: Carrier Pigeon Press, 1992.

SCRIPTURE INDEX

AUTHOR AND TOPIC INDEX

The Editor

John C. Nugent is Professor of Old Testament at his alma mater, Great Lakes Christian College in Lansing, Michigan. His Ph.D. is from Calvin Theological Seminary where he wrote a dissertation on John Howard Yoder's appropriation of the Old Testament for ecclesiology. He holds additional graduate degrees from Duke Divinity School (Th.M.) and Emmanuel School of Religion (M.Div.).

John is the author of *The Politics of Yahweh* (Cascade Books, forthcoming) and the editor of *Radical Ecumenicity: Pursuing Unity and Continuity after John Howard Yoder* (ACU Press, 2010). He has also published articles in books, academic journals, and popular level magazines in Bible, theology, Christian ethics, church planting, Yoder studies, and Stone-Campbellite history. John currently heads the John Howard Yoder Indexing Project and regularly writes Bible lesson commentaries for Standard Publishing. Additional ministry experiences include youth and pastoral ministry, camp directing, campus ministry, church planting, and house church ministry.

John and his wife Beth have been happily married since 1993. They have been blessed with three daughters: Alexia, Sierra, and Alissa. They are committed members of Delta Community Christian Church in Lansing, Michigan.

CPSIA information can be obtained at www.ICGtesting.com
Printed in the USA
BVOW051306061011

272896BV00004B/2/P